Gerard Delanty
Senses of the Future

T0366456

Gerard Delanty

Senses of the Future

Conflicting Ideas of the Future in the World Today

DE GRUYTER

ISBN [Hardcover] 978-3-11-124050-3
ISBN [Softcover] 978-3-11-124221-7
e-ISBN [PDF] 978-3-11-124060-2
e-ISBN [EPUB] 978-3-11-125391-6

Library of Congress Control Number: 2023951257

Bibliographic information published by the Deutsche Nationalbibliothek
The Deutsche Nationalbibliothek lists this publication in the Deutsche Nationalbibliografie; detailed
bibliographic data are available on the Internet at http://dnb.dnb.de.

© 2024 Walter de Gruyter GmbH, Berlin/Boston
Cover image: "The Last Man" (1849) by John Martin,
© National Museums Liverpool
Printing and binding: CPI books GmbH, Leck

www.degruyter.com

Preface

This is a book about the idea of the future. It is not about the future in the sense of what is going to happen but about how it can be known and what it means to speak of the future. It is also not a venture in futurology or in prediction. My approach is largely through the lens of social theory, in particular, critical social theory.

I look at the main ideas and theories of the future in modern thought, such as utopia and dystopia, the ideas of progress, prophecy and prediction, catastrophes, the long-term future of humanity, posthumanism, hope, and possibility.

While the idea of the future is not only a temporal concept – it is closely linked to space and is integral to the human condition itself – it does require a consideration of the philosophy of time and an account of developments in the natural sciences, from physics to biology and geology. I have tried to keep this discussion, in Chapter Two, as focused as possible. Without it, we cannot understand the nature of time, the implications of evolution for the human condition, technology such as AI, and planetary changes, as in the arrival of the Anthropocene. All of these are relevant to the idea of the future, which looms large in the imagination of the present. The future for long was seen as not much different from the present and that it could be known; or to the extent to which it was viewed as different, it was generally seen to be better than the present. We no longer see the future in such optimistic terms. The idea of normality and even the comforting illusion of sustainability has been shaken by the recent pandemic, by war, and by all too visible climate change and growing inequality. These experiences have inevitably shaped our view of the future, which is also inflected by ever-greater uncertainty and indeterminacy.

The approach I have taken is in part an exercise in reconstruction – reconstructing the many different conceptions of the idea of the future in modern thought, such as those of prophecy, utopia, and progress – but it is also a work of critique in that I have a critical position on a number of trends in current theories of the future. As will be clear from the Introductory chapter, I am broadly critical of approaches that see the future only through the lens of catastrophe or dystopia. It is true that today dystopias are more threatening and disturbing than those of the past, perhaps because they are more real and the potential for catastrophe is very great, including existential threats to humanity. Yet, the future is open and should be understood in terms of possibilities that are very real as well as unrealized potential. I also don't see technocratic approaches to the future based on prediction or probability really coming to terms with the challenge of

https://doi.org/10.1515/9783111240602-001

the future and the famous question Immanuel Kant posed as one of the most important questions of philosophy, 'for what should I hope?'

Until recently, at least in social science, a concern with the future was seen as unfashionable, due in part to the influence of postmodernism, which tended to equate the idea of the future with outmoded notions of utopia. Postmodernist thought shifted the focus to the past and to memory. This led to a pervasive presentism but no sense of a future. Within sociology today, there is a new interest in the sociology of the future in terms of imaginaries and social practices, while complexity theory offers a different perspective. So, my book is an attempt to clarify what it means to speak of the future, which touches on many important questions, from economy and technology to ecology and the state and democracy. As will be clear from Chapter Six, I take my point of departure from the critical theory tradition, which in my view offers something that is missing in the dominant phenomenological approaches.

Such an endeavor does not aim to say what the future will be but is a way to make sense of the clash of very different ideas of the future that are emerging today, ranging from extremist positions such as antinatalism and deep adaption to what I call techno-optimism and the misguided philosophy of longtermism. As I see it, the notion of the future is a multileveled concept and an interpretive category in that it is a form of sense making guided by references to structures inherent in both the human condition and the natural world. So it is neither purely subjective nor objective. In emphasizing the openness of the future, I am also mindful of the fact that the future is not entirely open, but perhaps best seen as uncertain and indeterminate.

I am grateful to those who read earlier drafts. Neal Harris, William Outhwaite, and Bryan S. Turner kindly read an earlier version of the entire manuscript. Piet Strydom provided immensely helpful suggestions on the theoretical framework in Chapter Six. Frederic Vandenberge provided useful comments on Chapter One. The discussion on transhumanism and AI in Chapter Seven has benefited from invaluable advice by Neal Harris, whose detailed comments on other chapters have helped to improve the work. I am also grateful to the editors at De Gruyter, Gerhard Boomgaarden, Antonia Mittelbach and Maximilian Gessl, and the copyeditor Nikhil Kumar. Needless to say, I am alone responsible for any errors.

Some of the ideas presented here were the basis of lectures at the Alberto Hurtado University, Santiago, Chile, in May 2022, where I was a visiting professor and, in October 2022, at the East China Normal University, Shanghai, where I was a guest professor for the Autumn term. I am grateful for comments from those who attended the talks.

Many of the ideas developed here go back to my older interest in critical theory, developed most recently in *Critical Theory and Social Transformation* (Palgrave,

2020), and cosmopolitanism, as in *The Cosmopolitanism Imagination* (Cambridge University Press 2009), but also to earlier work going back over thirty years. Without realizing it at the time, the idea of the future was central to such concerns.

I am grateful to the Walker Art Gallery of the National Museums Liverpool for kind permission to use for the cover of this book John Martin's 1849 painting, 'The Last Man.' The painting depicts an apocalyptical world in the future with only one person left in it alive. It shows a deserted city across a stormy sea inlet. Gesturing across the desolate landscape is an old man with the bodies of a woman and a child at his feet. As with Martin's many other paintings, which were in the Romantic and prophetic tradition, the painting expresses the sublime and the visionary and poignantly here the sense of a damaged world.

The book is dedicated to my children, Tristan and Dario, and my wife, Aurea.

Gerard Delanty
Barcelona, November 2023

Contents

Chapter One
Introduction: Conflicting Visions of the Future

It is clear that today the question of the future is one of the major problems facing contemporary societies. The future has become a problem for the present across a range of critical issues, such as climate change – which is the really major challenge, but not the only one – the economy (future supplies of energy, the viability of capitalism, growing inequality), security (as highlighted by the Russo-Ukrainian war and the renewed threat of nuclear war), developments in relation to artificial intelligence,[1] and governance with the growing instability of liberal democracy. Each of these crises taken separately presents grave risks of varying magnitude for the future, but it is the totality of them and their interrelations that is new and significant. This in essence is what makes a 'permacrisis,' a multiplication of interlocked crises that creates an apparently permanent situation of crisis out of polycrisis.[2] It is the point of orientation for how we relate to the future, which is in danger of being reduced to the permacrisis of the present.

An interesting development, the concern of this book, is what appears to be a transformation in how the human world is experienced in its spatial and temporal horizons: the future, now more than at any previous time in history, is a way of experiencing the world. Almost everything is now understood and experienced through the prism of the future since this is the primary focus for the playing out of crises. The overcoming of a crisis is always in the future, but it begins in the present. We live in the present but we are always oriented toward the future, whose shadow falls across the present. The greater the crisis, the more we are drawn into the future, but it can result in a sense of being stuck, as the notion of permacrisis suggests, that there is no way out, and we lose faith in the future.

In this book, I argue that the future is also more than a way that the world is experienced; it is a way the human condition is constituted, since humans are future-oriented beings. The future is both constitutive of humanity and also constituted by humanity in a historically unfolding process. But more than this, it should be seen in terms of potentiality and possibility, rather than as something to be predicted or withdrawn from into the past or into a futureless eternal present. This requires a shift in the view of the future as something that will happen and be-

---

1 For instance, the possible emergence of Artificial General Intelligence (AGI), a super artificial intelligence whereby robots have acquired the ability to learn and are no longer confined to performing logistical tasks given to them by humans (Elliott 2022). I discuss this in Chapter Seven.
2 https://theconversation.com/permacrisis-what-it-means-and-why-its-word-of-the-year-for-2022-194306

https://doi.org/10.1515/9783111240602-002

come a new present to one in which the future will be shaped by the present. It requires seeing the future less as a fate that is largely determined, allowing only its prediction, to one in which it is a product of foresight and willed. The latter requires a capacity that is moral, political, and cognitive in order to transcend the present.

There has been a seismic shift from the view of the future that prevailed for much of the previous century as essentially under the control of the present to a view of the future as unknown and thus out of control, since the unknown cannot be controlled and easily governed. The idea that there may not even be a future, at least not a desirable future, is now becoming a way in which the world and the human condition itself is viewed and experienced. That shift in perspective, along with new political spaces that are now emerging, has led to a sense that the future is 'now' (Anderson 2010; Monticelli 2023). This is reflected in, for example, the Fridays For Future movement, founded by Greta Thunberg, and Extinction Rebellion, both founded in 2018 and now global movements that seek to reopen the present to future possibility. It is also central to the notion of the Anthropocene, which is now widely regarded as a term to describe our present as one in which humans have changed nature itself. The future is therefore also planetary in that it is intertwined with the planetary crisis of the earth.

The future has become a category of historical experience. But it is also inscribed in the logic of history to the extent to which historical logics cannot be entirely abandoned and we return to a point before things started to go wrong. No such time existed. However, as I see it, we cannot separate future developments from, for example, the steady increase in societal complexity, digitalization and AI, democracy, and human rights. Additionally, there are now new societal goals that shape our approach to the future, for example, reducing greenhouse emissions and finding alternative sources of energy to fossil fuels. In the course of their 200,000-year history, humans have also evolved capacities that determine their future, such as intelligence, the capacity for empathy, reason, and solidarity. To be sure these capacities, acquired over thousands of years, are in conflict with other aspects of human nature, such as selfishness and self-preservation.

The future is not something that temporally arrives after the present, but it is a part of the present and consequently may become the past when our present time comes to an end. However, in the case of such eventualities, not everything is left behind. The future is not only a temporal concept but is also one that is located in space, due to the fact we live in a planetary habitat, without which the future would be nonexistent. Even theoretical physics, to be discussed in Chapter Two, recognizes that time and space are not separate but aspects of the same phenomenon, space-time. The relation to the future is bound up with the very possibility of society and is entangled in almost every way with the political. In this situation, the future has become a contested domain, with many different visions ranging from notions of the end times and proclamations of the death of the future to a new interest in the long-term survival of humanity. There is not one but a plurality of ideas of the future. There is also the problem that in the near future humans may be posthumans: Humans have already changed themselves as a result of biotechnology and digital technology, but with artificial intelligence a new relation to the future is taking shape, divesting it of its wonder and majesty. We may be entering a new posthuman age in which the future and humanity may be entirely shaped by forms of technology that have acquired human forms of intelligence.

However, it is far from clear what is the significance of these developments for the future and which are advantageous and which are dangers. The prospect of an unknown future instills anxiety, even dread, but it is also a source of hope insofar as it signals possibility. There is a diversity of positions and orientations, including ones that are emerging from new kinds of experiences. We cannot of course know the future in the way we can know the past. As Bertrand de Jouvenel wrote in a classic work on the future in 1964, *The Art of Conjecture*, knowledge of the future is a contradiction in terms since we cannot know what has not yet happened (Jouvenel 2017). Yet, as he acknowledged the only really useful knowledge is one that relates to the future. Before the heyday of futurology, this was already a key insight into the philosophy of the American pragmatists, such as John Dewey and William James, for whom knowledge must be useful for action. But what kind of knowledge is this?

Despite the difference between the past and the future, between what has happened and what is to come, it can be suggested, to begin, that our sense of the past has always been influenced by our view of the future. Revolutionaries have always looked to the past to frame their future cause, as is amply illustrated by examples from nationalism to communism. The future has often been seen as variously a recovery of a lost time, as a replication of what is established, or as a model bequeathed by a heroic age long gone. The writing of history is based on understanding or explaining future outcomes that were not known to contemporaries, since the historian has the benefit of hindsight and the past is nothing more than the accumulation of futures that are now our past. So, rather than see the hand of the past always shaping the future, perhaps it can be seen in reverse, with the past – in the sense of our understanding of it – being shaped by our orientation to the future.

In this book I explore the future as a field of tensions that is revealed in narratives, utopian desires, imaginaries, and, crucially, social struggles concerning the potential possibilities of the present – the future does not just arrive; it has to be fought for, as in Auden's poem 'Spain', inspired by the Spanish Civil War, and its hope of 'tomorrow perhaps the future.'[3] Of the many senses of the future that prevail today, I argue that an important one is a field of possibilities, a topic of recent interest in social theory.[4] Possibility presupposes potentiality. Human beings have potential resources to draw upon, which gives rise to various outcomes including ideals and desires that provide inspiration. What is potential is not necessarily realized – it is often just latent – but gives rise to concrete possibilities, such as specific goals to be pursued and realized. The future is formed from the infinitive potentials that humanity possesses and the possibilities that emerge from such potentials. This framework of temporal modalities will be discussed in more detail in Chapter Six. It will suffice to mention here that it entails a view of the future as open and contested, since it takes shape from the relatively open space of human potentiality and the field of possibilities that results from attempts to pursue various goals. While the future is not determined, it is also not entirely open, since many aspects are determined, such as those relating to the physical structure of the universe, and others are indeterminate.

Just as the study of the past is now generally seen in terms of contested histories, I emphasize the idea of contested futures, for there is not one narrative but many. This is also why the future can never be entirely predicted, since it is always subject to the pursuit of new possibilities and our knowledge is limited, including the capacity for prediction (see Stainforth 2023). In physics, quantum mechanics effectively replaced prediction with probability, with the result we can never know what the future holds in store for us other than calculating the odds of certain events happening (Clifford 2017: 84). It is also necessary to go beyond the models of thinking about the future that emanated from western societies in the nineteenth and twentieth centuries and the unquestioned assumptions about the nature of historical time. I also engage in a critique of the plurality of views of the future that characterize both popular and academic debate.

The idea of the future has also always been very much shaped by how the present has been understood. While I argue this is a key dimension of the future, the dominance of the past over the present – imagining the future in terms of past futures – needs to be challenged in order to give a more central place to the future. Knowledge oriented toward the future should be more interesting than knowing the past; it is certainly more important, but the allure of the past prevails as a place of refuge. It has also influenced too much our understanding of the future, even if the future was in fact the beacon.

---

3 https://sites.google.com/a/upr.edu/modernpoetry/Student-Blogs/ivan-andres-rodriguez/spainby whauden
4 Berardi (2017), Strydom (2023), Jeanpierre and Guégen (2022).

I am convinced that ideas of the future today are very different from those that prevailed in the past, even the relatively recent past, and that we need to go beyond a purely temporal concept of the future, which is also an epistemic and existential category. The old ideas of the future – such as those that go back to the Enlightenment with Condorcet, Kant, Sant-Simon, Comte, Marx – are in any case now part of the past, not the future. That is not to say that they have vanished entirely, for they left in their different ways an indelible mark on modernity and helped to shape new structures of consciousness, such as the view of the future as something that can be made by the present.

The future is also potentially longer in temporal terms than the past. While the history of human societies is not more than about 12,000 years old, with the earliest state-centered civilizations emerging around 6,000 years ago, the future is very likely to be longer, stretching out in theory infinitively, but in reality until the end of our planetary system – in about 5 billion years. This is the case even if we include the much longer and equally interesting deep prehistory of human society, going back to about 200,000 years ago when the human species emerged in Africa and when other hominid species also existed until they became extinct (Graeber and Weingrow 2018).

Most attitudes to the future concern the immediate future – what is going to happen in the next few years or possibly within the space of a generation – which implies a conception of the future as not too much different from the present. Peter Turchin's analysis (see Chapter Three) of the waves of instability that began almost ten years ago, c. 2012, leading to the current crisis of major societal and political instability, belongs to this broad view of the near future as a product of recurrent crisis tendencies (Turchin 2023). Then, there is the sense of the distant future of, say, from fifty years or to the end of the century, taking our current time in the mid-2020s as the reference. Other time spans begin with a sense of the long-term future, which can be from a century from now to as long as it is possible to imagine life itself lasting on the planet or in other terrestrial settings (Roser 2022). These temporalities of the future, essentially different time spans, are not necessarily in opposition to each other, nor are they successive, for time is not sequential; they can also be seen as a plurality of existing temporalities, each with very different future trajectories. In everyday life, we see this when we look at the twinkling stars in the night sky and see what in fact is their past – for we see only the light they emitted, perhaps millions of years ago. The future of major climatic change as a result of carbon dioxide and methane gas released into the atmosphere is in a way also paradoxically the past, for the carbon burned today as fuel is nothing but the heat of the sun absorbed by plant life millions of years ago.

The concept of the future does not then come already defined, nor is it an empty space that the present moves into. Whatever order or coherence it has comes from how we construe it and from how we experience time itself. The subject is always oriented to the future in many different ways, for example, through hope, despair, fear, fantasy, and wonder. Once we go beyond the immediate future, towards the deep future, it becomes increasingly open and consequently unknown. On the one side, there are trends that can be anticipated depending on our current situation, imaginaries, expectations; on the other side there is the open future of possibilities that are contingent on events yet to come, including potential mega-catastrophes, bringing the idea of the future into the infamous domain of 'unknown knowns.' It is undoubtedly a fact of our current historical condition that we can think of time in such terms as pertaining not to those living in the present but to future generations and possibly forms of human life that do not yet exist.

In premodern societies the future was unproblematically based on the past. The dominant conceptions were providence, prophecies, destiny, divination, fate. Premodern societies lived in a perpetual present, with only a limited perspective on the future as different from the present (see Chapter Three). The future was predetermined by what happened in the past. Oracles, prophets, druids, soothsayers, obelisks, etc. provided predictions of the future, but nothing could be done with the knowledge they produced on what might happen, as in the hapless fate of Casandra. We are today approaching this condition of a universal Casandra syndrome – as with Hegel's Owl of Minerva, knowledge often comes too late, and with the result we can only look back on what we already know. There is also the related problem that while today our knowledge of the human and natural world is vastly greater than in earlier times, there is the sense that we know less, simply because there is greater uncertainty and indeterminacy, and unlike our ancestors, we no longer see the world as unchanging.[5]

With modernity, the future was a product not of the past but of a present no longer bound by the past. Modernity was defined by the 'now,' the present moment, and signaled a rupture with the past (which was reappropriated by the new ideas of the modern era, thus making possible some continuity). This opened up the future to new possibilities. Prognosis replaced the dominance of prophecy. With the Enlightenment, science played a role in the new orientation to the future. The main new ideas of the future were those of utopia and progress, as the two master narratives that replaced the eschatological conception of the future. But as I argue in Chapter Four, prophecy did return in a new and largely secular guise in the 1790s and remained an important current in future thinking, from the romantics to modern science fiction. There were counternarratives, but on

---

5 This was already noted by Hans Jonas in 1979 (Jonas 1984: 119). See also Chapter Six for a discussion of Jonas' conception of the future.

the same theme, for example, as in the revolutionary tradition. The USSR had its own such narratives of the future, as Susan Buck-Morss outlined in *Catastrophe and Dreamworld* (2002).

Modernity entailed a great belief that the future could be mastered by human will and design. The great ideologies of the nineteenth century, socialism, communism, even nationalism, etc., all made a claim to the future; their claims were different but they all had a vision of a future society and proclaimed to be able to bring it about through political will. The future was yet to come, but it was deemed to be achievable through political action and guided by science. Unbounded optimism in the future was accompanied by critiques of what it promised, as in conservative critiques of the end of civilization, especially from the 1920s to the 1950s, on the themes of 'man versus machine' and elites versus the masses. Despite these countercritiques, the belief in the future prevailed. As the intellectual historian Reinhart Koselleck wrote in a seminal essay in 1976, the future became tied to a new 'horizon of expectation' that was not limited by 'the space of experience' – it drew on other sources, ones that transcended experience and history (Koselleck 2004). However, the reality of these visions of the future in the twentieth century was, as Alain Badieu has claimed in his book *Century*, disasters. They sought to create 'a new type of man' but left in their wake nothing but inhumanity (Badieu 2007 [2005]: 177). The century, moreover, was a ceaseless 'waiting' for the future.[6]

The post-1945 era in the western world witnessed the rise of a new era of scientific prediction and forecasting. As Jenny Andersson has shown in her authoritative *The Future of the World* (2018), the new science of prediction was a response to the Cold War situation, which led to a concern with controlling the future, which was increasingly seen as open and thus available for control. However, futurism was not hegemonic, for there were different positions, for example, the contrasting stances of the American sociologist Daniel Bell in *The Coming of Post-Industrial Society: a venture in social forecasting* in 1973 and the French political philosopher Bertrand de Jouvenel's *The Art of Conjecture* (2017 [1964/1967]). But the ideas of the era all invested great faith in the belief that the present could master the future, which was generally the immediate future of the next three or so decades. There were of course exceptions, a notable voice being the British economist E. F. Schumacher, who in a book in 1973, *Small is Beautiful: Economics as if People Matter*, questioned the dominant social forecasting approach to the future. Other visions that gradually emerged were inspired by imaginaries of an alternative future that could be realized through human agency, as in pragmatist philosophy and

---

6 The century has been a century of 'waiting': 'This century has been the century of a poetics of the wait, a poetics of the threshold' (p.22).

utilitarianism, but also in the various proponents of radical politics since the 1960s and in the rise of more critical and alternative currents in futurology.

These ideas of the future, which were all based on hope for a better world, were a product of an era of stability and lost their appeal from the end of the twentieth century with the emergence of a sense of a new era beginning marked by multiple crises. The American dream became a nightmare. The shock of the future, as in Alvin Toffler's 1970 book, *Future Shock*, no longer shocked (Toffler 1970). Punk culture proclaimed, 'No Future,' the phrase of a generation of British youth culture who thought they had no future (Worley 2017). The presuppositions upon which those optimistic ideas were based ceased to exist by the mid-1970s and new intellectual and political currents offered different ideas of the world. In many cases, there was a retreat to the past. In this time, the latter decades of the previous century, there was a revival of nationalism, collective memory, and identity politics, which are focused on the past rather than the future. The response to the future was one of disappointment, which nurtured variously denial, nostalgia, and fear. Neoliberalism, in cultivating an individualistic ethos, led to a survivalist mentality and the notion only some can have a future worth having. Margaret Thatcher's much-cited remark in 1980, 'there is no alternative,' captured the ethos of that movement and time.

The late modern period, from c. 1990, gave rise to new doubts about the received modernist ideas of the future, which became increasingly contested and pervaded by a fundamental sense of the unknown. Consequently it could not be easily mastered or predicted. The horizon of expectation shrank and there was a return to the space of experience, which had meanwhile widened to encompass possibilities that in earlier times were unimaginable. The idea of the future became absorbed into a new presentism – the idea that there is only an unending present into which we are doomed but can make the best of – but with the specter of catastrophe ever present (Nowotny 1994: 51). It is also possible that liberal democracy leans in this direction of shrinking the future to the relatively short space of electoral cycles, as Jonathan White has suggested (White 2024b).

So, in this period there has been a shift in the sense of the future as something going to happen to a sense that sees it as largely having already arrived: Postmodern thought wiped out the idea of the future and led to a new concern with critical histories of the past that had no place for the future; the post-Cold War context led to a pervasive presentism; critical social science challenged the positivist assumptions of prediction and control; in recent times, climate change raised the specter of the death of the future; and neoliberalism led to a survivalist mentality, a privatization of the future as something only for the isolated individual, and the notion that only some can have a future worth having. Nationalism and identity politics are predominantly focused on the past. In other words, on one reading of the current situation, we are witnessing a closing of the open horizon of the future today. However, there are also countercurrents.

A closer look at current theories of the future is in order as a point of departure for this book.

Contested Visions of the Future Today

There is a new interest in the idea of the future across a range of disciplines, as reflected in a large number of recent publications.[7] In my book, I seek to contribute to this burgeoning field with a theoretical reconstruction. I also aim to offer a different account of the idea of the future from some of the dominant trends in recent literature that variously reduce it to a category that can be predicted or understood in terms of catastrophe. In the following, I discuss some of these with a view to identifying some shortcomings.

One distinctive theme in recent literature on the idea of the future is that it is now a redundant concept. Two versions of this argument can be found in the writings of left-wing critics, such as Slavoj Zizek and Franco Beradi, for whom the future has been effectively killed by neoliberalism and an all-dominant capitalism. In his book, *Living in the End Times*, the Slovenian philosopher Slavoj Zizek (2011) says 'global capitalism is approaching an apocalyptical zero point' resulting from the 'four riders of the Apocalypse': the ecological crisis, the consequences of the biogenic revolution, imbalances within the capitalist system (for instance, the energy crisis), the explosive growth of social divisions and exclusions. This situation leads in turn to five stances on the future: denial, anger, bargaining, depression, and acceptance. Zizek offers a compelling analysis of the current situation under these headings. His analysis is based on the general thesis of the collapse of the utopian impulse, which is no longer able to sustain the vision of a viable future.

Writing in a similar vein, the Italian Marxist-anarchist philosopher Franco Berardi, in *After the Future*, also declares the end of utopia. The twentieth century was the century that believed in the future, which was tied to the idea of utopia, which in turn was linked to the idea of progress and reached a high point in 1968. The future was also connected to capitalism, 'in the experience of the expansion of the economy and knowledge' and also in the celebration of speed (Berardi 2011: 18). In his account, it declined from 1972 with the reversal of the progressive notion

---

7 Good examples are the volume *Futures*, edited by Anderson and Kemp (2021), Innerarity (2012), and White (2024a).

of progress following the influential Club of Rome's book, *The Limits to Growth* (Meadows *et al.* 1972). Then in 1977, the Punk movement declared 'No Future.' What was left of the idea of the future is devoid of a normative, desirable ideal.

Both Zizek and Berardi are correct in their analysis of the death of a particular conception of the future; for example, as aptly summarized by Berardi, the modernist utopian notion that the future will be not only better, but that it can be known and can be transformed by human will (p. 51). However, the shortcoming of this position is that it refers only to one conception of the future. As Berardi acknowledges: 'When I say "the Future," I am not referring to the direction of time. I am thinking, rather, of the psychological perception, which emerged in the cultural expectations that were fabricated during the long period of modern civilization, reaching a peak in the years after the Second World War' (p. 18). This period has long come to an end and, with it, the relative stability that it established.

In a later book, Berardi gave more prominence to the idea of the future as one of possibility, but did not develop the idea. Despite the darkness of the times and the sense of political impotence that is widely felt, possibility remains immanent in the present: 'I call possibility a content inscribed in the present constitution of the world (that is the immanence of the possible)' (Beradi 2017: 1).

It is true that the 'end times' is one of the most common ways the future is seen, as reflected in the turn from utopia to dystopia, the revival of eschatological visions, doomsday scenarios. Leonard Cohen's song of 1992, 'The Future' captured the mood: 'I've seen the future, baby. It is murder.'[8] Much of contemporary popular culture reflects this mood, as perhaps most vividly illustrated in the surge of post-apocalyptical films and dystopian science fiction, which have a particular appeal for young adults. The specter of the end times was always part of the modernist imagination, as Eva Horn (2018) has documented; it is a pervasive force in right-wing popular culture signaling the death of the established narratives (Nilges 2019: 81). Right-wing culture and thought – as reflected in Trump, Brexit, the Alt-Right, Dugin and Putin – generally has no place for the future, other than a reactionary and nostalgic appeal to what was once the future – and thus to the past. It is now a powerful movement in the USA with the growth of Christian apocalyptic sects, such as the New Apostolic Reformation movement.[9] But dystopian literature can also express a critical function as in the post-Trump popularity of the *Handmaiden Tale*, originally published in 1986. Its author, Margaret Atwood has been referred to a 'prophet of dystopia' (Munoz-Gonzalez (2022). Rather than see dystopia

---

8 In a 1992 album.
9 https://www.theatlantic.com/ideas/archive/2023/06/christian-movement-new-apostolic-reforma tion-politics-trump/674320/

and utopia as opposites, they might be seen as different temporal visions: dystopia appears to be a concern with the present while utopia reflects a view to the future. Post-apocalyptical and dystopian fiction can be a way of viewing the world beyond the limits of the present, as in for example Paul Lynch's *Prophet Song* (2023). As Manjikian has argued, such fiction is a way of talking about the present and the sense of catastrophic loss but also of future possibility (see also Lillyet *et al.* 2012). It is also a powerful current in the environmental movement, as Cassegard and Thorn (2012) argue.

It is true that historically fascism was based on futuristic thinking, and today there is a new brand of right-wing neoliberal utopias that are future oriented, as in the ideas of Elon Musk, combining big data, transhumanism, eternal life, and space travel. There is the intimation of humanity 'hacking' itself in a race for ultimate performativity and eternal life. Some of these prognoses, which have the flavor of fascism and futurology, have been explored by Ray Kurzweil, who thinks that humanity will converge with the technologies it created (Kurzweil 2005). I consider the implications of AI and big data for the future in the last chapter of this book. A related albeit fringe movement in contemporary philosophy is accelerationism, which argues for the radical overcoming of the present not by radical politics and opposition but through a fast-forward movement to the future through technological innovation.[10]

But does this mean that the utopian imagination is dead? Judith Shklar wrote in a classic work: 'Utopianism is dead, and without it no radical philosophy can exist' (1957: 268). In a lecture in 1970, 'The End of Utopia', Herbert Marcuse made a similar announcement. Utopia, as once understood, may be dead but the imagination that gave rise to utopia is still there. The classical visions – those programmatic visions to restructure state and society or the aspiration to create an ideal society – are quite clearly dead. However, as Claeys (2020) argues, the utopian imagination is still there in the sense of an aspiration to create something better and persists in new guises. E. O. Wright made a convincing case for real utopias (Wright 2010). Following Levitas, who distinguishes utopia as a method from a goal, we can see how our political present is still inspired by utopia for the exploration of alternative futures (Levitas 2013). It is also relevant to alternative spaces in contemporary society and alternatives to capitalism (Cooper 2014, Harvey 2000, Featherstone 2017). Much of Green political thought is inspired by the idea of utopia. Claeys and Thaler have demonstrated their relevance for climate politics (Claeys 2022, Thaler 2022).

---

10 https://www.theguardian.com/world/2017/may/11/accelerationism-how-a-fringe-philosophy-pre dicted-the-future-we-live-in

In this book, I am also suggesting that a different perspective on the future beyond the question of the end of utopia is possible. This does not entail a return to the older notions of utopia but of identifying new sources of possibility. Engaging with the philosophy of time (as I do in Chapter Two) and other theoretical positions in social theory can offer a different perspective on future possibility. So we are not facing the total obsolescence of utopia in face of dystopia (see also Gordon *et al.* 2011). According to Albrecht Wellmer, the great historical utopias of the Marxist tradition, Reason, idea of progress are all 'endgames,' by which he means they have come to an end, but something can still be salvaged from them (Wellmer 1993). The fact that a tradition ends does not mean that it has no further consequences, since its heritage remains. Dystopia is not confined to our present or something yet to come: the past is replete with examples of dystopia, including utopias that went wrong. In 1868, in an age that believed in utopianism, J. S. Mill used the term 'dystopians' to refer to British government policy in Ireland. Indeed, the utopian imagination could be seen as a response to the reality of dystopia. On a more pessimistic reading of the current situation, it may be the case that utopia is possible today only as the prevention of the worst, for example, climate catastrophe, rather than the creation of an ideal society. To confine the idea of utopia to the goal of keeping global warming or to within 1.5 c of pre-industrial levels, which will probably not be possible, is perhaps to empty the concept of its central meaning, the aspiration for a better world.

Related to the end times, there is a new interest in the sociology of catastrophe and disaster as a way of thinking about the future (see Chapter 3). While not necessarily always sharing the doomsday mentality, it is characterized by a sense of the future as increasingly the domain of the unknown. The future is seen as containing the specter of major global catastrophes, ranging from asteroid impacts and gamma ray bursts to nuclear war and biological warfare (Bostrom and Cirkovic 2008). The future that beckons portends the potential collapse of civilization and warnings of the need to be prepared to rebuild it from scratch (Servigne and Stevens 2020; Dartwell 2015). This conception of the future includes a new concern with the possibility of the extinction of humanity (Boulter 2005, Leslie 1998, Moynihan 2020). It is also an inspiration for climate trauma in dystopian science fiction (Kaplan 2016). The specter of catastrophe does not necessarily stand for an apocalyptical end, the total extinction of humanity, even life itself, but a gradual descent to doomsday, as in the notions of 'slow disasters' or 'slow catastrophe.'[11] One such example is the prospect that the Gulf Stream, now at its weakest in its 1,600-year history, will shut down in the next few years or at some point this century as a

---

11 See Jones (2017) and Knowles (2020). The concept is particularly pertinent to climate change.

result of the collapse of air currents – the Atlantic Meridional Overturning Circulation (AMOC) – that regulate it.[12] The result would be catastrophic, in particular for North Western Europe.

The specter of catastrophe has also given rise to very fruitful notions of emergency governance that complement in important ways the idea of risk (Aradeu and van Munster 2011; Opitz and Tellmann 2015). Amoore (2013), for example, detects a shift since September 11, 2001, from a politics of probability based on risk assessment to a politics of possibility whereby what was once seen as a low probability but high-impact event now becomes normalized as a possibility and can be controlled by new digital technology. Such approaches show how catastrophes open up new visions of the future and lead to progressive change, but they can also simply result in new kinds of political control.

An extreme position is the preference for an 'ahuman future' (MacCormack 2020) or a no future, as in 'antinatalism,' the belief that human life is a form of harm and should cease through zero births, as advocated by the South African philosopher David Benatar (2008).[13] Fear of the future is reflected in the relatively new phenomenon of eco-anxiety or climate anxiety, a chronic fear of environmental doom.[14] This trend toward climate trauma as a way to view the future has acquired a new relevance with notion of 'climate adaptation,' a much-discussed and now influential concept proposed by the British psychologist Jem Bendell in a 2018 paper that has been widely discussed on the internet. In view of the likelihood, he believes, of 'a near time collapse in society' and the apparent abandonment of any hope for the future, we have to look elsewhere for meaning.[15] A 'deep adaption' to the external reality of climate tragedy, including the possible extinction of much of life, is needed. One of the key implications of an argument that is not devoid of vagueness is the transformation of personal grief into 'climate grief.' In essence, the future is replaced by grieving for its loss.

It cannot be denied that grief – the feeling of an irrevocable loss – is an important orientation to the future and a legitimate prerequisite for facing the future;[16] however, it cannot be the only response as this would lead to a pathological condition of melancholy. It is a current in contemporary thought that is reflected in

---

12 https://www.nature.com/articles/s41467-023-39810-w; https://www.theguardian.com/environment/2021/aug/05/climate-crisis-scientists-spot-warning-signs-of-gulf-stream-collapse

13 https://www.newyorker.com/culture/persons-of-interest/the-case-for-not-being-born

14 https://www.theguardian.com/society/2021/oct/06/eco-anxiety-fear-of-environmental-doom-weighs-on-young-people; https://www.bbc.com/future/article/20200402-climate-grief-mourning-loss-due-to-climate-change and https://www.sciencedirect.com/science/article/pii/S2667278221000444

15 Bendell (2018). See also Bendell (2020) and Bendell and Read (2021).

16 See Cunsolo and Ellis (2018).

'doomism,' the view that the future is only bad news and nothing can be done to stop the worst or that there is yet worse still to come. A broader assessment of the experience of grief suggests a view of the emotional impact of catastrophe as opening a space for hope rather than pessimism or resigned fatalism. This sense of loss was already expressed in Rachel Carston's classic book, *Silent Spring* in 1962. Bryan Turner mentions the potential of intergenerational justice with respect to climate change as one response, another being the recognition of the vulnerability of all human beings (Turner 2023: 119, 130).

Isabelle Stegers sees the catastrophes of the present epoch as a basis for thinking about the possibility of thinking about a 'future that is not barbaric' (Stegers 2015: 15). It is clear that no account of the future can avoid the centrality of catastrophe. As I see it, the way this should be viewed is to see catastrophe as an external or exogenous force or event that can shape the future in specific ways. Catastrophes to be sure are very often internal as much as they are external in terms of their causes, since the cause is very often human induced. However, we still need a theory of the future to account for the internal or endogenous responses to the future that emanate from the human condition itself and from history. Catastrophes are not just recent occurrences but have been part of human history, especially natural catastrophes. So human beings – the chief cause of most catastrophes – have always had to deal with catastrophe. And they have dealt with them in many different ways, leading to new ways of relating to the future.

One of the most widespread positions on the idea of the future today is what can be called 'Presentism,' the idea that there is no future as such, only an endless present. Anything that could be in the future is already contained within the present, which never comes to an end. In many ways, this approach to the future was a product of postmodern thought. Postmodernism, despite its critical intervention as in Derrida's critique of the 'metaphysics of presence' in *Writing and Difference*, effectively wiped out the idea of the future as a normative alternative to the present (Derrida 1978). The future was dismissed as an illusion of Enlightenment thinking. The writings of Michel Foucault, above all, led to a new concern with critical histories of the past that had no place for the future. As he wrote in 1966 in *The Order of Things:* 'It is no longer possible to think in our day other than in the void created by man's disappearance' (1994: 342). It is true that he saw this void as opening up a space for thinking about how we have come to be what we are. However, it is fairly clear that his work was more about the past than the future. Yet, in a late interview shortly before his death in 1984 he said, 'I say study history, not the future. Study history to prepare for the future.'[17]

---

17 Jamin (1984).

Derrida's philosophical project, in contrast, had a more specific concern with the future and arguably went against the general tendency in poststructuralist thought in opposing the privileging of the present – as in his critique of the 'metaphysics of presence' – as the site of the past in order to open up alternative possibilities for thought. As he wrote in the introduction to *Of Grammatology:* 'The Future can only be anticipated in the form of an absolute danger. It is that which breaks absolutely with constituted normality and can be proclaimed, presented, as a sort of monstrosity.' (Derrida 1976. [1967]: 5). For Derrida, the real radical sense of the future is to be understood as *l'avenir* and not as *le future*, that is, a sense of the future as something that cannot be predicted, a future yet to come. It has indeed been said that all his concepts and work were devoted to the future, understood as some permanent condition immanent in the present that is revealed with the passing of time.[18]

In contemporary thought these ideas led to a pervasive presentism, namely the idea the future is an extended present. Francois Hartog's *Regimes of Historicity* is a good example of this approach (Hartog 2015 [2003]; see also Fritzsche, 2004). Hartog sees a conflict of different 'regimes of historicity' between past, present, and future regimes. Future-oriented regimes overcame past-oriented ones, while today a presentist one is dominant: 'The twentieth century, in retrospect, combined futurism and presentism. It started out more futurist than presentist, and ended up more presentist than futurist.' It led to a view of history as written in the name of the future (p. 107). But now, 'futurism has sunk below the horizon and presentism has taken its place. We cannot see beyond it. Since it has neither a past nor a future, this present daily fabricates the past and future it requires, while privileging the immediate' (p. 113). He sees this presentism as consuming the orientation to the future that was the preoccupation of the left and has become swamped by memory and heritage. Much can be said about his critical and far-reaching analysis of the rise of memory which has claimed the future. His notion of regimes of historicity captures the shifting waves of time consciousness.

While Hartog's book has the undoubted merit of drawing attention to competing temporalities, it is limited in its portrayal of presentism as the dominant one and leaves very little scope for other concepts of the future and alternative currents in time consciousness.[19] In this book I try to show that there is still a space for the future.

---

18 See the various interpretations of Derrida's writings on the future, Cornell (2005), Gaston (2011), Martinon (2007), Simmons (2016), Trebeznik (2019), and Wood (2006).
19 See also Simon and Tamm (2021: 13) for an alternative account of 'historical futures.' The basic idea of the vanishing future was already introduced by Helga Nowotny in her book on time (Nowotny 1994 [1989]).

At this juncture, it is helpful to recall Zygmunt Bauman's last book, *Retrotopia*, in which he discussed in a similar vein the rise of a culture of nostalgia for a time when there was a future. Utopia now is simply projected backward to the recovery of something lost (Bauman 2017). But the past that is appealed to here has no potential for the present.[20] Bauman's work keeps open the space for a different response to the future beyond the decline of certain narratives of utopian thought and politics.

The sense of the future as an eternal present is not entirely a product of our time. In the eighteenth century, Jean Baptiste Rousseau – poet and dramatist not to be confused with his contemporary Jean-Jacques Rousseau – captured this mood with a famous aphorism in one of his Odes, 'The moment passed is no longer; the future may never be; the present is all of which man is master.'[21] This sense of the loss of the future later became a defining feature of the left in the second half of the twentieth century with the loss of utopia and disillusionment with the revolutionary hopes for the future. As summed up by Enzo Traverso in *Left-Wing Melancholia:* 'The utopias of the past century have disappeared, leaving a present charged with memory but unable to project itself into the future' (Traverso 2016: 7). Milan Kundera wrote words to this effect in the *Book of Laughter and Forgetting:* 'We must never allow the future to collapse under the burden of memory' (1983/1980 [1979]: 187).

Other approaches to the future take a much more optimistic view of the capacity of humanity to shape the future in what may be called 'techno-optimism.' Such positions generally display considerable optimism about the capacity of science and technology to create the future, even in possibly other planetary settings, as in W. Patrick McCray's book, *The Visioneers*, which gives an account of visionary scientists who pursued utopian imaginaries of creating technologies to bring about entirely new futures, including space colonies. Some of their visions were failures, while others did lead to major successes, as in nanotechnology (McCray 2012). Another example of what I call 'techno-optimism' is the phenomenon of geoengineering or climate engineering as the solution to the problems of climate change through, for example, carbon dioxide removal from the atmosphere or solar engineering reflecting sunlight back into space (Hamilton 2013, Oomen 2021). Wenger *et al.* (2020) propose the concept of 'prevision' to analyze technologically driven measures to shape the future across a range of societal sectors in the context of unpredictability, complexity, and uncertainty. Undoubtedly a good deal of future research will be dominated by these approaches to the future, especially as they relate to AI.

---

20 See also Boyn (2001) on the rise of nostalgia.
21 https://fr.wikisource.org/wiki/Ode_XIII_(Second_livre_des_Odes_de_J.-B._Rousseau)

The future envisioned in these accounts is largely the immediate future, but with glimpses of the distant future. Another strand in current future thinking is 'Longtermism,' as espoused most comprehensively by William MacAskill in his book, *What We Owe to the Future* (2022). MacAskill, a moral philosopher, has made what appears to be a compelling case for looking at the very long term-future. Longtermism 'is the idea that positively influencing the longterm future is a key moral priority of our time. Longtermism is about taking seriously just how big the future could be and how high the stakes are in shaping it. If humanity survives to even a fraction of its potential life span, then, strange as it may seem, we are the ancients: we live at the very beginning of history, in the most distant past. What we do now will affect untold numbers of future people' (MacAskill, 2022: 3). However, the long-term he has in mind is, as conveyed by the subtitle of his book, a 'million-year view.' An earlier position on this was put forward by Steward Brand for a notion of a 10,000-year present, effectively incorporating a sense of the future as long as the history of civilization (Brand 1999).

These concerns about future people are present in another important assessment of possible future human extinction. Toby Ord's book *The Precipice* offers the most systematic probability analysis of human extinction through existential risks and catastrophes (Ord 2020). Ord's analysis touches on the relatively new field of population ethics, which is concerned with the consequences of our action on future people, and draws on the moral philosophy of Derek Parfit, who laid the foundations for population ethics and our responsibility for future people in relation to people currently living.[22] The key question here is how much value should be placed on the long-term survival of humanity as a moral value in itself in order to secure the conditions of future people. Future people are people who do not yet exist but will in the future. Parfit was interested in our duties to them and if it was relevant that they were not yet born. Do future people matter more than people who now exist? His moral philosophy was based on the argument that just as we have obligations to people far away, we have similar obligations to people in the future. Just as one should not discriminate against someone because of *where* they were born, one should not discriminate against *when* someone is born: a future person is as valuable as one who now exists. On this controversial premise, that time and distance are the same for morality, it is as bad to harm a future person as it is to harm a living one. His moral philosophy raised many important questions about future people but also led to many problems, for instance,

---

22 His main work was *Reasons and Persons* (Parfit 1984). The four chapters in Part 4 discuss his theory of future people and our obligations to them. See for an invaluable guide to his thought and life, Edmonds (2023).

the basic problem of the unknowability of the future and thus of the uncertain consequences of plans made in the present for a very distant future. Also people separated from us in space are closer to us than people separated from us in the vastness of time.

For moral philosophers such as Ord and MacAskill these concerns do not matter: the key challenge for them is the survival of humanity in the very distant long term. Ord's overall conclusions are that the greatest existential risks are human caused rather than natural, for example, nuclear war, and these risks are unacceptably high as well as being avoidable. His impeccable analysis cannot be faulted, but the danger of a concern with the need to guarantee the existence of future people – those who may live more than 200,000 years from now or more – is that it can be to the detriment of people living now and those in very near future. There is also the problem that the survival of humanity may not require the survival of everyone but could be accomplished by the survival of an elite. In my view, the idea of the future as a critical concept cannot be only a question of survival. The proponents of longtermism and the related school of population ethics ultimately rest on very dubious foundations that are essentially about concern for people who do not yet exist and little regard for those who now exist. They do not see it that way, but it is the outcome of a position that equates future persons with existing ones. Longtermism is not just an argument for responsibility for future generations, but an argument for ensuring that there will always be people whose welfare is what we need to be concerned about. Rather than see current suffering as the problem, they see the relatively small risk of human extinction as a result of a future catastrophic occurrence as the problem since their objective is to ensure that for the very distant future, there will not just be people but happy ones.[23] Inevitably the realization of these concerns brings longtermism into the domain of space travel. Longtermism and the related political philosophy associated with it, effective altruism, rest on deeply problematical assumptions given its lack of concern for the present and its preference for non-political solutions, such as personal altruism. In general, this is a theory of the future that I reject.

The 'deep future,' the preoccupation of evolutionary biology, on future biological evolution of humans is another influential conception of the future, as in Scott Solomon's *Future Humans* (2016). This is related to long life/longevity and includes discussions around transhumanism/posthumanism[24] and also pertains to extinc-

---

23 See Kieran Setiya's incisive review of MacAskill's argument https://www.bostonreview.net/articles/the-new-moral-mathematics/

24 Posthumanism can imply simply a critique of classical humanism and the Enlightenment's emphasis on humanity as the maker of history, but it also has a different and stronger implication of a

tion studies, including the prospect of the extinction of humanity, a topic that the Covid pandemic has opened up (Lynteris 2020). Relevant in this context is the 'future of humanity' literature, as in Ord's *The Precipice*, Martin Rees's books, *Our Final Century* and *On the Future of Humanity* (Rees 2003, 2018), and other contributions by astrophysicists exploring space travel and life beyond the planet earth, for example, Kaku (2018) and the relatively new science of astrobiology, a development of exobiology.[25] The question here is of how distant into the future it is really sensible to go; for example, what will humanity look like at the point of the end of the sun in about 5 to 6 billion years? As Martin Rees succinctly puts it: 'Any creatures witnessing the Sun's demise won't be human – they'll be as different from us as we are from a bug' (Rees 2018: 178).

Other conceptions of the future relate in different ways more specifically to ecological politics. The notion of sustainable development is one such response to the future. This is based on the pursuit of new ends, for example, the notion of a 'green economy' or low carbon futures, and has become one of the main policies for most states and international organizations. One can locate this in this wider context of the notion of risk, as a way of relating to the future. However, the notion of 'a risk society' has been mostly absorbed into the pursuit of policies of sustainability, which has become a more all-embracing term. There are of course different and conflicting conceptions of sustainability (Adloff and Neckel 2019). The notion of sustainability implies a very limited embracing of the future, since it seeks the continuation of the present and thus the sustainability of what has become unsustainable. Yet, it is difficult to see how a politics of the future could not entail at least some degree of policies of sustainable development, which are best seen as restrictions of uncontrolled growth and the need for non–fossil fuel energy.

More radical conceptions of the future are also in evidence in contemporary writing on the future that seek to reveal a shift from the dominant imaginary of *homo economicus* to a second or counter imaginary, *homo ecologicus*, as, for example, in de Bruyn and Lütticken's *Futurity Report* (2020). Across a range of writing on contemporary culture, from artificial intelligence, Afrofuturism,[26] and cultural politics, the future has been reinserted into the analysis of our time to reveal different expressions of the creative imagination in, for example, reinventing utopia.

---

more intensified form of transhumanism, by which is meant the transformation of humanity by technology. In this case, posthumanism amounts to symbiosis of humans and technology.

25 https://www.nationalgeographic.com/astrobiology/

26 Coined in 1993, Afrofuturism is both a philosophy and an aesthetic which combines sci-fi and future imaginations to challenge notions of 'Afro-pessimism.' https://www.architecturaldigest.com/story/what-is-afrofuturism

It is a key idea in the cultural analysis of science fiction (Jameson 2008). Works such as Octavia Butler's 1993 prescient novel on a dystopic United States, *Parable of the Sower* and its sequel *Parable of the Talents*, or the recent *Ministry of the Future*, can exert an important critical function (Butler 2014a and 2014b; Robinson 2021).

The new critical literature makes much of the notion of the imaginary and narratives (see Bazzani 2022). This can be the basis of productive research on contemporary culture – as well as on capitalism as Jens Beckert (2016) has demonstrated – but is limited in that neither the notion of imaginary nor the narratives it leads to can on their own create new realities. However, they can influence their formation and, as Beckert shows very well, in the form of forecasts, scenario models, etc., imaginaries create fictions which are ways in which uncertainty is managed.[27] To be sure, in a sense, this is a kind of reality creation, but in a more general perspective it is difficult to see how fictions on their own will solve all problems. An image of a future is not in itself enough to bring it about. For this reason, in Chapter 6, I argue for a need to go beyond this kind of sociological theory, valuable as it is, and incorporate perspectives in critical theory.

This is just a sketch of some major themes and debates on the idea of the future which are not just academic topics but also themes in the public sphere. In this short critical review, I have not considered the main philosophical and sociological theories of the future, a wide and somewhat disparate literature that has not yet been brought together. This is the purpose of the following chapters. The aim of this book is to advance the debate on the future by bringing a more comprehensive sociological and philosophical contribution to its theorization (see especially Chapters Four, Five, and Six). This will also entail engaging with the philosophy of time including contributions from physics, which I do in Chapter Two.

Return to the Future

The book begins with the recognition that notwithstanding the general drift toward the 'death of the future' and the previously mentioned new visions, there is an emerging concern about the future today. These visions are an expression of such concerns, but in themselves they are inadequate when it comes to understanding the ways in which the future is disclosed. I argue that in the present day, despite the apparent closure of the open horizon of the future, we are in fact experiencing a shift away from the sense of the death of the future. Pessimism about

---

27 See also Esposito for a related but different approach to finance (Esposito 2011).

the future – with a shift from utopia to catastrophe and the end times – was an outcome of more critical assessments of the structural conditions of contemporary society and the capacity of the institutions of modernity to create the conditions for a better world. Yet, the idea of the future persisted in a variety of counterhegemonic projects, which created new desires and hopes. These include cosmopolitics and climate politics, but much else.

My argument is that in our time the present is being redefined by the future: contemporary societies are beginning to see themselves through the lens of the future. This is in stark contrast to the dominant twentieth-century tendency for the future to be defined by the present and the outcome of present trends that can be largely foreseen. Rather than controlling or predicting the future, we have lost control in the permacrisis of the present. Consequently, notions such as autonomy and democracy are in crisis (see Zielonka 2023). Depending on how the experience of permacrisis unfolds, new expectations can arise, along with the disclosure of possible futures. It is these that need further investigation.

So, the future is being both lost and rediscovered today, but in ways that are very different from the modernist belief that it can be mastered by the present. It is unlikely that control can be reestablished in the ways that were once considered orthodox. However, it is plausibly the case that other ways of relating to the future are taking shape. There is the possibility, for instance, in a not-too-distant future, that death will be considerably postponed, and as a result of removing or reducing the centrality of death to the human condition though supralongevity. However, whatever changes may occur in the nature of death, birth first needs to occur. Shana Swan has raised the specter of a future in which there are no births due to the end of human fertility (Swan 2022).

The crisis of contemporary societies – climate, water, capitalism, energy, democracy, security – is now so great that it is possible to venture the claim that our societies are being defined by the orientation to the future and not by the past as such. The future has now become a problem for the present because the received ideas of the future no longer fit into the space of human experience, which has been widened to encompass responses to a range of major crises that constitute an overall permacrisis. This amounts to a possible ontological shift in the nature of the social world and in the nature of historical time which can be characterized as a shift in emphasis from the older dominance of the present to one in which the present is being reframed by the future. The key insight that underlies the book is that this has led to a different orientation to the future. It is no longer a case of the space of experience opening up expectations of a better future (to paraphrase Koselleck) that could then be pursued to improve the present; instead new experiences are leading to the realization that expectations cannot be realized by the present.

The significance of the idea of the future today is not in the facts of the future or what will happen in the future – but in the form of knowing it, a form that is also something experienced. This rationale recalls Henri Bergson's theory of the future as *becoming* when he wrote in *Time and Free Will* in 1889: 'The idea of the future, pregnant with an infinity of possibilities, is thus more fruitful than the future itself, and this is why we find more charm in hope than in possession, in dreams than in reality.'[28] Bergson is without a doubt one of the most important philosophers of time. I consider some aspects of his work in Chapter Two. Put differently, the question is less about what the future is or what will happen in the future than how we know it and in what ways the future can be known. To know something is, in part at least, to take responsibility for it. We cannot be responsible for the things that we do not know. So the future is something we have responsibility for, to the extent of our knowledge of the world. Since we also have responsibility for the injustices and mistakes of the past, that too requires a future-oriented consciousness (to be discussed in Chapter Six). Perhaps that is the significance of Walter Benjamin's famous interpretation of Paul Klee's painting of 1920, *Angelus Novus*, an angel who is moving toward the future but with its face turned backward (Benjamin 1970).

The challenge is to understand the new opening into the future, which is now becoming a way of experiencing the world. The critical task is to investigate the ways in which the future is used to understand the present: rather than the present controlling the future, the shadow of the future is now shaping the present. The Austrian poet Rainer Maria Rilke had some sense of this idea of the future when he wrote in a letter in 1904 in a much-cited sentence: 'The future enters into us, in order to transform us, long before it happens.'[29]

While we cannot go back to the older projects to control the future, we can recover a sense of responsibility for the future. There is also the question of what legacies we want to leave for the future, including the very deep future. What kind of future fossils will we leave behind? (Farrier 2020). Unlike earlier civilizations, the ruins and traces of our present will, as a result of the Anthropocene, leave an indelible mark on the earth. There will be more than footprints left, such as those that have been left on the moon following the Apollo missions of the early 1970s, but long-life plastic engraved into the rock surface of the earth, carbon and other toxic substances released by our civilization, and waste of all kinds. The future not only then is important as a project of survival but also relates to the work of future memory and the question of the meaning of heritage in the context of the

---

28 Bergson (1910, Chapter One, P.10).
29 His 8th letter, 1904. https://rilkepoetry.com/letters-to-a-young-poet/letter-eight/

Anthropocene, which suggests that it is also related to nature and not only the ruins left behind by humans (see Cameron and Neilson 2014, Harrison *et al.* 2020, Harrison and Sterling 2020). The question that this raises is less about the preservation of the ruins of the past than what we want to pass on to future people. Heritage, normally backward looking, is also necessarily a form of future making in linking past, present, and future. A future-oriented heritage would be very different from the traditional understanding of heritage as the preservation and conservation of the ruins and relics of the past.[30]

The argument I am advancing in this book is that the main conceptions of the future, such as those mentioned above and others to be discussed in the course of the book, do not provide sufficient direction. There is not yet a fully developed theory of the future in the human and social sciences. What an adequate theory of the future is far from clear, especially as it has various inflections. It must at least be able to offer a different reading of the current situation than, for example, the apparent dominance of the end times or presentist positions. The parsimonious simplicity of longtermism is a false if seductive solution. There are promising new developments in sociology and in related fields that emphasize possibility, the imagination, anticipation, and expectation as modalities that have a constitutive role in shaping the future. These developments, some of which are influenced by the social phenomenological tradition and pragmatist philosophy, offer fertile ground to advance a social theory of the future. I argue that these approaches need to be complemented by a stronger emphasis on learning mechanisms (as in the work Habermas). Future possibilities do not simply just happen or emerge from the legacies of the past but are products of learning by individuals and collectively by society. People do not just orient themselves to the future on the basis of past experiences, drawing from history, but also draw from the potentials of the present and imagined futures as well as reference systems that transcend mere experience and self-understanding. The historical process has been marked by moments when certain characteristics, beliefs, and forms of social organization were selected and stabilized through institutionalization, cultural worldviews, and epistemic and cognitive structures (Strydom 2023). These are also the essential building blocks of the future. The future is also a capacity inherent in the human condition itself; as Seligman *et al.* show (2016), it is a unique feature of humans to be able to imagine alternatives stretching into the future, a capacity they term 'prospection.' In that sense, the future is internal to humans, which means that it is in part hidden; as Wittgenstein remarked toward the end of *Philosophical Investigations,*

---

30 I refer here to important new work in the field of critical heritage studies, especially the work of Rodney Harrison, cited above.

'"What is *internal* is hidden from us." The Future is hidden from us. But does the astronomer think like that when he calculates an eclipse of the sun?' (1963 [1953]: 223). That which is hidden can be disclosed, but for this to be possible we need the right kind of concepts. It is true that the notion of the human condition is something of a construction. The term arose following Andre Malraux's novel *La Condition humaine* in 1933, which provided the inspiration for Hannah Arendt's book, *The Human Condition* in 1958.[31] In invoking the notion, I am not attributing to it an unchanging essence while recognizing that there are abiding constants in human nature that make possible a sense of the future. These constants and other universals confer upon human existence and nature itself a degree of necessity, which does not mean absolute determinism since change and contingency is also at work.

In Chapter Six I make the case for a conception of the future that draws from the critical theory tradition. I argue that the future is not to be viewed only as simply the outcome of external shocks, such as catastrophes, but it is also shaped by historical legacies and by the human condition itself, which is inherently future oriented. That does not mean that it is entirely open, such that anything can happen, for it is also structured and limited by reason, evolutionary outcomes, and temporal modalities of various kinds of possibility. There are five main ways in which the future is disclosed. In brief, the key ideas are the following.

First, the future is something existential; it is at first an emotional relationship and manifests on the level of the individual psyche. It can take, for example, the form of chronophobia, fear of the future, which is an anxiety disorder about the passing of time,[32] or as discussed earlier grief following traumatic climatic change. The future is an expression of human experience and can express itself in the form of hope and desire as well as fear and foreboding. People project their fears on to the future, as Marc Augé (2014) wrote, but they also seek in it redemption.

Second, the future is disclosed in the form of imaginaries of desirable futures, a projection emanating from the creative imagination of an ideal to be pursued. In this case, it is closer to the language of expectation and anticipation. Such expressions of the future are expressed in various cultural models including the very idea of the future itself, which can be seen as a general cultural model. On their own, such cultural models do not create the future but provide the potential resources by generating ideals to be pursued though more specific goals.

---

31 Translated into English as *Man's Fate* in 1934, it exerted a strong influence on post-1945 social and political thought.
32 For an application beyond psychiatry to cultural analysis, see Lee (2006).

Third, the future is also shaped by universal normative principles and structures of consciousness, which are the basic ideas that provide direction for future thinking and action. These are products of historical evolution – for example, those that can be attributed to the Axial Age breakthrough – and transcend the present in the sense that they are irreducible to cultural systems. In the language of philosophy, they are abstract expressions of reason, i.e., reference systems and regulative principles – justice, peace, truth, responsibility for future generations, empathy, etc. – cognitive structures (as in modal forms of reasoning such as possibility, probability, potentiality) and include knowledge (science) that gives form and direction to social possibility. Such ideas also include the very idea of the future itself, for the future is in itself an idea that invites interpretation, that is to say the idea of the future is first of all *an idea* and as such it opens up a field of possible interpretations.

Fourth, the future is also disclosed in the domain of actuality, including the latent and unrealized potentials within the present. The future is not entirely a rupture from the present but is in part immanent in present social arrangements. For example, democratic orders, despite the limitations of the electoral cycle, are more likely to be able to create viable futures than authoritarian ones due to the large space they allow for political contestation. Thus, the future is related to the spatial relations of the present and is also a product of evolution.

Fifth, the future is an epistemic construct in that it is disclosed through knowledge, including scientific methods of forecasting, prediction, and modeling. Such forms of knowledge are not to be dismissed, for they can provide an essential basis for future knowledge. However, we still need a normative idea of the future, that is, a view of the future based on a moral view of what kind of society we want to have and what kind of future for which we can hope.

All these dimensions of the future are furthermore mediated by social struggles going on in the present. The future thus does not just happen on its own or is simply the product of an external shock such as a catastrophe; it is not a case of just moving forward in time. It is in many ways a cognitive problem of how it is constructed and interpreted by the present. The temporal dimension of the future is bound up with normative, cognitive, and epistemic structures. For these reasons, the future is also not only a product of the space of experience or an imaginary. This is because the key aspect of the future is possibility, which necessarily requires an account of other dynamics and processes, such as evolution and learning.

This book is both a work of reconstruction and critique grounded in a historical and philosophical hermeneutics of the future. In the following chapters my aim is to reconstruct the main conceptions of the future in modern thought and provide a critical reading of some of the main contemporaries theories of the future.

Outline of the Chapters

The next chapter establishes the groundwork for a theory of the future by looking at the main conceptions of time in the physical world, in particular in physics, for it is here that we find the most advanced and important theories of the arrows of time. The chapter then deals with the transformation in time that has come from developments in the Earth Sciences with the notion of the Anthropocene. The chapter finally engages with debates in the theory of evolution around the future of humanity, for evolution does not just stop in the present but is open ended. While cautious of a strict application of notions of time in the natural sciences, I seek to reconstruct their significance for the idea of the future in society today.

Chapter Three is about history and the future; it deals with the problem of whether learning from past errors is enough to face the challenges of the present. I argue that the kind of problems human societies faced in the past are today in the context of the Anthropocene, with climate change endangering the viability of society and increased societal complexity, and vastly different in scale and severity from the problems that previous societies had to deal with. So learning from the past may not be entirely reliable as a guide for the future. It may also be the case that we have misunderstood the errors of the past, as in the assumption that the civilizations and societies of the premodern world perished because they lacked the knowledge that allegedly gave modernity the means to determine the future in its own image or the controversial view, also to be discussed later in this chapter, that they often got wrong the balance with the natural environment and as a result perished. The chapter offers a critical assessment of conceptions of the future in premodern societies, theories of civilizational collapse, and theories of catastrophe in history.

Chapter Four looks at how the idea of the future appeared in modern thought. As a point of departure, I take Hans Blumenberg's thesis that the modern age opened up a space for the idea of the future in the development of a time consciousness that considerably expanded the scope of human experience. This idea was developed by another major German intellectual historian, Reinhart Koselleck, who argued in a classic essay in 1967 that the modern idea of the future effectively goes back to Kant. This is followed by a discussion of another aspect of the idea of the future for which the notion of expectation does not fully grasp, namely as an imaginary, and is expressed in utopian thought as well as in Marx's sense of the future as a product of political struggle. The third section of the chapter considers the notion of the future in terms of possibility, as associated with the American pragmatist tradition (C. S. Peirce, William James, and George Herbert Mead). The final section looks at the idea of the future that emerged from the phenomenological tradition in modern philosophy as represented by Martin Heidegger, who gave an important new direction to the idea of the future as a category of experience that was formative of the human condition.

In Chapter Five I shift the focus to the idea of the future in social and political science from the middle of the twentieth century, looking in particular at sociological approaches to the future. First, I discuss two influential and very different conceptions of the future in political theory, namely F. A. Hayek and Bertrand de Jouvenel. Second, I discuss the rise of futurology in the post-1945 period, but with its origins from the end of the nineteenth century, as in the writings of H. G. Wells. Third, I look at the developments in sociological theory that were explicitly focused on new thinking about the future, especially the work of sociologist Daniel Bell and Niklas Luhmann, who wrote important work on the idea of the future and with some mention of the economist E. F. Schumacher. I also discuss later figures, such as the sociologists Ulrick Beck, John Urry, and other theorists of globalization who advanced new ideas about the future in terms of risk and complexity. Finally, I look at a specific and relatively recent strand within sociological theory that built on the phenomenological tradition, as revived by Alfred Schutz, to produce important theories of the future.

Chapter Six offers a reconstruction of the theory of the future in the critical theory tradition from its sources in Kant, Hegel, and Marx, and the early Frankfurt School (Adorno but also Benjamin and Marcuse), Ernst Bloch to the later theories of Habermas and K.-O. Apel and Honneth. The work of Hans Jonas is also considered in the context of the idea of responsibility for the future. I argue that the phenomenological approaches in sociological theory, while important, are insufficient and need to be complemented with perspectives from the critical tradition and critical theory more generally in order to account for the fundamental reality of transcendence. The key concept is the notion of possibility: present potentialities open up future possibilities. The chapter goes on to discuss the relevance of critical cosmopolitanism for the idea of the future.

In the concluding chapter, I address a number of questions that have been raised but not fully answered in the preceding chapters. These concern substantive topics that, while falling beyond the scope of a book on the conceptual aspects of the future, nonetheless need to be addressed at least in a rudimentary outline. The first is do we actually really need a theory of the future? Second, are we already in a new era? Third, is AI leading to a posthuman future, especially in light of the possible emergence of AGI? Finally, how should we see struggles for the future today?

References

Adam, B. 1990. *Time and Social Theory*. Cambridge: Polity Press.

Anderson, B. 2010. 'Preemption, Precaution, Preparedness: Anticipatory Action and Future Geographies.' *Progress in Human Geography*, 34 (6): 777–97.

Andersson, J. 2018. *The Future of the World: Futurology, Futurists and the Struggle for the Post-Cold War Imagination*. Oxford: Oxford University Press.

Andersson, J. and Kemp, S. (eds). 2021. *Futures*. Oxford: Oxford University Press.

Adloff, F. and Neckel, S. 2019. 'Futures of Sustainability as Modernization, Transformation, and Control: A Conceptual Framework.' *Sustainability Science*, 14: 1015–25.

Amoore, L. 2013. *The Politics of Possibility: Risk and Security beyond Probability*. Durham, NC: Duke University Press.

Aradeu, C. and van Munster, R. 2011. *Politics of Catastrophe: Genealogy of the Unknown*. London: Routledge.

Arendt, H. 1958. *The Human Condition*. Chicago: University of Chicago Press.

Augé, M. 2014. [2012] *The Future*. London: Verso.

Badiou, A. 2007. [2005] *Century*. Cambridge: Polity Press.

Bauman, Z. 2017. *Retrotopia*. Cambridge: Polity Press.

Bazzani, G. 2022. 'Futures in Action: Expectations, Imaginaries and Narratives of the Future.' *Sociology*, 57 (2): 382–97.

Beck, U. 1992. [1986] *The Risk Society*. London: Sage.

Beckert, J. 2016. *Imagined Futures: Fictional Expectations and Capitalist Dynamics*. Cambridge, MASS.: Harvard University Press.

Berardi, F. 2011. *After the Future*. Edinburgh: AK Press.

Berardi, F. 2017. *Futurability: The Age of Impotence and the Horizon of the World*. London: Verso.

Bergson, H. 1910. [1889] *Time and Free Will: An Essay on the Immediate Data of Consciousness*. London: Allen and Unwin.

Bell, D. 1999. [1973] *The Coming of Post-Industrial Society: A Venture in Social Forecasting*. New York: Basic Books.

Benatar, D. 2008. *Better Never to Have Been Born: The Harm of Coming into Existence*. Oxford: Oxford University Press.

Bendell, J. 2018. 'Deep Adaptation: A Map for Navigating Climate Tragedy.' *IFLAS* Occasional Papers 2. http://insight.cumbria.ac.uk/id/eprint/4166/18/Bendell_Deep%20Adaptation%202020%20update.pdf

Bendell, J. 2020. 'To criticise Deep Adaptation, start here.' Published online at openDemocracy: https://www.opendemocracy.net/en/oureconomy/criticise-deep-adaptation-start-here/

Bendell, J. and Read, R. (eds) 2021. *Deep Adaptation: Navigating the Realities of Climate Chaos*. Cambridge: Polity Press.

Benjamin, W. 1970. 'Theses on the Philosophy of History.' In: *Illuminations*. London: Fontana.

Boyn, S. 2001. *The Future of Nostalgia*. New York: Basic Books.

Bostrom, N. and Cirkovic, M. (eds) 2008. *Global Catastrophic Risks*. Oxford: Oxford University Press.

Boulter, M. 2005. *Extinction: Evolution and the End of Man*. New York: Columbia University Press.

Buck-Morss, S. 2002. *Dreamworld and Catastrophe: The Passing of Mass Utopia in East and West*. Cambridge, MASS: MIT Press.

Brand, S. 1999. *The Clock of the Long-Now: Time and Responsibility*. New York: Basic Books.

de Bruyn, C. H. and Lütticken, S. 2020. *Futurity Report*. Berlin: Sternberg Press.

Butler, O. 2014a. [1993] *Parable of the Sower*. London: Headline Publishing.

Butler, O. 2014b. [1988] *Parable of the Talents*. London: Headline Publishing.

Cassegard, C. and Thorn, H. 2012. 'Toward a Postapocalyptic environmentalism? Responses to loss and vision of the future in climate activism.' *Environment and Planning E Nature and Space*, 1 (4): 561–78.

Cameron, F. and Neilson, B. (eds) 2014. *Climate Change and Museum Futures*. London: Routledge.

Carston, R. 1962. *Silent Spring*. New York: Houghton Mifflin Harcourt.

Claeys, G. 2020. *Utopia: The History of an Idea*. London: Thames and Hudson.

Claeys, G. 2022. *Utopianism for a Dying Planet*. Princeton: Princeton University Press.

Clifford, T. 2017. *Gravity: A Very Short Introduction*. Oxford: Oxford University Press.

Cooper, D. 2014. *Everyday Utopias: The Conceptual Life in Promising Spaces*. Durham, NC.: Duke University Press.

Cornell, D. 2005. 'Derrida: The Gift of the Future.' *Differences: A Journal of Feminist Cultural Studies*, 16 (3): 68–75.

Cunsolo, A. and Ellis, N. 2018. 'Ecological Grief as a Mental Health Response to Climate Change Related Loss.' *Nature, Climate Change*, 8: 275–81.

Dartwell, L. 2015. *The Knowledge: How to Rebuild our World after an Apocalypse*. London: Vintage.

Derrida, J. 1976. [1967] *Of Grammatology*. Baltimore: Johns Hopkins University Press.

Derrida, J. 1978. *Writing and Difference*. Chicago: University of Chicago Press.

Edmonds, D. 2023. *Parfit: A Philosopher and His Mission to Save Morality*. Princeton: Princeton University Press.

Elliott, A. 2022. *Making Sense of AI: Our Algorithmic World*. Cambridge: Polity Press.

Esposito, E. 2011. [2009] *The Future of Futures: The Time of Money in Finance and Society*. Cheltenham: Edward Elgar.

Farrier, D. 2020. *Footprints: In Search of Future Fossils*. London: 4th Estate.

Featherstone, M. 2017. *Planet Utopia: Utopia, Dystopia and Globalization*. London: Routledge.

Foucault, M. 1994. [1966] *The Order of Things*. New York: Vintage Books.

Fritzsche, P. 2004. *Stranded in the Present: Modern Time and the Melancholy of History*. Cambridge, MASS.: Harvard University Press.

Harvey, D. 2000. *Spaces of Hope*. Edinburgh: Edinburgh University Press.

Gaston, S. 2011. 'Derrida and the End of the World.' *New Literary History*, 42 (3): 499–517.

Gordon, M. Tilley, H. and Prakash, G. (eds) 2011. *Utopia/Dystopia: Conditions of Historical Possibility*. Princeton: Princeton University Press.

Graeber, D. and Wengrow, D. 2021. *The Dawn of Everything: A New History of Humanity*. London: Penguin.

Hamilton, C. 2013. *Earthmasters: The Dawn of the Age of Climate Engineering*. New Haven: Yale University Press.

Harrison, R. *et al.* (eds) 2020. *Heritage Futures: Comparative Natural and Cultural Heritage*. London: UCL Press.

Harrison, R. and Sterling, C. (eds) 2020. *Deterritorializing the Future: Heritage In, Of and After the Anthropocene*. London: Routledge.

Hartog, F. 2015. [2003] *Regimes of Historicity: Presentism and Experiences of Time*. New York: Columbia University Press.

Horn, E. 2018. [2014] *The Future as Catastrophe: Imagining Disaster in the Modern Age*. Cambridge: Cambridge University Press.

Innerarity, D. 2012. [2009] *The Future and its Enemies*. Stanford: Stanford University Press.

Jameson, F. 2007. *Archaeologies of the Future: The Desire Called Utopia and Other Science Fiction.* London: Verso.

Jamin, R. 1984. 'Michel Foucault: A Last Interview of with French Philosopher Michel Foucault'. https://monoskop.org/images/5/54/Raskin_Jamin_1984_A_Last_Interview_with_French_Philoso pher_Michel_Foucault.pdf

Jeanpierre, L. and Guégen, H. 2022. *La perspective du possible: Comment penser ce qui peut arriver, et ce que nous pouvons faire.* Paris: Découverte.

Jones, R. 2017. *Slow Catastrophes: Living with Drought in Australia.* Clayton, Viv: Monash University Publishing.

Jonas, H. 1984. [1979] *The Imperative of Responsibility: In Search of an Ethics for the Technological Age.* Chicago: Chicago University Press.

de Jouvenel, B. 2017. [1964/1967] *The Art of Conjecture.* London: New York.

Kaku, M. 2018. *The Future of Humanity.* London: Penguin.

Kaplan, E. A. 2016. *Climate Trauma: foreseeing the Future in Dystopian Film and Fiction.* New Brunswick, NJ: Rutgers University Press.

Knowles, S. G. 2020. 'Slow Disaster in the Anthropocene: A Historian Witnessing Climate Change in the Korean Peninsula.' *Daedalus,* 149 (4): 192–206.

Koselleck, R. 2004. [1967] '"Spaces of Experience" and "Horizon of Expectation": Two Historical Concepts.' In: *Futures Past: On the Semantics of Historical Time.* New York: Columbia University Press.

Kundera, M. 1983/1980. [1979] *The Book of Laughter and Forgetting.* London: Penguin.

Kurzweil, R. 2005. *The Singularity is Near: When Humans Transcend Biology.* London: Penguin.

Lee, P. M. 2006. *Chronophobia: On Time in the Art of the 1960s.* Cambridge, MASS.: MIT Press.

Leslie, J. 1998. *The End of the World.* London: Routledge.

Levitas, R. 2013. *Utopia as Method: The Imaginary Reconstitution of Society.* London: Palgrave.

Lilley, S., McNally, D., Yuen, E., and Davis, J. 2012. (eds) *Catastrophism: The Apocalyptical Politics of Collapse and Rebirth.* Oakland, CA.:PM Press.

Lynch, P. 2023. *Prophet Song.* London: OneWorld Publications.

Lynteris, C. 2020. *Human Extinction and the Pandemic Imaginary.* London: Routledge.

MacAskill, W. 2022. *What We Owe to the Future: A Million Year View.* OneWorld.

MacCormack, P. 2020. *The Ahuman Manifesto: Activism for the End of the World.* London: Bloomsbury.

Manjikian, M. 2012. *Apocalypse and Post-Politics: The Romance of the End.* Lahnhan, MD.: Lexington Books.

McCray, W. P. 2012. *The Visioneers: How a Group of Elite Scientists Pursued Space Colonies, Nanotechnology, and a Limitless Future.* Princeton: Princeton University Press.

Marcuse, H. 1970. 'The End of Utopia'. In: *Five Lectures: Psychoanalysis, Politics and Utopia.* Boston: Beacon Press.

Martinon, J.-P. 2007. *On Futurity: Malabou, Nancy and Derrida.* London: Palgrave.

Meadows, D., Meadows, D., Randers, W., and Behrends III, W. 1972. *The Limits to Growth: A Report for the Club of Rome's Project on the Predicament of Mankind.* New York: Universe Books.

Monticelli, L. (ed.). 2023. *The Future is Now: An Introduction to Prefigurative Politics.* Bristol: Bristol University Press.

Moynihan, T. 2020. *X-Risk: How Humanity Discovered its Own Extinction.* Cambridge, Mass.: MIT Press.

Munoz-Gonzalez, E. 2022. *Posthumanity in the Anthropocene: Margaret Atwood's Dystopia.* London: Routledge.

Nilges, M. 2019. *Right-Wing Culture in Contemporary Capitalism: Regression and Hope in a Time Without Future.* London: Bloomsbury.

Nowotny, H. 1994. [1989] *Time: The Modern and Postmodern Experience.* Cambridge: Polity Press.

Oomen, J. 2021. *Imagining Climate Engineering: Dreaming of the Designer Climate.* London: Routledge.

Opitz, S. and Tellmann, U. 2017. 'Future Emergence: Temporal Politics in Law and Economy.' *Theory, Economy and Society,* 32 (2): 107–29.

Ord, T. 2020. *The Precipice: Existential Risk and the Future of Humanity.* New York: Hachette.

Parfit, D. 1984. *Reasons and Persons.* Oxford: Oxford University Press.

Rees, M. 2003. *Our Final Century: Will Civilization Survive the Twenty-First Century?* London: Arrow Books.

Rees, M. 2018. *On the Future of Humanity.* Princeton: Princeton University Press.

Robinson, K. S. 2021. *Ministry of the Future.* London: Orbit.

Roser, M. 2022. 'The future is vast – what does this mean for our own life?' Published online at OurWorldInData.org' Retrieved from: https://ourworldindata.org/the-future-is-vast

Schumacher, E. F. 1973. *Small is Beautiful: Economics as if People Mattered.* London: Blond and Briggs.

Seligman, M., Railton, P., Baumeister, R. and Sripada, C. 2016. *Homo Prospectus.* Oxford: Oxford University Press.

Servigne, P. and Stevens, R. 2020. *How Everything Can Collapse.* Cambridge: Polity Press.

Shklar, J. 1957. *After Utopia: The Decline of Political Faith.* Princeton: Princeton University Press.

Simmons, L. 2016. 'Reasoning the Disaster.' *Filozofski vestnik,* 37 (2): 213–34.

Simon, Z. B. 2018. 'History begins in the Future: On the Historical Sensibility in the Age of Technology.' In: Helgesson, S. and Svenungsson, J. (eds) *The Ethos of History: Time and Responsibility.* Oxford: Berghahn.

Simon, Z. B. and Tamm., 2021. 'Historical Futures.' *History and Theory,* 60 (1): 3–22.

Solomon, S. 2016. *Future Humans: Inside the Science of our Continuous Evolution.* New Haven: Yale University Press.

Stainforth, D. 2023. *Predicting our Climate Future.* Oxford: Oxford University Press.

Stegers, I. 2015. *In Catastrophic Times: Resisting the Coming Barbarism.* London: Open Humanities Press.

Strydom, P. 2023. 'The Critical Theory of Society: From its Young Hegelian Core to the Key Concept of Possibility.' *European Journal of Social Theory,* 26 (2): 153–79.

Swan, S. 2022. *Count Down: How Our Modern World is Threatening Sperm Counts, Altering Male and Female Reproductive Development and Imperiling the Future of the Human Race.* New York: Scribner.

Thaler, M. 2022. *No Other Planet: Utopian Visions for a Climate-Changed World.* Cambridge: Cambridge University Press.

Toffler, A. 1970. *Future Shock.* New York: Random House.

Turchin, P. 2023. *End Times: Elites, Counter-Elites and the Path of Political Disintegration.* London: Allen Lane.

Turner, B. S. 2023. *A Theory of Catastrophe.* Berlin: De Gruyter.

Traverso, E. 2016. *Left-Wing Melancholia: Marxism, History, and Memory.* New York: Columbia University Press.

Trebeznik, L. 2019. 'Being on the Brink of the Future: Jacques Derrida and Poetics of Waiting.' *Theological Quarterly,* 79 (2): 347–56.

Wellmer, A. 1993. [1988] *Endgames: The Irreconcilable Nature of Modernity: Essays and Lectures.* Cambridge, MASS.: MIT Press.

Wenger, A., Jasper, U., and Dunn Cavelty, M. (eds) 2020. *The Politics and Science of Prevision.* London: Routledge.

White, J. 2024a. *In the Long-Run: The Future as a Political Idea.* London: Profile.

White, J. 2024b. 'Technological Myopia: On the Pitfalls of Depoliticizing the Future.' *European Journal of Social Theory,* 27 (2).

Wittgenstein, L. 1963. [1953] *Philosophical Investigations.* Oxford: Basil Blackwell.

Wood, D. 2006. 'On Being Haunted by the Future.' *Research in Phenomenology,* 36: 274 – 98.

Wright, E. O. 2010. *Envisioning Real Utopias.* London: Verso.

Worley, M. 2017. *No Future: Punk Politics and British Youth Culture, 1976 – 1984.* Cambridge: Cambridge University Press.

Zielonka, J. 2023. *The Lost Future: And How to Claim it Back.* New Haven: Yale University Press.

Zizek, S. 2011. *Living at the End of Times.* London: Verso.

Chapter Two
When is the Future? The Problem of Time and the Human Condition

The future is primarily a temporal concept. A big emphasis is placed in this book on other dimensions to the future than the strictly temporal one, but an adequate theory of the future must begin with the category of time. Time pervades all things and life itself is inseparable from time, which along with space is the most fundamental aspect of reality. Yet, it is difficult to say exactly what is time. The elusiveness of time is reflected in grasping the future. When does the future begin? Human perception of time requires the categories of the past, the present, and the future. These are fundamental to human experience of the world and of life itself. That one is born, lives, and dies is the reality of existence and the future is simply a point beyond the present as 'the now.' This suggests that time is a way we experience the world, but it is also more than a mode of experience. The remorseless passage of time, as in the life of a living being from birth to death, is an aspect of the physical reality of the world and so would appear to have an objective dimension: we can't delude ourselves that we are not going to die.

Human life in both its biological forms and its social organization has been shaped in accordance with the cycle of day and night, which in turn is determined by the earth's rotation and orbit. The resulting structure of the calendar and clock time has given human societies a reasonably objective structure for the organization of time, which has of course been shaped by many other forces, including those that emerged in the course of human history. Capitalism itself is based on time, as in the notion that time is money.[1] Norbert Elias, in an important work on the social construction of time, wrote that the experience of time 'is based on people's capacity for connecting with each other two or more different sequences of continuous changes, one of which serves as a timing standard for the other (or others)'.[2] He showed that social time is a symbolic reworking of processes in the physical world. In the next chapters, I look in more detail at sociological and philosophical theories of time. This chapter is focused more on the philosophy of time in the natural sciences.

Philosophers and scientists concerned with the problem of time have grappled with the subjective and objective view of time: time as we experience the world

---

1 According to Marx, wage labor is in the final analysis based on buying time from the worker.
2 Elias (1992: 72; see also 78–91). For a very good interpretation of Elias, see Tabbonis (2001).

https://doi.org/10.1515/9783111240602-003

and the objective reality of nature or the physical world in all its dimensions. I will argue in this chapter that this distinction must be questioned in so far as it represents an absolute dichotomy, but it is probably necessary as an analytical distinction in order to make sense of two different perspectives, the human one and the physical or natural one. It is possible that much of our sense of time is a product of our cognitive makeup and does not fully correspond to the physical order of the natural world of which we are a part. This will be discussed in more detail in the next section. To begin, let us note that the category of time is rooted in human experience without being entirely subjective. It is central to human consciousness. Kant regarded it, along with space, as part of the structure of human sensibility. According to the French philosopher, Henri Bergson, in one of the most important philosophies of time, there is a distinction between objective clock time, *temps*, and time as duration, *la durée*. The latter is a category of consciousness and is a product of human experience. As such, it is not fixed, it can be changed; it is a category of becoming, and can take variable forms. While constrained by clock time, as that attempts to mirror the physical structure of the world in the social order of time, time as duration is very much lived time, something that is experienced in the here and now. It also extends into the future as an open field of possibilities because the human mind is not constrained, even if limited, by clock time.[3] The future is thus to be understood as a process of becoming; it is being continuously made in the present. For Bergson, time is real; it is not an illusion of consciousness and has effects, for it is part of the process of change but also makes possible continuity. In his early work, *Time and Free Will* [1889], he tried to show that because time is open, there is no determinism, thus making possible free will (Bergson 1910). The future cannot be known, for if it could be it would be determined and this is incompatible with the nature of time. According to Barry Allen, 'Bergson is without doubt the most profound thinker about time since antiquity'; he demonstrated that time is always an interval, not something instantaneous, and it is effective in bringing about change (2023: 61).

This basic insight is important to relating the concept of time to the nature of life and consciousness of life. Heidegger in *Being and Time* in 1927 related time to human existence and, as with Bergson and others in the phenomenological tradition, he saw time as 'lived time' *Erlebnis* (Heidegger will be discussed in more detail in Chapter Four). So, time is essentially a way in which the world is experienced and it is what makes it possible to create new realities. However, we do not normally experience time directly, unless we look at the clock and see the time passing or in the way people in earlier times noticed the night sky changing.

---

3 See Jancsary (2019).

But this is only an illusion, as clock time is also an artifact of social institutions. Perhaps the most important institution is the International Bureau of Weights and Measures in Paris. Established in 1875 it is responsible for an international system of time measurement as well as other metrological standards. It ensures through a system based on atomic clocks that all clocks keep to the same temporal standards, known as Coordinated Universal Time. The structure of time in the physical universe and the human experience of time are mediated through various processes, of which five can be mentioned. The most important ways we experience time are through change, memory, action, space, and the mind.

Time is not normally directly experienced as such but is indirectly experienced through the experience of change itself. According to Aristotle in the *Physics*, time is essentially about change. More specifically, he saw time as the actualization of possibility, which is what makes the future possible. We experience the passage of time through a sense of things changing, including our own lives. This sense of time as movement can be the experience of transience, flow, and movement. Rather like the distinction between climate and weather, we experience the former through the latter. It is a position that necessarily requires that time is not just continuous but ruptured since nothing flows without rupture. It is also what opens up the possibility of the future as a condition of becoming that derives from the fact of movement. The Stoic philosopher and Roman Emperor, Marcus Aurelius, in his *Mediations*, written between AD 161 and 180, saw time as a river: 'Time is a sort of river of passing events, and strong is its current; no sooner is a thing brought to sight than it is swept by and another takes its place, and they too will be swept away' (Book IV: paragraph 43).

The sense of temporal continuity with the possibility of change in turn requires a capacity for memory. Without memory, there is no way for time to be experienced, as Paul Ricoeur has shown (Ricoeur 2000). The capacity for individuals and societies or cultures to recall is what makes possible the past. Without this cognitive capacity we would live in an eternal present. Memory is experience organized as a narrative, as in a biography or an autobiography; it is an ordering device based on selection and interpretation. It makes possible continuity as well as change. But it is not all about change, which makes sense only as a relation to continuity. Neither individuals nor collective actors see themselves as eternally in change without any continuity. One is the same person that one was when born and at other various points in one's life despite whatever biographical changes one makes in the course of one's life, but age bears the marks of time. The work of memory makes possible that balance between continuity and rupture and gives rise to the sense of permanence in a world of transience.

Time is not only past directed as in memory and a time consciousness but it is also bound up with action. A fundamental feature of action is intentionality: we are oriented to the future in that we are seeking to achieve a result in doing anything. This means that the future is bound up with the present and can be immediate. In this sense, the future is being continuously created in everything that is done. It is not therefore something that comes after the present but is the basis of the possibility of the present.

It follows from this reasoning that time is also spacialized. It is located in a present that exists in a spatial context. It is not simply a flow – as in the movement of water in a river as a metaphor of time – that occurs through its own temporal dynamics, but is a material reality and constitutive of social being. A river is not just the flow of water but is also a physical entity. The notion of space-time has been given increased importance in social theory and in physics in the twentieth century, with sociological notions such as space-time flows, virtual space, and space-time compression and in physics the four-dimensional concept of space-time. The link between space and time also points to a conception of time that suggests multiple temporalities. This idea is not just a product of theoretical physics but is also central to the geographical coordinating system of latitude and longitude for the measurement and communication of positions of direction on the earth.[4]

We are also temporally oriented by virtue of the nature of our mind in that humans are creatures endowed with intelligence and possess universal concepts – such as justice, freedom, truth, and the dignity of the person – enabling them to have the capacity for self-transcendence, a reaching out beyond the present, and for imagining alternative realities. This is what makes possible a sense of the future as a basic cognitive orientation (Strydom 2023).

All these dimensions of temporality make possible history and evolution, which are also temporal processes. In these processes, time does not just simply flow or unfold carrying the world and its contents with it, as a river flowing toward the sea carrying objects in its stream. The passage time is also a dynamic and transformative process in which space and existence are in constant creation. There is nothing deterministic or mechanical about this, as Darwin also held about evolution; evolution does not advance toward a goal; chance plays a role, as does human creativity and the desire to always reach beyond the present.

---

4 The earth rotates 360 degrees of longitude in 24 hours. For one degree changes in longitude, there is a corresponding change in time of four minutes.

Time in the Physical World: Lessons from Physics

The concept of time in the human and social sciences cannot be entirely separated from the idea of natural time in the natural sciences, in particular in physics. Social time and natural time are indeed very different orders of temporality and many other processes are bound up with them. However, they are connected in important ways and it is helpful to begin with some discussion on the concept of time in the natural sciences.

It was in the natural sciences that the first attempts were made to understand the nature of time, first with Parmenides and Heraclitus and then Aristotle. The major developments since Isaac Newton to Albert Einstein fundamentally altered our understanding of time, as did in a different way the theory of evolution since Charles Darwin (to be discussed separately later in this chapter). It is clear that in the twentieth century, developments in theoretical physics have undermined the nineteenth-century positivistic assumptions of the social sciences, which sought to emulate a conception of nature that the natural science was about to discard, namely the view of the physical world as fixed, immutable, and objective. This conception of nature was not only wrong but it was also wrong for the social sciences as a model for society. When the interpretative social sciences, since Max Weber discarded the positivist approach for sociological analysis, they wrongly assumed that the natural science retained many of the assumptions of Newtonian science, especially relating to the nature of reality. The social and human sciences have since caught up with the theory of time, but they did so only after the revolution in the natural sciences in the early twentieth century, as was also the case with the theory of evolution, which had a long-lasting impact on the social sciences where it was often misunderstood or misappropriated.

One of the most important lessons of modern physics is that time is not a physical phenomenon. That does not mean it does not exist but that it does not take the form often attributed to it and does not necessarily correspond to the way it is experienced by human beings. The philosophy of time has been divided between the view normally attributed to Parmenides that the natural world is unchanging and the view associated with Heraclitus that everything is in flux, and all is change. Aristotle held to a view, as noted, closer to Heraclitus that time is based on motion[5] but retained a notion of permanence in that for something to change there must be a phenomenon that undergoes change. The perspective of Parmenides was not necessarily entirely the contrary in that he saw the natural world to be less variable

---

5 More specifically, time is the measurement of motion, which equally changes and takes a numerical form.

than what our view of things suggests whereby things perish when they die. The experience of human life is that it is short and the passage from birth to death therefore does not capture the true nature of the physical universe where past and present give the illusion of things being in constant change while we inhabit a defined present from which we view the passage of time. It is clear, for instance, that the basic elements of life – the amino acids that constitute the molecular structure of life – do not undergo much if any change, nor do the fundamental laws of the physical universe change, for example, the Periodic Table or the particle structure of atoms. The atoms out of which the molecular structure of life is composed were created after the origin of the universe and remain unchanged and will remain unchanged for the life of the universe: atoms do not age and cannot be created or destroyed. It is true that Isaac Newton complicated things with a claim later rejected by Einstein that there is an absolute dimension to time that lies outside the domain of human experience and is in contrast to relative time (as for example the solar day, which is variable). Newton held that there is a flow of time that moves at a constant speed and consequently time passes uniformly regardless of space. This so-called Newtonian concept of time was discarded by Einstein.

Albert Einstein followed Hermann Minkowski, his high school teacher in Zurich and an accomplished mathematician, with the famous notion of space-time which did away with Newtonian time, which had separated space and time. Einstein, who was intrigued by the phenomenon of movement and especially the speed of light, showed that everything in the universe is moving and therefore due to this fundamental fact there cannot be an absolute measurement of time. Contrary to Aristotle, he showed that there is no state of rest in which objects would be if they were not forced into motion. All is motion. It is impossible to say what is moving and what is stationary. Everything is moving and is moving in relation to everything else. The earth is moving around the sun, which is moving within the galaxy, which itself is moving in the universe, which is expanding. The old view of time presupposed a stationary location, a fixed point, from which movement could be measured. Time in this view was the duration of the movement from one point to another. But this is based on an illusion, as in the experience of seeing a train moving from a position within another train that is also moving. Galileo had already made the crucial step toward a theory of the relativity of movement with the insight that movement at a constant speed is indistinguishable from standing still (Wooton 2010: 63),

According to what later became known as the Special Theory of Relativity, based on a scientific article by Einstein in 1905, the passage of time is relative to an observer's given position in space, which is not a fixed one. Two events that appear to be simultaneous are so only in one frame of reference, but to an observer in another frame of reference they may not be simultaneous. It is not possible to say what body is in motion and which is at rest. It is only possible to say that they are moving relative to each other and they are also moving in relation to other bodies because everything is in a state of motion (since we live on a rotating and orbiting planet and in a cosmos that is in motion). So, according to the Special Theory of Relativity there is no unique measure of time that all observers can agree on. This is not just an effect of perspective, but if the observers were accompanied by atomic clocks they would record different time, assuming that the speed they were traveling was ultra-fast. The Special Theory of Relativity showed that objects or a closed system moving at a constant speed will experience a slowing down of time.

It is important to note that the theory of relativity does not state that everything is relative or subjective; it has nothing to do with relativism; it means only that measurements of time are relative to the speed of an observer. Einstein insisted on the universal validity of the laws of physics. By relativity, Einstein meant invariance, and originally intended to term his theory 'invariance theory' but followed Max Plank's lead and named it relativity theory (Isaacson 2007: 131–2). In other words, the physical laws of the cosmos are invariant rather than relative. For this reason, he also agreed with Max Planck that while the past and the future of the universe is the outcome of chance, necessity is also at work – as he put in a much cited sentence, 'God does not play dice with the universe.'

A conception of the physical world in which everything is in motion fundamentally changed the understanding of time, which henceforth had to be relative, in the specific sense Einstein stipulated. It is often said that Einstein discarded the notion of time as such. He was certainly aware, as a patent officer in Bern, that the perfect clock did not and could not exist (Galison 2003). No matter how accurate a clock is, it can never be entirely correct, since there is no objective order of time. It seemed that he had got rid of the notion of time, which was in part the outcome of the theory that time vanishes once the speed of light is reached. This is a misunderstanding in that what he showed was that our human perception of time does not capture the reality of time in the physical universe since it is based on the illusion of a fixed point (there are no fixed points) and a fixed present (which also does not exist). There is also no 'now,' no present, that is the reference point for determining the passage of time and his conception of space-time is also not in terms of a flow of time. The problem in essence is that there is no state of rest that can be the basis of a measurement of the movement of time. Yet, time does exist and it is related to motion without which there is no time, but it is not linked, as was the case with Newton, in a mechanical way changing only with respect to location. Paradoxically, motion or movement makes possible time but also eradicates it at the point when the speed of light is reached. Time is now seen to change its form and is affected by other forces, such as gravity, as the later General Theory of Relativity in 1915 demonstrated. It showed how space-time is shaped by the interconnection between gravity and time, with gravity (akin to 'weight' exerting a force on time). According to Lockwood: 'Nothing in the physics of special relativity actually forces us to abandon the common-sense picture, according to which there is an objective, albeit constantly shifting, boundary that separates the real, and wholly fixed, past from a currently unreal, and partly open, future' (Lockwood 2005: 57).

So, what Einstein did was to demonstrate the relativity of time in relation to space by showing the effects of the speed of light. A basic tenet of the Special Theory of Relativity, which built on the discoveries of Ole Roemer and James Clerk Maxwell, is that light, which has no intrinsic mass, has a constant speed and cannot be exceeded; nothing can exceed the speed of light. The fact that time cannot be defined by absolute criteria as it is relative to speed, does not mean that it does not exist. It is just that it does not exist in the way that we perceive it, which is just one way of understanding time. Einstein showed that time is not just relative to space, to location, but it is relative to motion. In that way he connected time and space. Time moves slower at higher speeds than lower ones. The faster the speed, the slower time will pass. The fastest speed possible, i. e. the speed of light, if approached would experience zero time, as time cannot travel faster than light, which travels at a constant of 300,000 km per second approximately. Additionally, time moves more quickly at higher altitudes than lower ones. This is because mass slows down time due to gravity, which is always higher where mass is greater. It follows from this principle of gravitational time dilation that at higher altitudes gravity is weaker and thus time, however much imperceptibly, passes faster. Thus, astronauts in the International Space Station will experience (theoretically at least, for the real time is imperceptible short) time passing more quickly than people on earth (due to less gravity a few hundred kilometers into space) and due to their increased velocity of 28,000 km per hour as they orbit the earth (which they do every 90 minutes approximately) they will experience time moving more slowing (the latter being a more powerful force means they will return after their six-month sojourn a fraction of second younger). So, time is slowed down by gravity and by speed. Einstein further claimed that motion under the influence of gravity bends the fabric of time and space, including light itself.

Following Minkowski's lead, Einstein developed the new notion of time-space, which Minkowski introduced, as a four-dimensional concept in which time is the fourth dimension to the three dimensions of space. Space-time is bent by gravitational force and is not as previously thought akin to a flat surface. Theoretical physics gives a central place to space in relation to time, with the idea in quantum theory that space may have given rise to time itself. However, this claim has an unclear relation to Einstein's theory of relativity for which space and time are co-terminus.[6] According to Lockwood: 'By far the most natural way of thinking of time, in the context of contemporary physics and cosmology, is to regard it as one dimension of a multidimensional space-time manifold' (Lockwood 2016: 449).

While the arrow of time points forwards, opening up the future, when we gaze into the starry sky it should be bore in mind that what we see there is only the past, for there is a fundamental time lag between event – the source of light – and its perception by us at a specific location on earth. The light the sun emits reaches us eight minutes after it leaves the sun and it is more than four years for light to reach us from the nearest stars. In many cases, the stars emitting the light have ceased to exist millions or even billions of years ago.

We can finally mention the implications of developments in thermodynamics for our understanding of time. Thermodynamics concerns energy and its transformation within closed systems. The first law states that energy is conserved when it changes form; the second law states that there is an increase in entropy, for while energy is not lost its transformation results in its dissipation. An implication of the first law is that future states are simply changes in the nature of energy. An implication of the second law is that there is a direction to time, the so-called arrow of time, which accords more closely with the human perception of time. According to this law, a fundamental characteristic of the universe is the increase in entropy. All closed systems, which include the universe, move from low to high entropy because when an event occurs, energy is released due to the acceleration involved. However, this is a theory about entropy, in essence the increase in randomness, rather than time as such. It postulates that things move from order to disorder, simply because – according to the Austrian physicist Ludwig Boltzmann, a pioneering figure in the science – there is always a greater statistical probability of a transformation leading to a different and more complex order.

The British physicist Arthur Eddington, following Boltzmann, argued that the arrow of time, a term he popularized, leads to an increase in randomness, a universal tendency for entropy to increase. In other words, there are more ways to make disorder than to establish order. To the extent to which this is a concept of thinking about the future, it is one that suggests ever more complexity due to increased movement. It accords[7] with Darwin's theory of evolution through natural section that the evolution of forms of life occurs through the random occur-

---

6 It is also unclear if Einstein's theory applies to the speed of the expansion of the universe, which may be greater than the speed of light, since it is a theory only about the movement of objects and theoretical observers, whereas the expansion of the universe is the expansion of space.

7 Despite the problem that life is not a closed system. Life evades this second law, as Erwin Schrödinger (2012 [1944]) argued in *What is Life?*, since living entities are not closed systems (they are in interaction with their environment through exchange of matter and energy).

rence of a mutation and that more complex forms of life emerge from more basic ones (though in this case, basic forms of life, such as bacteria, continue to exist, for not everything evolves). Thus, the theory also requires a view of the arrow of time as one directional, in the sense that once something begins, it cannot be reversed to its previous state. Einstein's theories also had a strong resonance in Bergson's writings, as in his 1922 work *Duration and Simultaneity*, and he was familiar with Bergson's ideas. In this work Bergson wrote: 'Immanent in our measurement of time, therefore, is the tendency to empty its content into a space of four dimensions in which past, present, and future are juxtaposed or superimposed for all eternity' (Bergson 2014: 215). At this time Einstein's theory of relativity was seen to belong as much to epistemology as to theoretical physics, which perhaps accounts for its enthusiastic reception by philosophers (Allen 2023: 40–2). Please add this sentence. Erwin Schrödinger, one of the founders of quantum mechanics, believed the fundamental problems of physics were philosophical questions concerning the nature of consciousness (Moore, W. 2015).

According to Alexander North Whitehead, in one of the major works on the philosophy of nature, the human understanding of time is limited by what can be perceived through the senses, as in the sense of time as duration. In *The Concept of Nature*, and in other works, he argued for a notion of nature that emphasized the centrality of a creative process that includes human existence. This offered an alternative to dualistic accounts of time, as in J. M. E. McTaggart's famous 1908 essay, where he postulates two kinds of time series, A and B. The A series is the common sense 'tensed' understanding of the time as determined by the moving present, which constantly repositions the past and the future when the present moves into the future and what is now present becomes the past. The B series refers to the specific points in the series that do not change, as in dates. While both concepts of time are always at work – in that our notion of the present changes from one moment to the next and yet we have a specific time referents that do not change – his elegant model of time has been challenged by other notions of time, including the theory of relativity and Whitehead's work.

Whitehead's work instead sees nature as a process than as a series, a notion which effectively amounts to time, a position he shares with Bergson, but he prefers to talk about the 'passage of nature' rather than time (Whitehead 1920: 54). The core of nature is 'the creative force of existence' and it is this that gives rise to the mystery of time. It cannot be said that the human experience of time in which things are born and eventually die has no place in the cosmic order. The notion of extra-terrestrial life, popularized by the cosmologist Carl Sagan in the 1970s and early 1980s, is itself an application of the human conception of life for imagining other forms of life. As cosmologists, such as Stephen Hawking in his *Brief History of Time* argued, the very fact that the expanding universe, discovered in 1929 by Edwin Hubble who observed distant galaxies moving away from us, had an origin some 14 billion years ago and will eventually end is itself a conception of time that assumes a past and a finite future. He claimed that this discovery was one of the great intellectual revolutions of the twentieth century (Hawking [1988] 2017: 40). It meant that the universe was expanding in all directions and that galaxies were moving further and further from each other. This in effect meant too that time was being produced (see also Lockwood 2005; Rovelli 2019; Prosser 2016). However, the notion of the expanding universe suggests a conception of time as infinite in this specific sense of continuous expansion. As Hawking explained, while the laws of science do not distinguish between forward and backward directions of time, they do recognize three arrows of time: the thermodynamic arrow (the direction by which disorder increases), the psychological one in which we remember the past and not the future, and the cosmological arrow pointing in the direction of an expanding rather than a contracting universe (Hawking 2017: 154). Recent notions of the universe structured more in terms of a giant loop might require some rethinking of the notion of the arrow of time as far as the expanding universe is concerned.[8]

The theories of time discussed here do not have direct applications for the human and social sciences. The Theory of Special Relativity, for instance, was confined to the analysis of very large amounts of mass and ultra-fast movement that have no empirical application in social and historical conditions. It was named 'special' since it concerned only the theoretical case of observers moving at a constant velocity and in a straight line, which cannot have any bearing on social life.[9] Einstein, who was not a religious believer, once reassured an archbishop that his theory is purely scientific and has no implication for religion (Isaacson 2007: 279). Yet, these theories are immensely important in shaping our view of time, since they made it possible to think of time in new ways beyond those that prevailed in the past and which restricted the scope of the human mind to explore the nature of existence and the physical underpinnings of the human condition. While the human understanding of time does not directly correspond to the order of time in the physical world, it is the basis for any appreciation of the nature of time. This was also one of the key arguments of the philosophy of Immanuel Kant in *The Critique of Pure Reason* in 1781/7, namely the claim that the concepts of space and time are senses intrinsic to human sensibility and which enable us to gain knowledge of the external physical world in imperfect ways that do not

---

8 https://www.scientificamerican.com/article/is-the-universe-a-giant-loop/
9 Even for the later General Theory this was very abstract in that it did not accommodate accelerated velocity.

offer a perfect mirror. But they are not just intrinsic to the human mind, they are also intrinsic to social organization and help us to understand the idea of an instantaneous present, the nature of acceleration, complexity, and virtual reality, all of which are central to contemporary sociology.

The concept of time in theoretical physics and in the philosophy of nature demonstrates that there is not just one order of time but many. In similar ways, some of the great discoveries in other domains of thought in the late nineteenth and early twentieth centuries, ranging from Darwin to Marx and Freud, showed that human life also unfolds according to dynamic processes rather than being predetermined or fixed but has no specific direction. A famous example is Werner Heisenberg's axiom of uncertainty – also known as the indeterminacy principle – in a 1927 paper, which states that it is not possible to know simultaneously the exact position and the exact movement of a given body, for only one – either location or movement – can be determined. Kurt Gödel's incompleteness theorem can also be mentioned as an example of uncertainty in modern mathematics and physics. The theorem, published in 1931, states that there will always be true statements that cannot be proven (Budiansky 2021 Chapter 5).

In this period, first in the natural sciences and in the philosophy of science, a new emphasis emerged on ideas such as indeterminacy, chance, contingency, multicausality, and relativity. Some of these ideas had a direct impact on the human and social sciences as well as a more general impact, leading to new directions in social and historical inquiry. As most vividly captured by Whitehead, rather than see reality as a preordained material entity, it should be seen as a creative process that unfolds through interaction with other processes, an idea that has had many parallels with later developments in philosophy and sociology that stress the centrality of relational accounts of the social world. However, as noted earlier, relativism in the human and social science does not accord with the scientific theory of relativity, which is consistent with universality, as the laws of physics are universally valid, unlike the 'laws' of the social world, which are more akin to conventions. Wittgenstein was almost certainly influenced by Einstein when he wrote in 1929, 'When we think about the future of the world, we always have in mind its being at the place where it would be if it continued to move as we see it moving now. We do not realize that it moves not in a straight line, but in a curve, and that direction constantly changes.'[10]

A further implication of these theories about the physical world is that the human sense of time and the time of the natural world are interlinked. Both Berg-

---

10 Wittgenstein (1998 [1929]: 20).

son and George Herbert Mead[11] attempted to link these orders of temporality. These interrelated temporalities – encompassing the time of human life, the history of human societies, and the cosmic order of the physical universe including the history of the planet earth – have today come to the fore of contemporary critical thought. These theories have opened the notion of nature and with it the idea of naturalism to wider approaches, such as critical realism, which is based on Roy Bhaskar's version of naturalism, as in *The Possibility of Naturalism* (1979), the weaker version of naturalism, so-called weak naturalism, in the work of Habermas (2003b: 27–8, 2008)[12], and the Gaia hypothesis, namely the argument of James Lovejoy that living beings interact with the inorganic physical order of the earth to make possible the conditions for life itself (Lovejoy 2000 [1979]). All these theories in their different ways express a relational conception of the world whereby the human order of the social world is interlinked with the natural order of the earth.

Has the Future already Begun? Time and History

The future is often seen as something that comes after the present or as something that is yet to come. In the first case, the future effectively flows from the present in the way the present emerged from the past. It suggests continuity while in the second sense there is the anticipation of rupture, where the future marks a point at which something new emerges. Both senses of the future have been powerful forces in modernity and have reflected positive as well as negative views about the future as something that can give rise to hope or something to be feared. Views of the future have generally been influenced by how the present is evaluated and how the past has been viewed. Today, new conceptions of the future are taking shape that respond to the incorporation of timescales that reflect the natural history of the earth in its relation to the history of human societies, 'the world,' and the biochemical processes of the web of life itself.

Our time is increasingly being viewed as the Anthropocene, the era of human-induced climatic change. Initially a contested concept in geology, it entered the earth sciences more generally to refer to the wider impact, beyond the strictly geological, of human action on the planet (on the oceans, the atmosphere, *etc.*). Despite efforts to have it an officially named Era in the geological timescales of the

---

11 Mead (1932). See also Chapters Four and Five.
12 For Habermas, 'weak naturalism contents itself with the basic background assumption that the biological endowment and the cultural way of life of Homo sapiens have a "natural" origin and can in principle be explained in terms of evolutionary theory' (2003b: 27–8).

history of the earth, the current geological Age, named in 2018, is the Late Holocene Meghalayan Age, the third Age of the Holocene. The Holocene Epoch, which began c. 12,000 years ago, after the end of the last ice age, approximates to the history of human societies, since the advent of agriculture and settlement of the earth with permanent dwellings. The early civilizations, based on cities and agricultural economies, emerged c. 6,000 years ago, in Mesopotamia, the Indus Valley, Egypt, and China. In geological time, the Late Holocene Meghalayan Age began over 4,200 years ago following a period of cooling that led to the collapse of some of the first civilizations due to mega droughts in those regions. In the longer perspective of human history, this is a very long time but in the 4.5 billion geologic history of the earth it is a tiny slice of time. Yet, it is this short time period that major planetary change is occurring due not to the natural history of the planet as such but to a form of life that developed on it. It should be noted that climate change does not only refer to global warming but also to other aspects of planetary change, such as rising sea levels, the growing acidification of the oceans, weather turbulence, etc. It is of course the case that many of these aspects of climate change are effects of planetary warming.

Human-induced climate change can be regarded as one of the major moments of historical rupture since the advent of settled societies and will determine the future of society. Since the term Anthropocene first began to be used c. 2000, it has undergone a discursive shift from a temporal term in geology to one in the earth sciences to, more generally, what it has now effectively become, a social-political term – even a cultural model – to designate the time of human climate change. In that sense, it is a way to interpret critically the global challenges facing humanity as a whole as a result of climate change, which is now incontrovertibly caused to a large degree by the release into the atmosphere of carbon as a consequence of human activity. It is thus a temporal term, but also one that encompasses the dimension of space – in its initial rendition in geology, it refers to the physical structure of the earth – in that it now refers to the planetary level and to human subject-formation (Delanty and Mota 2017).

If this assessment of our historical situation is correct, it means that the future has already begun in the sense that whatever major changes will occur, let's say, in the course of the next hundred years as a result of climate change will be as a consequence of what has already taken place. If we look at the Anthropocene in such terms, the major moment of rupture has occurred, for the Anthropocene is a term to refer not just to our present but also to the imprint of our past. It is a further question of when that moment actually happened.

The answer is a matter of agreeing on the timescale of the Anthropocene. If the notion of an Anthropocene era, in nongeological terms, is more or less the equivalent of the era of human-induced climate change, we have to agree that it has already begun and that this roughly coincides with the massive release of CO_2 and other greenhouse gasses, such as methane, into the earth's atmosphere. Since 1880, global average temperatures have risen by just over 1 °C, with the greatest increase since 1975. We can discount arguments that would place the origin of Anthropogenic action prior to the modern era on the grounds that human activity never reached a point at which it led to greater variability in climate change than what can be attributed to natural changes. The Anthropocene refers to more than human influences on the earth, a much-researched topic in historical geography, but to humanity as a geo-climatic force. This period, taken as a whole, can be said to coincide with modernity and the rise of industrialism. However, the Anthropogenic impact of industrialism and modernity did not set in until the twentieth century. Capitalism in some general and undefined way played a role, but it was not the primary agent, as much of the world undergoing industrialization was not all capitalist. At this time, the major example of noncapitalist industrialization was the USSR. According to the Great Acceleration thesis, the decisive moment was the immediate aftermath of the Second World War, which itself contributed to climate change, due to the increased amounts of energy that the war necessitated (see Steffen 2011; McNeill and Engelke 2014). Even in the capitalist world, capitalism itself was not the primary causal agent in the increased usage of fossil fuels. This was also a period in which massive population growth occurred and when societal advancement led to more advanced societies, which had greater needs for energy in order to satisfy the expectations of improved quality of life. Mitchells (2011, 2013) has related the need for increased energy to the expansion of social development and mass democracy – modern democracies need more energy than premodern agricultural societies and this has mostly come from fossil fuels: 'fossil fuel allowed the reorganization of energy systems that made possible, in conjunction with other changes, the novel forms of collective life out of which late- nineteenth- century mass politics developed' (Mitchell 2011: 119).

The Great Acceleration began c. 1950 in the western world and gradually spread to much of the rest of the world, especially to East Asia in the latter decades of the previous century, such that we can speak of a 'Second Great Acceleration' or an 'Asian Great Acceleration' (see Wagner 2023). While it is clear that Anthropogenic activity is the cause of climate change, it is a further question what is the nature of the activity that has inaugurated the Anthropocene. Capitalism is one aspect of a wider phenomenon, while modernity in general is too all encompassing (Chakrabarty 2009, 2014; Moore, J.W. 2015). In many ways, the notion of an Anthropocene is inaccurate, since while postulating humanity as the cause, this makes sense only in relation to natural causation, which has been scientifically refuted. To invoke humanity in general risks depoliticizing climate change, as not all members of the human species caused climate change even if all experience the detrimental consequences. Some societies more than others have been prime causal agents at specific points in history. What then is the specificity of the Anthropocene?

From a long-term sociological and historical perspective, I suggest, the cause of climate change has to be seen primarily in terms of energy usage. The need for energy is the fundamental fact of the material basis of all societies. It was the need for ever greater amounts of energy that came with modernity that led to the release of greenhouses cases, since until the present day energy usage on a great scale has been almost entirely carbon based, whether coal, oil, or gas (if we exclude nuclear power, which currently is not more than 10 percent of global energy). If the focus is put on energy, we have a clear picture of historical and planetary transformation. This begins with modernity and reaches a climax in the second half of the twentieth century as a result of worldwide modernization leading to an explosion in energy usage, first in the west and then in Asia. To be sure, energy usage does not directly account for all aspects of climate change and other factors have to be taken into account, such as the cutting down of rainforests and the melting of permafrost leading to the release of methane gases. However, the forces behind such factors are arguably indirectly related to the massive demands for energy. In this case, the transformation of the Amazon for food production is itself an instance of the need for energy, as food is energy. But more generally, population expansion which now stands at 8 billion – and the related increase in domestic animals, which now includes around 900 m dogs and 600 m cats – and improved living standards in much of the world translate into increased demands for energy, without which societal development is not possible. Until now, especially in the developing world or the recently developed world in Asia and above all in China, this need is met largely by carbon sources. It is true that some of this is mitigated by nuclear energy, which does not entail carbon emissions of much significance and, as mentioned, accounts for a relatively small amount of global energy. In any case, nuclear energy also gives rise to a future-oriented problem in that it postpones for future generations the problem of the disposal of dangerous long-life radioactive waste.

My argument, in a nutshell, is that energy usage is the key to the Great Acceleration – the massive increase in carbon dioxide and other greenhouse gases – and that it is this that leads to the predicament of the Anthropocene and a major rupturing in timescales. There is little point in attributing the cause to humanity in general, modernity or capitalism, or industrialism. If this makes sense, we can see some interesting links with the discussion earlier in this chapter around the dynamics and processes at work in the physical world. Following from the work of philosophers of science such as Henri Bergson and Alfred North Whitehead and the revolution begun by Einstein and others in the field of theoretical physics and thermodynamics, we can see some resonances if not applications of some of the key ideas concerning energy, acceleration, and entropy. It is beyond the scope of this chapter to explore in any detail direct links, but some of these perspectives are not irrelevant for understanding the temporality of the Anthropocene, especially since it is now more acceptable within the human and social sciences to see the human order of the world and human life itself as part of the physical world of the earth. If the condition of the possibility of society is the use of energy, then the Second Law of Thermodynamics – the tendency of energy conversion to lead toward high entropy – must also apply to society and would appear to be pertinent to the Great Acceleration (as well as to other aspects of society). The task of reversing climate change, or at least preventing the further rise of global temperatures, is inextricably concerned with the problem of energy.

Bernard Stiegler (2018) is one theorist who has made the notion of entropy central to a radical philosophy that seeks to reverse the Anthropocene's nihilistic entropic destruction of the possibility of possibility. However, he appears to be oblivious to the fact that the overall tendency in all of nature, including society and all forms of life, toward an increase in entropy cannot be reversed, since this goes against the irreversible arrow of time: it is not possible to move backward from high to low entropy, which cannot be controlled. Reversing or controlling climate changes – a deacceleration – is not about overcoming entropy and nor is it about less energy but about different kinds of energy. It is probably not possible for our complex advanced societies to use less energy, in a sense other than devising more efficient forms that may require less and safer forms of energy; but rather to use different forms of energy – but these will not lead to less entropy, except possibly in reducing climatic disturbances. A further problem with the sociological application of the Second Law is that strictly speaking it applies only to closed systems.[13]

The Anthropocene is, in one sense, a future-oriented idea that highlights planetary transformation, at least as far as human societies are concerned (it is unlikely humans have the capacity to destroy the earth, but will probably succeed in making it uninhabitable at least for large numbers of people (Wallace-Wells 2019). Darwin, in *On the Origin of Species*, observed that 'no cataclysm has desolated the world' (Darwin [1859] 2008: 360). But, as we have seen, it is also a concept that refers to the recent past and our present. The dominant conception portends catastrophe, and is future directed, which is not surprising as the past of the Anthropocene is a very short one, not extending in any meaningful sense beyond the

---

13 Prigogine and Stengers (2018 [1978]) offer a different perspective in a classic work. For them, order emerges out of chaos as is reflected in evolution, diversification, and instabilities of different kinds. Order and chaos are not divergent concepts.

middle of the twentieth century. Since the future extends to an unknown but finite point in time – if we can take the remaining seven or so billion years the sun has until it ceases to exist – it is a realm of possibility. This question raises again what the future is in temporal terms as a time beyond the present. The future as infinite does not cast much light on the current situation, if this can be taken to have begun seven decades or so ago. We need a more meaningful timescale that accords with the self-understanding of the present in confronting the problems of climate change.

So, what would a meaningful timescale be for a future-oriented politics? We will not discuss here approaches that argue for the very long-term future of humanity in possibly other terrestrial settings, as in for example MacAskill (2022). In view of the need to take account of the present time, letting aside for now the question of when the present begins and when it ends, and the need to address planetary transformation for future generations, including those yet to be born, a case can be made for what Elise Boulding has called a 'two-hundred year present', a concept that does not designate an endless present devoid of a future but one that incorporates the perspective of the future into it: 'On the one hand are such great sweeps of time that individual human events seem insignificant; on the other is such a brief present that it is gone before we know it. Between these two extremes there lies a medium range of time which is neither too long nor too short for immediate comprehension, and which has organic quality that gives it relevance to the present moment. This medium range is the 200-year present' (Boulding 1988: 3–4). This long present begins one hundred years ago with the birth of people who are one hundred years old today and extends to 100 years from the birth of people born today.[14] The two-hundred-year present incorporates both the present as normally understood and the shadow of the future, while leaving open the deep future. As a variable timescale, it shifts with time.

ʹThis is an invaluable concept that is highly pertinent to the Anthropocene. Since the future has already begun, we need a sense of the future that addresses both the current crisis and the prospects of more severe problems yet to come. A feature of climate change is that however severe the current situation is, there is worse to come if CO_2 emissions are not drastically curtailed. Viewed in such terms, the Anthropocene can also be viewed not only as a catastrophe but also through the lens of a 'Good Anthropocene', in the sense of an adequate response to the climate catastrophe. Never before in human history has political self-understanding been defined so explicitly in temporal terms. The Anthropocene is a temporal term

---

14 See a 2003 interview https://www.beyondintractability.org/audiodisplay/boulding-e-3-future-studies2. Originally, Boulding (1988).

– the age of humanity – and the urgency of the political situation of its time is a temporal one, as in the Doomsday Clock, the 'minutes to midnight' scenario. On 23rd of January 2023, the Bulletin of the Atomic Scientists set the Doomsday Clock at 90 seconds to midnight to highlight the threat the Russian invasion of Ukraine presents. This is the closest to midnight the clock has been since it was established in 1947 to draw attention to global existential threats at the dawn of the nuclear weapons age.[15]

Time, Life, and the Human Condition: Biology, Evolution, and Culture

In this chapter, I have argued for an interconnected conception of human and natural history, a perspective that has been much emphasized in recent years. The later work of Bruno Latour did much for the re-linking of what had been previously severed in much of the human and social sciences (Latour 2013). Remarkably, it was the hermeneutical and critical traditions in the social science that were the most fervent in forging the discord between the human and natural worlds. This tendency was also reflected in a hegemonic conception of time that excluded other ideas of time, as Johannes Fabian showed in a classic work, *Time and the Other* (Fabian 1988). With modernity, humans created the illusion that they escaped from nature through its mastery. Paradoxically, this illusion emerged in the aftermath of the demotion of humanity's centrality to the world and universe as a result of the revolution in science from Copernicus and Galileo to Darwin and Einstein. This myth has taken an additional paradoxical turn in the Anthropocene with the destruction of the natural life of the planet by humans who become subservient to nature as a result of their domination, an idea that was foretold by Adorno and Horkheimer in *Dialectic of Enlightenment* in 1944 (Adorno and Horkheimer 1979). Fortunately, today, especially in light of the politics of nature and climate change, there is a greater recognition of the need to see the human and the natural as connected in multiple ways (see for example Constanza *et al.* 2007). But how should we understand those connections?

The discussion of the Anthropocene in the foregoing drew attention to the history of human societies – the world – and the planetary history of the earth. A fuller account would have to include the biochemical history of human life, as part of the wider context of what has been referred to as the 'web of life' (Capra 1997). The

---

15 https://www.theguardian.com/world/2023/jan/24/doomsday-clock-at-record-90-seconds-to-midnight-amid-ukraine-crisis

question of time and the orientation to the future is very much connected with recent transformations in what it means to be human. Human life is not an unchanging constant, for human beings, *Homo sapiens*, evolved through significant change before reaching their present condition sometime between 300,000 and 150,000 years ago, with c. 200,000 generally being the consensus. According to the theory of evolution, to be discussed later in this chapter, human life is not fixed but is an adaptative and selective process and has been very much the outcome of chance, due to natural selection based on genetic mutations generating genetic variations. As the Gaia thesis states, there is a coevolution of the human and the biological as well as the geological/biosphere. In this context, Barbara Adams has drawn attention to the biorhythms that connect human time with biological time (Adam 1990: 70 – 90). However, there is an unresolved problem with these positions.

The connectivity of humans to the natural world, despite the dislocations of modernity, suggests a fairly settled conception of the human condition as shaped by the relation to nature. This seems to be confirmed by Darwin's theory of evolution, which on one reading says that once a 'form of life' – a term Darwin introduced – has evolved, it remains in that condition until a mutant appears that is more adaptive to the environment and which then is selected by the process called natural selection. Darwin's *On the Origin of Species* in 1859 had in fact very little to say specifically on human beings, who are hardly mentioned in the book, concerned as it was with more generic features of inheritance and adaptation through natural selection. It was one of the most influential books ever written. In recent times its originality has been somewhat questioned, since it is clear Darwin was influenced by others – including Alfred Russell Wallace who was a co-discoverer of natural selection and independently used the term – and many of the insights were already emerging in the work of his contemporaries (see Ruse 2009; Bowler 2009). Indeed, Wallace was more imaginative than Darwin when it came to speculating on human life on other planets, as he did in *Man's Place in the Universe* in 1904, but concluded that life could not exist beyond the earth due to the apparent absence of water elsewhere (Wallace 2012). However, Darwin succeeded whereas others failed in advancing the theory of evolution in a book that ranks as one of the great works of science. But aside from demolishing the theory of divine creation, what does it really tell us about the human condition, how much change does it allow, and what of the future?

Toward the end of the book there is just one single mention of humanity where he speculates about future fields of research opening up when: 'Light will be thrown on the origin of man and his history' (Darwin 2008: 359). One reads this great book in vain for a clue as to an answer to this question. There appears to be a general consensus that Darwin sought to avoid too much focus on humanity in the work and aimed to get his ideas accepted with examples from less advanced forms of life, and more empirical evidence was available at this time about earlier forms of human life than of earlier human life. This perhaps explains some of the elusiveness of the work in respect to some key issues and no scientific advantage would have resulted from focusing on humans as his main specimens. It also comes as a surprise to the modern reader that Darwin did not use the term evolution, which in his time was not in common currency in English,[16] but used such terms as 'descent with modification' or the 'process of modification' or simply 'descent.' The book ended with a famous sentence about endless forms of life now being 'evolved,' the closest he got with the term evolution. His understanding of evolution, to retrospectively apply the term, effectively was 'descent with modification through natural selection.'

Darwin's *Origin of Species* nonetheless offered a glimpse of a new perspective on the future in relation to the deep past of life itself. His insights were far reaching in revealing the limits of the taken-for-granted view of history as of relatively short duration, which created the illusion of the present being more significant than what it really was: 'The belief that species were immutable productions was almost unavoidable as long as the history of the world was thought to be of short duration' (2008: 354). In this time it was believed by many that the universe was created in 4004 BC. Evolution for Darwin is a very slow process of 'infinitesimally small inherited modifications' and it is this that makes the deep past imperceptible since it works through tiny changes: 'We see nothing of these slow changes in progress, until the hand of time has marked the long lapse of ages, and then so imperfect is our view into long past geological ages, that we only see that the forms of life are now different from what they formerly were' (2008: 66).

Darwin is not normally seen as a theorist of time, but the theory of evolution was in fact a theory of time – of slow and deep time – and one that reduced the significance of the present: 'The whole history of the world, as at present known, although of a length quite incomprehensible by us, will hereafter be recognized as a mere fragment of time, compared with ages which have elapsed since the first creature, progenitor of innumerable extinct and living descendants, was created.' In this passage he goes onto speculate that all forms of life eventually become extinct: 'Judging from the past, we may safely infer that not one living species will transmit its unaltered likeness to a distant futurity. And of the species now living very few will transmit progeny of any kind to a far distant futurity' (2008: 359). This suggests that future humans and their successors will be very different from *Homo sapiens*. The book closes with a benign view of natural selection working 'to a se-

---

16 Jean-Baptiste Lamarck used the term.

cure future of equally inappreciable length.' However, the future of all forms of life must reckon with their eventual extinction. So, much for the Kingdom to Come whose entrants will perish one day.

While in the later *Descent of Man* in 1871, there are more clues about the evolution of *Homo sapiens* through sexual selection, which works through mate choice, rather than through natural selection, which works through mutations, Darwin himself had very little to say on the future (as opposed to the past) of human evolution other than what can be inferred from his view that all forms of life become eventually extinct, which he explicitly states in *On the Origin of Species* (p. 97) as a logical inference. Sexual selection in humans suggests a stronger emphasis on selection as a product of will or design than natural selection. From a strictly Darwinian evolutionary perspective, it appears that humans have undergone little evolutionary change in their c. 200,000 history, perhaps with some evolutionary change c. 50,000 years ago with developments in the human brain (Mithen 1998). The influential evolutionary theorist Stephen Jay Gould claimed that there has been no evolutionary change in the past 40,000 years. If this is correct it is unlikely there is going to be much evolutionary change in the future, though it is not clear what the future timescale here is.[17] It appears that human beings today, despite considerable genetic variation, are more or less the same as they were 150,000 to 200,000 years ago in their genetic makeup. Yet, they are still undergoing bodily change and human life has changed and is changing in fundamental ways. In Darwinian terms, and in line with Gould's reasoning, future humans would not emerge for at least another 50,000 years.

There is no scientific consensus on whether changes to the human body in the last 150,000 or so years amount to evolutionary change in biological terms. This is largely a question of how evolution is defined – how much weight is given to selection and to adaptation – and what evidence might be used. From a Darwinian perspective, evolution is very slow and incremental and is, on some accounts, strictly genetic. It is also highly contingent in that evolutionary adaptation is ultimately only a matter of chance and is not ordained or engrained. It is contingent of whether a form of life with specific characteristics will adapt or not to its environment. Natural selection is the key cause of change but it rests on the fact of chance i. e. a mutation occurring to generate a variant that might or might not be selected. So, a chance occurrence – in this case, a genetic change – plays a huge and undoubtedly too big a role in the theory. Chance is produced by history, which generates variety; evolution is a process that solves problems produced by history by making selections, which subsequently stabilize through adaptation to create

---

17 In an Interview in 2000.

new forms of life or modified version of previous forms. It is through this process that the future is produced.

Darwin himself did not have knowledge of genetics as such, but effectively his emphasis on inheritance amounted to a theory of genetic inheritance. It does not seem to be helpful to say that nongenetic bodily changes are not evolutionary, especially as Darwin ultimately does not provide a firm guide on what counts as evolution. In *The Descent of Man*, he extended the vision of evolution to include morality and emotion, which he saw as emerging from learning and thus as a form of adaptive behavior (see Lewens 2015). In doing so, he opened up the complicated question of cultural and cognitive evolution.

One of the problems with seeking a firm guide on what evolution might have in store for humanity in the future is that Darwin in *On the Origin of Species* was in effect presenting his theory of natural selection as an alternative to the theory of divine creation. This explains why he made some concessions for divine creation on matters that lay outside the scope of the theory he was advancing, for example a creator could conceivably create the fundamental laws of the world but not the forms of life itself since these are always ultimately contingent on circumstances and cannot be determined. However, the theory of natural selection still remains influential in social science (Blute 2010; Turner and Maryanski 2008).

A less rigid definition of evolution as bodily change in relation to the social and natural environment avoids some of the problems associated with the Darwinian legacy and the requirement for genetic evidence of evolutionary change. Stephen Jay Gould developed a theory of evolution that emphasized 'fits and starts' rather than a continuous process of slow change (Gould 2002). Cockran and Harpending (2011) argue the opposite of the Darwinian position but also do not accept Gould's position, with the argument that biological human evolution has continued over the past 10,000 years, basically the era of human society. The argument is not without controversy since it strays into the domain of cultural evolution while making strong claims for the continuation of genetic evolution. Russell brings a different and important perspective to these debates with an account of evolution that emphasizes the coevolution of human and nonhuman forms of life. His account of evolution does not limit evolution to the formation of species and any change in traits qualifies. 'It does not require millions of years because a population can evolve in just one generation. It does not involve natural selection because the mechanism for change in traits goes unspecified' (Russell 2011: 8). He makes the important point that for much of recorded history, essentially the history of civilization since the advent of farming c. 12,000 years ago, there was the constant alteration of inherited traits and genes in all human and nonhuman forms life, due to their interaction, as in the domestication of plants and animals by humans. Human and nonhuman populations have coevolved in response to each other.

The definition of traits in this account includes those transmitted by culture and reduces the place of natural selection, since selection in many cases is not 'natural' but the result of the hand of humanity.

Human evolution will very probably continue to undergo bodily change, but for this to be discernible, a long timescale will probably be needed. There is much interesting inquiry into what human beings will look like in 10,000 years from now and even further timescales (see for a discussion, Solomon 2016). This is today all complicated by the fact that chance may be less important in determining evolutionary change, effectively ending one aspect of the Darwinian theory, since life can be designed by human intervention raising major normative questions about the future of human nature, as in its most basic elements it is prior to society (Habermas 2003a). It may be the case that adaptation today for humans is more about adaptation to the demands of technology (Kahn 2011). In this view, technology has replaced nature, and is now itself a form of nature, as 'technological nature,' opening up possibilities of posthuman forms of human life. In his insightful survey of the question of future human evolution, Peter Ward (2009) succinctly summed up the possible routes of humanity's evolutionary future as stasis (more or less staying as we are now, perhaps with minor modifications as a result of cultural evolution), speciation (the evolution of a new human species) or symbiosis (evolution through integration with machines following the emergence of machine superintelligence). There is widespread consensus that there is less human evolution determined by chance than by human direction through sexual selection. This is related to the argument that culture is taking over the role once performed by biology, as Richard Dawkins suggested in *The Selfish Gene* with 'memes' replacing the function of 'genes' (Dawkins 1978). So, it may be the case that our evolution is now more cultural than biological, where biological refers to natural selection based on genetic mutations. This has also been argued by Inglehart (2019) who claims that once the primary challenge for human life is no longer survival, other factors play a role in shaping the evolution of values and behavior. Yet, we cannot exclude long-term biological evolution.

The inescapable conclusion is that evolution must be seen in terms of a dual model of inheritance through genetic and cultural selection (see Zhao 2022). However, where the genetic dimension is still a factor, the element of randomness through mutation is less important due to selection and genetic engineering, itself influenced by cultural determinants. Despite the undoubted importance of the cultural logic of evolution, it is unlikely that genetic mutations as in the classic Darwinian theory will vanish, since a feature of human biology today is considerable variation, which is a necessary basis for selection (since without it, there is nothing to select). If there is one aspect of Darwin's theory that is less relevant for future human evolution, it is 'survival of the fittest' defined in biological terms. However,

Darwin's emphasis on human evolution through sexual selection suggests that his own position was less rigid and his account of sexual selection does not exhaust the wider category of cultural and cognitive evolution. Warring and Wood (2021) attempt to resolve some of these issues with the argument that human culture – in language, beliefs, institutions, technology, *etc.* – constitutes a secondary system of adaptive inheritance in humans (see also Runciman 2009). Culture replaces genetics as a system of inheritance. Group-level cultural evolution is more rapid and more selective than genetic evolution in humans (Laland 2017: 217). In addition, as a further layer, Strydom following Habermas (1979 [1976]) argues for the separate dynamic of cognitive evolution in terms of learning capacities and universal meta principles that have evolved in history (Strydom 2015, 2017).

Letting aside the problem of genetic change and whether it is a requirement for evolution, an argument can be made that the human body has undergone a major change since the middle of the twentieth century, in the period that coincides with the Anthropocene as the Great Acceleration. It would appear that there has been an acceleration also in life itself with a worldwide trend toward increased life expectancy, which will conceivably be further extended, as mortality rates continue to fall. This is not due to genetic change, but is a result of improved health care, hygiene, and nutrition for much of the world's population. Globally, life expectancy has risen from the mid-1940s to early 70s and since the 1950s and today there is a growth in super-old people, with Japan leading the way (Moreland 2022: 129 – 31). Thomas has argued that it is possible that the chemical acceleration of human life has brought about a significant physiological difference between people today and pre-1950 human beings (Thomas 2022). Life itself is no longer fixed and can be genetically modified raising a further question about the meaning of the continued relevance of the notion of the human (Carrigan and Porpora 2021). Bryan S. Turner (2017) claims that as a result of major neurological, biotechnical, and physiological changes to the human body, the age-old concern that defined the human condition of the experience of suffering and unhappiness may be waning. Then, there is the phenomenon of the toxic body and the possibility of pandemics yet to come arising from new kinds of pathogens, which is a reminder that nature cannot be fully mastered. We now know all too clearly since the COVID-19 pandemic that the virus that caused so much destruction is not entirely natural but a product of societal transformation (Delanty 2021).

The time of the Anthropocene may also be the age of sociocultural and cognitive shifts in society through changes in subject formation: 'humans…have begun to reflect on and re-articulate their commonly taken-for-granted cognitive presuppositions in a way that facilitates the construction of new directing and guiding cultural models of nature, of their sociocultural world and of themselves as agents' (Strydom 2017: 76; see also, 2015). As a cultural and cognitive process, evolution entails the creation of innovation with the potential for human progress, as Bowler argues (2020). Darwin himself clearly thought that natural selection was benign, even if the specter of extinction of our form of life cast a shadow from a very distant the future: 'Natural selection acts solely through the preservation of variations in some way advantageous, which consequently endure' (2008: 84). His notion of 'the struggle for existence' strongly asserted the 'dependency of one being on another' and was part of the 'economy of nature' (2008: 50–1). So, while natural selection works by competition, it leads to improvements and favorable variations. This is far from the erroneous applications to economic and social life, which was contrary to Darwin's reasoning, for he saw the separate process of sexual selection at work especially in the life of humans and that this takes a different course. However, a note of caution on applications of Darwin's ideas for human society is in order: In *On the Origin of Species*, Darwin was writing principally about less advanced forms of life and not about complex societal organization. Contrary to later uses of his work for sociological analysis, Darwin himself did not see any direct application to society and there is no basis in his work for a teleological 'stages' theory of historical development.

Evolutionary progress cannot be entirely determined, for it is an open process. Henri Bergson's notion of creative evolution captures this wider sense of future evolutionary possibilities.[18] As Jacques Monod argued in an influential work, *Change and Necessity,* the role of chance played a major role in human existence in determining the evolution of all forms of life (Monod 1972). The notion of evolution encompasses a wide range of processes beyond genetics. While the relationship between the biological evolution and cultural evolution is not fully understood, due in so small part to differing notions of what evolution actually is and the place of genetics in it, there appears to be widespread agreement that future human evolution is no longer determined by the fundamental problem of survival. Other forces are also at work, for example, the development of collective learning, empathy, and social cooperation. Zhao (2022) refers to this level of evolution as 'human self-selection.' Such a view would suggest that evolution has speeded up, not slowed down or stabilized. Some stabilization has occurred in the course of the development of human civilization, allowing other changes to take place and thus opening up future possibilities. In this way, the logic of evolution creates the conditions for the possibility of the future. A relevant consideration in this context is the argument of Suddendorf et al. (2022) that the development of foresight radically transformed humans into thinking beings capable of seeing the future in multiple ways. Insight was essential to the capacity for innovation upon which evo-

---

18 One of his major works was *Creative Evolution* in 1907 (Bergson 1911).

lution depends. Humans have learned not only to think about the future but also acquired the ability to think about thinking about the future. They are actually more interested in the future than in the past.

Conclusion

In this chapter I have endeavored to reconstruct the orientation to the future that is implicit in the temporal concepts of the natural sciences. While cautious of a strict application of notions of time in the natural sciences, I have tried to reconstruct their significance for the idea of the future in society today. Conceptions of time in physics since Einstein, suggest a notion of time as *process* rather than as something fixed and absolute, concepts that are perhaps best captured by the philosophy of Henri Bergson. More generally, a case has been made to see human or social time and natural time as interlinked. This would appear to be confirmed with developments that initiated in geology and the earth sciences around the idea of the Anthropocene, an idea that is now a wider cultural model by which contemporary societies reinterpret themselves in terms of a new relationship between the planetary level of the earth and the social order of the world. Such a perspective suggests a conception of time interwoven with space.

Bergson additionally established a basis for thinking of the future as possibility: that which does not exist, could exist as a possibility. When something comes into existence, it can be said that it was possible even if it was not conceivable before it existed. Because of the future, possibility is present in the past, since when something happened it was possible for it to happen, as otherwise it would not have happened. From a Bergsonian perspective, some things are potentially possible (because they are latent in the present or partly actual), while others are only possible.

This does not mean that everything is possible, for there is always chance and necessity conditioning future possibilities. The future is always the outcome of chance, that is occurrences resulting from the fact of contingency. Contingency can be understood to be a condition of openness in which something emerges, whether by chance or as a result of a cause (and following Aristotle there are different kinds of causes, material, formal, efficient and final causes). While everything is the result of chance at some level – the universe, life, the world – it is also not a product of chaos or occurring in a vacuum. Chance is also conditioned by necessity, as well as possibility and actuality, which result in various gradations of determinism since they produce causes (and everything that exists has had a cause). The Greek pre-Socratic philosopher Democritus expressed this basic truth with the statement 'Everything existing in the universe is the fruit of chance and necessity' (Monod 1979). Determinism is an outcome of the simple fact that everything has a cause. So, to say something is determined or that a future event or state of affairs is determined is to say that there are causes that can explain it, at least in principle (as the causes may be unknown). To invoke necessity is to say something similar, but more specifically it means that an outcome could not be other than what it is. Determinism and necessity are thus not in opposition to chance, contingency and to free will. For these reasons, the future while being open, is also limited by the structure of causality and the nature of reality which includes the modalities of necessity, possibility and actuality (see also Strydom 2024).

Finally, the relevance of these ideas was discussed with respect to theories of evolution – as a future-oriented process – and in relation to subject formation: the self-understanding of humanity today is very much bound up with a relationship to the earth that is expressed in cultural notions of time and guided by evolutionary processes and learning thresholds that have been reached.

While the idea of the future should not be subordinated to the past, in some senses the deep past does hold sway over the future. If humans had never used fossil fuels, the problem of climate change would not exist. Once the use of fossil fuels began – going back to ancient times but on an industrial scale since the eighteenth century – the fate of civilization was sealed, not least because their negative consequences were not known until relatively recently. This knowledge may have come too late; yet it is not easy to imagine civilization without ever having had fossil fuels. Early societies solved much of their energy needs through the abhorrent practice of slavery. Had fossil fuels not been invented for energy use (or if they did not exist in a hypothetical thought experiment), civilization would not have advanced much beyond what it was by the eighteenth century when world population was under one billion, and might not have gotten that far. Paradoxically, this suggests that civilization is based on what may destroy it.

This problem is also relevant to the question of advanced extra-terrestrial life, whether it is possible for advanced forms of life to exist without fossil fuels; if not, it is hypothetically possible that this may be one reason why we will not discover them, as such worlds may have existed and perished. If advanced forms of life do exist in other parts of the universe, it must be because they invented other forms of energy. It remains to be seen if humans will make the transition from carbon to alternative sources of energy. If they do, as Mitchell (2011) has argued, they may also achieve a more democratic future, for this is connected with finding alternatives to carbon energy.

References

Adam, B. 1990. *Time and Social Theory.* Cambridge: Polity Press.

Adorno, T. W. and Horkheimer, M. 1979. [1944] *Dialectic of Enlightenment.* London: Verso.

Allen, B. 2023. *Living in Time: The Philosophy of Henri Bergson.* Oxford: Oxford University Press.

Bergson, H. 1910. [1889] *Time and Free Will: An Essay on the Immediate Data of Consciousness.* London: Allen and Unwin.

Bergson, H. 1911. [1907] *Creative Evolution.* New York: Holt.

Bergson, H. 2014. [1922] 'Concerning the Nature of Time.' In: *Henri Bergson: Key Writings*, edited by Answell-Pearson and O' Maoilearca. London: Bloomsbury.

Bhaskar, R. 1979. *The Possibility of Naturalism.* London: Routledge.

Blute, M. 2010. *Darwinian Sociocultural Evolution: Solutions to Dilemmas in Cultural and Social Theory.* Cambridge: Cambridge University Press.

Boulding, E. 1988. 'Expanding our Sense of Time and History: The 200-Hundred Year Present.' In: *Building a Global Civic Culture: Education for an Independent World.* New York: Teacher's College Press.

Bowler, P. 2009. *Evolution: The History of an Idea.* Berkeley: University of California Press.

Bowler, P. 2020. *Progress Unchained: Ideas of Evolution, Human History and the Future.* Cambridge: Cambridge University Press.

Budiansky, S. 2021. *Journey to the Edge of Reason: The Life of Kurt Gödel.* Oxford: Oxford University Press.

Capra, F. 1997. *The Web of Life.* London: Penguin.

Carrigan, M. and Porpora, D. (eds) 2021. *Post-Human Futures: Human Enhancement, Artificial Intelligence and Social Theory.* London: Routledge.

Chakrabarty, D. 2009. 'The Climate of History: Four Theses.' *Critical Inquiry*, 35: 197–22.

Chakrabarty, D. 2014. 'Climate and Capital: on Conjoined Histories.' *Critical Inquiry*, 41: 1–23.

Cochran, G. and Harpending, H. (eds) 2011. *The 10,000 Year Explosion: How Civilization Accelerated Human Evolution.* London: Basic Books.

Costanza, R., Graumlich, L., and Steffen, W. (eds) 2007/2011. *Sustainability or Collapse? An Integrated History and Future of People on Earth.* Cambridge, MA.: MIT Press.

Darwin, C. 2008. [1859] *On the Origin of Species.* Oxford: Oxford University Press.

Dawkins, R. 1976. *The Selfish Gene.* Oxford: Oxford University Press.

Delanty, G. (ed.) 2021. *Pandemics, Society and Politics: Critical Reflections on the Covid-19 Crisis.* Berlin: De Gruyter.

Delanty, G. and Mota, A. 2017. 'Governing the Anthropocene: Agency, Governance and Knowledge.' *European Journal of Social Theory*, 20 (1): 9–38.

Elias, N. 1992. *Time: An Essay.* Oxford: Blackwell.

Fabian, J. 1988. *Time and the Other: How Anthropology Makes its Other.* New York: Columbia University Press.

Galison, P. 2003. *Einstein's Clocks, Poincare's Maps.* London: Norton.

Gould, S. J. 2002. *The Structure of Evolutionary Theory.* Cambridge, MASS.: Harvard University Press.

Habermas, J. 1979. [1976]. *Communication and the Evolution of Society.* London: Heinemann.

Habermas, J. 2003a. *The Future of Human Nature.* Cambridge: Polity Press.

Habermas, J. 2003b. *Truth and Justification.* Cambridge: Polity Press.

Habermas, J. 2008. *Between Naturalism and Religion: Philosophical Essays.* Cambridge: Polity Press.

Hawking, S. 1988. *A Short History of Time.* New York: Bantam Books.

Inglehart, I. 2019. *Cultural Evolution: People's Motivations are Changing, and Reshaping the World.* Cambridge: Cambridge University Press.

Isaacson, W. 2007. *Einstein: His Life and Universe.* London: Simon and Schuster.

Jancsary, J. 2019. 'The Future as an Undefined and Open Time: A Bergsonian Approach.' *Axiomathes,* 29: 61–80.

Kahn, P. 2011. *Technological Nature: Adaptation and the Future of Human Life.* Cambridge, MASS.: MIT Press.

Latour, B. 2013. *Facing Gaia: Six Lectures on the Political Theology of Nature.* Cambridge: Polity Press.

Laland, K. 2017. *Darwin's Unfinished Symphony: How Culture Made the Human Mind.* Princeton: Princeton University Press.

Lewens, T. 2015. *Cultural Evolution.* Oxford: Oxford University Press.

Lockwood, D. 2005. *The Labyrinth of Time: Introducing the Universe.* Oxford: Oxford University Press.

Lovejoy, J. 2000. [1979] *Gaia: A New Look at Life on Earth.* Oxford: Oxford University Press.

Mead, G. H. 1932. *The Philosophy of the Present.* London: The Open Court Company.

Mithen, S. 1998. *The Prehistory of the Mind.* London: Phoenix.

Monod: J. 1972. [1970] *Chance and Necessity: An Essay on the Natural Philosophy of Modern Biology.* New York: Vintage.

Moreland, P. 2022. *Tomorrow's People: The Future of Humanity in Ten Numbers.* London: Picador.

Moore, J. W. 2015. *Capitalism and the Web of Life: Ecology and the Accumulation of Capital.* London: Verso.

Moore, W. 2015. *Schrödinger: Life and Thought.* Cambridge: Cambridge University Press.

Mc Neill, J. R. and Engelke, P. 2014. *The Great Acceleration: An Environmental History of the Anthropocene.* Cambridge, MA: Harvard University Press.

McTaggart, J. 1908. 'The Unreality of Time.' *Mind,* 17 (68): 457–474.

McTaggart, J. 1921 and 1927. *The Nature of Existence,* vols 1 and 2. Cambridge: Cambridge University Press.

MacAskill, W. 2022. *What We Owe to the Future.* London: Basic Books.

Mitchell, T. 2011. 'Hydrocarbon Utopia.' In: Gordon, M. Tilley, H. and Prakash, G. (eds) *Utopia/Dystopia: Conditions of Historical Possibility.* Princeton: Princeton University Press.

Mitchell, T. 2013. 2nd edition. *Carbon Democracy: Political Power in the Age of Oil.* London: Verso.

Prigogine, I. and Stengers, I. 2018. [1978] *Order Out of Chaos: Man's New Dialogue with Nature.* London: Verso.

Prosser, S. 2016. *Experiencing Time.* Oxford: Oxford University Press.

Ricoeur, P. 2000. *Memory, History and Forgetting.* Chicago. University of Chicago Press.

Rovelli, C. 2019. *The Order of Time.* London: Penguin.

Runciman, W. G. 2009. *The Theory of Cultural and Social Selection.* Cambridge: Cambridge University Press.

Ruse, M. 2009. 'Charles Darwin on Human Evolution.' *Journal of Economic Behaviour and Organization,* 71 (1): 10–9.

Russell, E. 2011. *Evolutionary History.* Cambridge: Cambridge University Press.

Schrödinger, E. 2012. [1944] *What is Life?* Cambridge: Cambridge University Press.

Solomon, S. 2016. *Future Humans: Inside the Science of our Continuous Evolution.* New Haven: Yale University Press.

Steffen, W. *et al.* 2015. The Trajectory of the Anthropocene: the Great Acceleration.' *The Anthropocene Review,* 2 (1): 81–98

Stiegler, B. 2018. *The Neganthropocene.* London: Open Humanities Press.

Strydom, P. 2015. 'Cognitive Fluidity and Climate Change: A Critical Social-theoretical Approach to the Current Challenge.' *European Journal of Social Theory*, 18 (3): 236 – 56.

Strydom, P. 2017. 'The Sociocultural Self-creation of a Natural Category: Sociotheoretical Reflections on Human Agency under the Temporal Conditions of the Anthropocene.' *European Journal of Social Theory*, 20 (1): 61 – 79.

Strydom, P. 2023. 'The Critical Theory of Society: From its Young Hegelian Core to the Key Concept of Possibility.' *European Journal of Social Theory*, 26 (2): 153 – 79.

Strydom, P. 2024. 'Towards a Sociology of the Future: An Exploration in Cognitive Social Theory,' *European Journal of Social Theory*, 27 (2).

Suddendorf, T. Redshaw, J. and Bulley, A. 2022. *The Invention of Tomorrow: A Natural History of Foresight.* New York: Basic Books.

Tabbonis, S. 2001. 'The Idea of Social Time in Norbert Elias.' *Time & Society*, 10 (1): 5 – 22.

Thomas, J. A. 2014. 'History and Biology in the Anthropocene: Problems of Scale, Problems of Value.' *American Historical Review*, 119 (5):1587 – 1607.

Turner, B. S. 2017. 'Ritual, Belief and Habituation: Religion and Religions form the Axial Age to the Anthropocene.' *European Journal of Social Theory*, 20 (17): 132 – 45.

Turner, J. and Maryanski, A. 2008. *On the Origins of Societies by Natural Selection.* London: Routledge.

Wallace-Wells, D. 2019. *The Uninhabitable Earth: A Story of the Future.* London: Penguin

Wagner, P. 2023. 'The Triple Problem Displacement: Climate Change and the Politics of the Great Acceleration.' *European Journal of Social Theory*, 26 (1): 24 – 47.

Wallace, A. R. 2012. [1904] *Man's Place in the Universe.* London: Chapman and Hall. https://www.gu tenberg.org/cache/epub/39928/pg39928-images.html

Ward, P. 2009. 'What Will Become of Homo Sapiens?' *Scientific American.* 300 (1): 68 – 73.

Warring, T. and Wood, T. 2021. 'Long-term Gene-Culture Coevolution and the Human Evolution Transition.' *Proceedings of the Royal Society B.* 288: 20210538. https://doi.org/10.1098/rspb.2021. 0538

Whitehead, A. N. 1920. *The Concept of Nature.* Cambridge: Cambridge University Press.

Wittgenstein, L. 1998. [1929/1977] *Culture and Value: A Selection from the Posthumous Writings.* G. H. von Wright (ed.). Translated by P. Winch. Oxford: Blackwell.

Wootton, D. 2010. *Galileo: Watcher of the Skies.* New Haven: Yale University Press.

Zhao, S. 2022. 'Human Self-Creation as a Mechanism of Human Societal Evolution: A Critique of the Cultural Selection Argument.' *European Journal of Social Theory*, 25 (3): 386 – 402.

Chapter Three
Lessons from the Past: What Does the Past Tell Us about the Future?

The past is one obvious place to look for a guide to the future. As the previous chapter showed, the evolution of the human mind, culture, and societies created the conditions of the very possibility of the future. In many ways the possibility of the future is a product of the human capacity to learn from history and the Darwinian conception of evolution is itself a process of cumulative learning. This obviously does not mean that there were no errors in the past. The history of political thought can be read as the history of failure.[1] But learning from past mistakes has been a key feature of human progress throughout history, even if much of that learning has been unconscious. According to Karl Popper, the possibility of error is always built into scientific knowledge, which is based on the principle of falsification, but we learn from our errors.

It therefore follows that the past gives us a certain sense of how to prepare for the future, as in the much-quoted phrase attributed to the American philosopher George Santayana in *The Life of Reason* in 1905: 'Those who cannot remember the past are condemned to repeat it.'[2] Another version is the phrase Winston Churchill used in a speech in 1948, 'Those who do not study history are doomed to repeat it,' by which he meant to repeat its errors. In *Reflections on the Revolution in France* Edmund Burke in 1790 wrote in a similar vein: 'In history a great volume is unrolled for our instruction, drawing the materials of future wisdom from the past errors and infirmities of mankind.' It seems to be self-evident that the errors of the past will be repeated if we do not learn from history. However, it is questionable if history repeats itself anyway and that past errors are simply perpetuated in the present. The question I am raising in this chapter is a different one. It is whether learning from past errors might be enough to face the challenges of the present. Is it enough to know the errors of the past as a guide to the future?

An argument I am making in this book is that the future is looking increasingly unknown, in contrast to much of modernity when the future was seen as something that the present can master. The kind of problems human societies faced in the past are today in the context of the Anthropocene, with climate change endan-

---

1 See Freeden (2009).
2 These were not his words and the phrase an invention: Santayana in fact wrote: 'remember, so that you don't make the same mistake again' (p. 89) and 'mistakes are often discovered too late' (p. 54).

https://doi.org/10.1515/9783111240602-004

gering the viability of society, the as-yet uncertain implications of new technologies such as AI, and increased societal complexity very different from the problems that previous societies had to deal with. The past does not provide much of a guide when it comes to anthropogenic risks, which are now generally regarded as the most likely cause of existential threats to humankind, since the major catastrophes that occurred in human history were predominantly natural. In that sense, learning from the errors or even the achievements of past may not be entirely reliable as a guide for the future. Our sense of the future today may then be very different from the older and established views of the future.

It may also be the case that we have misunderstood the errors of the past, as in the assumption that the civilizations and societies of the premodern world perished because they lacked the knowledge that allegedly gave to modernity the means to determine the future in its own image or the controversial view, to be discussed later in this chapter, that they often got wrong the balance with the natural environment and as a result perished. Accordingly, in this chapter I aim to assess the degree to which the past offers a guide to the future. I neither want to write past historical experiences with catastrophe off as the history of error nor see those histories as times of lost opportunities.

The Future in the Past

In Greek mythology Cassandra was a Trojan princess, the daughter of the Priam, King of Troy. She had the power of foresight but it came with the curse that no one would believe her prophecies. Thus, her prediction of the defeat and destruction of Troy was not believed. She also foresaw her own death but could do nothing to prevent it. The figure of Casandra has come to symbolize those who see catastrophe but are not believed. There is something universal about Casandra as an aspect of the human condition that refers to the failure to face the future which stares one in the face but the subject responds with disbelief and helplessness. While in a sense we are all Cassandras, in seeking comfort in the illusion that the future will not be different from the present, it is a condition that is more characteristic of the premodern world than the modern in that it was a predisposition nurtured by a time consciousness that no longer exists. The modern age was born of the belief that the future would be different from the present. Nonetheless, we still suffer from the myopia of seeing catastrophe but not being able to do much about it.

The premoderns' view of the future was conditioned by their system of knowledge which led them to understand time and space as fairly fixed. The cosmos was relatively ordered and reflected the order of the Gods. In Greek mythology, Apollo was the God of prophecies, but mortals could not see into the future, nor could they believe those like Casandra who had that divine gift given to her by Apollo. Tiresias, a prophet of Apollo, was allowed to see the future after he was blinded for seeing her naked; according to another myth he was blinded for revealing the secrets of the gods.[3] Either way, his prophecies were to no avail. The future could therefore only be fate and its foresight from oracles produced prophecies that could not be altered. This was also the fate of Oedipus who was unable to escape his destiny of which he had foreknowledge to kill his father and marry his mother.

According to another Greek myth, Pandora's Box was opened by Pandora, who was the first woman on earth, having been tricked into doing so with the result that the evils that were put into it escaped as a curse to humanity by the gods. She managed to close the box but too late, for only one curse was kept inside – this was the curse of hope. The meaning of the myth is unclear. It could mean that humankind was not allowed to hope, or if it did hope it would be to its detriment. But it could also mean that the promise of hope could be preserved for the future.

The Greeks had two words for time: *Chronos* and *Kairos*. The former, which established the modern legacy of chronology, referred to sequential time and a product of creation myths, while the latter referred to the time as the moment, the now. Nonetheless, the ancient Greeks had an advanced understanding of time in many respects; they designed clocks and calendars, and time was central to the writings of Plato and Aristotle, for whom it signaled variously becoming, duration, change. However, unlike modern time consciousness, the ancient conception of time, despite enlarging the space of reflection, left little room for human agency to change the course of history, since the world and the structure of reality cannot be effectively changed. The future was a matter of fate or destiny, revealed by oracles, by prophets, or in ancient books. According to Agnes Heller, there is no time in Platonism. Premodern thought was hierarchical, so the immutable had to be given priority over a view that sees in time a force of destruction and change. In her analysis, the Greek and Roman concept of time was in essence a conception of motion and emphasized the eternal repetition of the same (Heller 1999).

In ancient China, the *I Ching*, one of the oldest known books, was used to predict the future. Confucius said, 'Study the past if you would define the future.' In Hindu thought, the Sanskrit book 'Bhavishya Purana' was a prophetic text on the future, meaning 'History of the Future' ('Bhavishya' means 'the future' in Hindi). It can be located as part of the prophetic tradition and concerned among other topics

---

3 See Alfred Schutz's interpretation (Schutz 1959).

the kings that were predicted to rule in the future. Time consciousness, however, was not necessarily entirely characterized by fatalism, at least in the writings of Aristotle, who opposed the position of the fatalist, and held that future was not predetermined but open. Another aspect of the future in ancient thought was that it could be known by looking backward into the past, as in the truths contained in mythology. The past thus offered the present a guide to the future. As Marcus Aurelius wrote in his *Mediations*, 'Never let the future disturb you. You will meet it if you have to with the same weapons of reason which arm you against the present' (Book VII, paragraph 8).

This is not to suggest that the ancients were not particularly interested in the future, even if it had a less important place in their time consciousness than the past. As Pollak has shown in a classic work, the image of the future existed throughout history (Pollak 1973). The birth of history writing with Herodotus, often regarded as the 'father of historians,' marked a different approach, one that stressed inquiry based on facts rather than received wisdom. At the end of the first chapter of Book 1 of *The History of the Peloponnesian Wars*, Thucydides, a contemporary of Herodotus, wrote in 431 BC: 'The absence of romance in my history will, I fear, detract somewhat from its interest; but if be judged by those inquirers who desire an exact knowledge of the past and aid to the interpretation of the future, which in the course of human beings must resemble if it does not reflect it, I shall be content.'[4] Along with the histories of Herodotus, this was one of the first works that reflected the modern practice of historical writing as a science that was not subservient to myth and story-telling. History, while telling a story, was supposed to be recording an accurate account of the past. In this passage we also see a clear orientation to the future, with history as an aid to the 'interpretation of the future.' This is perhaps one of the most direct statements in ancient thought on the idea of the future that challenges the hapless fate of Casandra. The quest for a 'good life' or, per Plato, the search for a perfect political system also reflected an orientation to the future.

In *The Decline of the West*, Spengler in 1918 claimed incorrectly that Plato had no conception of the future, which Spengler understood to be a dynamic force and part of the organic necessity of life. While this idea of the future was not present in Plato, for whom the analysis of the physical structure of the cosmos gives us a sense of our place in the greater scheme of things, and in many ways the future was a product of the present, he had nonetheless a conception of how the present can transcend itself. The world of what Plato called the *Ideas* transcended the

---

4 The book is accessible on the Gutenberg Project, https://www.gutenberg.org/files/7142/7142-h/7142-h.htm#link2HCH0002

human world but in a way that opens the human world to something larger (see Hausheer 1929). Thought is future oriented.

Despite these qualifications, it is difficult to disagree with Koselleck when he wrote: 'Until the early modern period, it was a general principle derived from experience that the future could bring nothing fundamentally different' (Koselleck, 2002: 112). The idea of an open future was not a characteristic of premodern thought. Unexpected occurrences, such as natural disasters, were seen as part of the order of things. This view pertained as well to political and social upheaval, which did not lead to a conception of a different future. Despite the attempt to escape the Casandra syndrome through historical inquiry, the ancients did not have the means that we have to determine the future through human agency or to imagine very different futures. The fact that modal logic was central to the thought of late antiquity and early medieval times did not alter this, as such modes of reasoning apparently were not extended to the political domain (Knuuttila 2021). The concept of an eternal time did exist, as in the idea of Rome as an 'eternal city,' but this was a belief that Rome will never perish. The ancients had a limited understanding of infinity, as in the Greek concept of *apeiron*. The notion of infinity was a modern development and related to the discovery of the cosmos as a place in which the human world was just a tiny speck. 'This was made possible by the fact that the moderns adopted a positive attitude to infinity and accepted the validity of infinite processes, instead of sequestering the problem of infinity, as did the Greeks, and instead of arresting endless sequences scholastically or theologically by assuming the absolute nature of the unlimited, as did Christianity' (Strydom 2017: 795; see also Alexander 2015).

Later, the Christian worldview led to a conception of time that was defined by creation (that is, in the past), revelation, and redemption (or salvation), which could be achieved in the present in order to enter a future world through the 'last judgement' (Heller 1999: 174). The world and the universe had a specific point of origin and, in the eschatological conception of time, prophecies foretold an apocalyptical end to all that was created. The notion of the apocalypse, which means revelation, was a powerful expression of the future for much of the history of western civilization. It signaled a conception of the future that would dawn on the last day, a meaning that as Habermas has remarked was still retained by Schelling in *Philosophy of the Ages of the World* (Habermas 1987: 5). Arguably the Christian faith was a future-oriented one, especially in the millenarian movements, even if its conception of the future entailed its final end (Cohen 1961, Hall 2009, Weber 2000). Before the end of the world, redemption is possible. The future could be conceived only through revelation, by which God's plan would be revealed to those who had belief. In that sense, as Koselleck also commented in the above mentioned essay, the history of Christianity is a history of expectations.

The key concept of the Christian notion of the future was redemption, the belief that the individual could redeem, i.e., gain salvation, themselves through atonement in order to enter the Kingdom of God. All modern ideas of the future were defined against this notion of the future, which also bequeathed the notion of the end of history. This became less important to Christianity, which settled with the individualization of redemption as personal salvation.

One of the main alternative conceptions of time before modernity to the Christian linear one was the cyclical theory of time. This was prevalent in most of the early civilizations and persisted in Chinese, Hindu, Egyptian, Mayan, Inca thought and was also present in Greek thought. The cyclical view of time was based on the recognition of occurrences in nature and that human life had a similar process of birth, death and rebirth. It made sense for a long time to many cultures as it was rooted in bodily experience (Fuchs 2018). While this view of time was also part of the Christian worldview, it was given a more pronounced linear direction in that the passage of time led to a final end. In contrast, the cyclical theory of time posited an eternal return.

Cyclical conceptions of civilization were revived in modern times by Giambattista Vico in *The New Science* in 1725, a work that sought to outline a systematic theory of history in terms of the rise and fall of cultures, and later by Oswald Spengler in *The Decline of the West* (Spengler 1926 [1918]). Arnold Toynbee in his 12-volume *Study in History* [1934–61] outlined the history of civilization in terms of a process of cycles of growth, decay, and collapse (Toynbee 1987). Nietzsche, influenced by the ancient Greek notion of becoming, had a similar theory of eternal recurrence, the idea that history will repeat itself over and over again. The concept in Nietzsche is certainly obscure and is related to his other notion of *amor fati*, love of fate, and has been interpreted to express the affirmation of life and existence, which never comes to an end and never had a beginning. Such an interpretation can be found in Milan Kundera's 1984 book, *The Unbearable Lightness of Being*, which was inspired by Nietzsche's notion of the eternal return and sought to give a deeper meaning to the present moment. The world was not created by a God, Nietzsche held, in contrast to Christian theology, but was eternally in a state of recurrence. To accept this was the challenge for the individual rather than to seek salvation. In *Human All Too Human* in 1898 he wrote, 'Our destiny exercises its influence over us even when, as yet, we have not learned its nature: it is our future that lays down the law to our today' (preface, paragraph 7).

Modernity has arguably been too dismissive of premodern ideas of the future, which were reflected in Nietzsche's notion of the eternal recurrence. We have lost the closer connection that they experienced between the human world and nature. This perhaps explains the interest in 2012 in the Mayan Long Calendar and its alleged prophecy of the end of the world on 21st December 2012, following the end of a 5126-year-old cycle. However, this was a modern invention and based on a mis-reading of the Mayan calendar.[5] Other Mesoamerican ideas of the future are less apocalyptical. It has recently been noted that the Armondawa, an Amazonian tribe, do not have a conception of time.[6] Danowski and Viveiros, two Brazilian anthro-pologists, also find in Amerindian thought a different time consciousness from the western philosophical tradition, which does not operate around the distinction between nature and culture or one that assigns animals to the past and humans to the future: 'What we call "environment" is for them a society of societies, an inter-national area, a *cosmopoliteia*. There is, therefore, no absolute difference in status between society and environment, as if the first were the "subject", the second the "object"' (2017: 69). The destruction of the Amerindian world by modernity gives them first-hand experience to tell us something about the future: 'we are on the verge of a process in which the planet as a whole will become something like six-teenth-century America: a world invaded, wrecked, and razed by barbarian for-eigners' (2017: 108). But with this insight, we are already in the domain of the mod-ern. According to Agnes Heller, time 'is the "imaginary institution" of modernity, primarily historical imagination, which places time at the centre point of philo-sophical reflection'; it is related to demise, disappearance, unsteadiness, motion, and change (Heller 1999: 173).

Modernity was born with the separation of the social world from the natural world and the declaration of a different temporality for human societies than the laws of nature. We cannot recover what has been lost; the clock cannot be reset. The ancient world of the classical civilizations was based on agricultural econo-mies and relatively rigid social organization that made natural time a premise of history, as Koselleck remarked (2002: 106). Luhmann also acknowledged this in his argument that the future, while not a modern invention, was more central to its self-understanding than was the case with premodern societies (Luhmann 1992). There was little space for an advanced conception of the future in societies that saw the world and the wider cosmos as relatively small and fixed and the human world at the center.

The appeal of simpler societies exerts an attraction for many people today when faced with the problems that complex modern societies have created, but de-spite the allure of the past it is not at all evident what it really has to offer the pre-sent. The ancient idea of the future remained limited and informed by how the present was experienced, and this in turn was the outcome of past events. The

---

5 https://www.nationalgeographic.com/science/article/111220-end-of-world-2012-maya-calendar-ex plained-ancient-science

6 See https://www.bbc.com/news/science-environment-13452711

rise of Christianity – which must be seen as a radical overcoming of antiquity and its forms of knowledge – led to a preordained conception of time that offered only the prospect of personal redemption by a savior. Christianity introduced a radical notion of the future as the end of human time. Even if the modern idea of the future broke with the Christian one, as Hans Blumenberg (1985 [1966]) argued in *The Legitimacy of the Modern Age*, it was very much influenced by the vision of a possible future world (see Chapter Three). The pursuit of redemption in Christian thought – and in its most radical form in the millenarian Protestant sects – gave the idea of the future a new and radical zeal. Christian thought was a product of the medieval age, but it was also a major force in the transition to modernity when the Protestant Reformation gave a long-lasting cultural impetus to modern society, as was most systematically analyzed by Max Weber with his theory of rationalization and the 'Protestant Ethic' providing modern capitalism with a spiritual foundation. Thus, the making of money, itself a future-oriented activity, had a close parallel with Christian ideas of the accumulation of salvation. There can be no doubt that the religion has played a significant role in shaping the idea of the future. It was a central insight of classical sociology that some notion of a reward in the future is essential to the present.

The notion that the past is a guide to the future survived well into modern times. Even a skeptical thinker such as David Hume wrote in his *Treatise on Human Nature* [1739]: 'The supposition that the future resembles the past, isn't based on arguments of any kind, and comes from a habit that makes us expect for the future the same sequence of events as we have been accustomed to in the past' (Book 1, Part iii, section 12).[7] However, he regarded habit or custom as the best guide for the future.

Yet, examples can be found in the Renaissance mind that saw the future as manifest in human will rather than fate or fortune. Shakespeare wrote in *Julius Caesar* in 1599: 'Men are sometime the masters of their fate. The fault, dear Brutus, is not in our stars, but in ourselves, that we are underlings.'[8] Another glimpse of the future is to be found in famous lines in *Macbeth:* 'If you can look into the seeds of time, and say which grain will grow and which will not speak them to me.'[9] Earlier in the century, Machiavelli in *The Prince* [1532] questioned the prevailing Renaissance idea of the dominance of fortune when he wrote, 'so as not to rule out

---

7 Available at https://www.earlymoderntexts.com/assets/pdfs/hume1739book1.pdf
8 These words of Cassius talking to Brutus in Act 1, Scene 11 have often been phrased as, 'It is not in the stars to hold our destiny but in ourselves.'
9 Act 1, Scene 3.

free will, I believe that it is probably true that fortune is the arbiter of half the things we do, leaving the other half or so be controlled by ourselves.'[10]

Failed Societies and Civilizational Collapse

One obvious way to understand how societies today or in the near future will bear up and cope with the many challenges that they face, as well as those yet to come, is to look back into history and examine comparable situations or ones that might cast some light on the predicament of the present. In the context of the Anthropocene today, the specter of civilizational collapse looms large. One of the major examples of civilizational collapse was in the the beginning of the late Holocene. As noted in the previous chapter, in geological time, the Late Holocene Meghalayan Age began over 4,200 years ago following a period of cooling that led to the end of some of the first civilizations due to mega droughts in those regions.

While it is unlikely that for now the entirety of human society will fail,[11] there is certainly the dire prospect of societal failure for many parts of the world as global temperatures soar and droughts turn many parts of the world into inhospitable wastelands. Some of these problems have been faced in the past, though the cause in these cases was not human-induced climate change on a global level. Then, there is question about the end of some of the great civilizations of the world, for reasons that cannot be attributed to changes in the natural environment. What lessons can be learned from some of the major critical junctures of the past when a social and political order – be it a state, empire, or civilization – came to end as a result of either internal or external shocks?

Some of the most striking examples of the collapse of a major social and political order that comes to mind are the end of the Roman Empire, the end of the Mayan civilization, or the end of the USSR. These examples are often characterized by a strong sense of collapse, though as will be argued in this chapter this is a somewhat questionable concept. Of the many other examples that one could consider are those associated with a revolution that brought about the downfall of the old order, for example, the French Revolution in 1789, the Russian Revolution in 1917, the Chinese Revolution in 1911, and, culminating in the formation of the People's Republic of China in 1949, the victory of the Khmer Rouge, who declared in

---

10 Machiavelli (1982) [1532] Chapter XXV, p. 130. He questions the view of the time that 'events are controlled by fortune and by God in such a way that the prudence of men cannot modify them, indeed, that men have no influence whatsoever.'
11 For a different view see Erlich and Erlich (2013).

the tradition of the French Revolutionary calendar a Year Zero on 17th April 1975 when they took over Cambodia.

Despite the fascination of these cataclysmic events, they are perhaps less relevant to us today in that it is less likely that we will see a revolutionary breakdown of one political order and the emergence of another in the way that was a feature of the great revolutions of the previous centuries whereby a revolutionary elite with a mass following swept to power and created a new social and political order. In all these cases the revolutionary elites gained control of the center of power – the central organs of the state and the removal of the sovereign. Today, power is generally less concentrated in the figure of the sovereign ruler, making revolutionary change difficult, though not necessarily impossible, as illustrated by the revolutions in central and eastern Europe in 1989/1990. However, arguably, these were the last such revolutions in western societies and have been referred to as 'catching-up' revolutions. The prevalence of authoritarian regimes in many parts of the world – particularly dictatorships such as Russia, Belarus, North Korea, and Myanmar, for example – undoubtedly offers more scope for revolutionary transformation. Since the Russo-Ukrainian war in 2022, and the consequent realignment of the world into liberal democracies and authoritarian regimes coupled with malfunctioning democracies, the future prospects of major revolutions should not be excluded. We are very far from the 'end of history' in that specific sense of the worldwide triumph of liberal democracy. As Turchin has argued, there are recurring patterns throughout history since the first states formed about 5,000 years ago that reveal cycles of political disintegration that brought about elite overproduction resulting in intraelite conflict, popular immiseration leading to mass mobilization potential, declining state legitimacy and fiscal crisis, and geopolitical factors. Of these the first has been the main driver of instability and potential cause of a revolutionary transformation (Turchin 2023). I return to this topic in the final chapter of this book.

In the present context, and with a view to lessons from the past, I am more interested in visions of collapse or the catastrophic end of a particular society rather than questions of revolutionary transformation arising from political disintegration (Turchin 2023). So, given that today we face such scenarios of collapse, as Servigne and Stevens (2020) argue in their book on collapse as the horizon of our present, we can consider how previous civilizations faced decline and even collapse. Is our predicament different?

Such discussions about the specter of collapse are not specific to our time (Butzer and Endfield 2012). As often remarked in the emerging popular literature on collapse, which has given rise to the semiscientific genre of 'collapsology,' Edward Gibbon's *The History of the Decline and Fall of the Roman Empire* (1776–1789) was a major reference for those interested in the notion of the collapse of civilization.

The Roman Empire is one of the famous examples of decline and, in the stronger sense, of collapse. Gibbon, a secular Whig, believed, undoubtedly erroneously, that the adoption of Christianity by the Roman Empire was one of the main internal causes of its decline (along with external causes, such as attacks from the Germanic peoples). That he was wrong on this did not stop his history from becoming one of the best-known accounts of the end of the ancient world. However, he did not invoke the notion of collapse but began a trend to see in the decline of the Roman Empire whatever one wanted to find – in his case the corrupting effects of Christianity.

The attraction that this powerful concept of collapse has is not unrelated to the modernist fascination with the ruins of a past anterior to the recent past. The notion that the modern age began after the end of the medieval age and an earlier Dark Age was accompanied by the rediscovery of antiquity as a model of a world that was lost but which the modern era can emulate. The repudiation of the recent past and the glorification of a long-lost past was central to the self-understanding of modernity that came with the Enlightenment. It was undoubtedly this romantic belief in a heroic age that inspired the search for lost cultures – Troy, Mycenae, ancient Egypt, etc. – and the investigation into their disappearance and descent into a long 'Dark Age.' Nonetheless, the modern age was characterized by a strong sense of its own future. It is possible that the preoccupation with the vanished world of antiquity and other classical civilizations was because they were deemed not to possess the advances in science and technology that were the basis of modernity. As the inheritor of the mantle of ancient Greece and Rome, those societies at the forefront of modernity could proclaim a certain superiority over those parts of the world perceived as premodern.

There was one major problem with the notion of the collapse of civilization. One of the most vivid examples of collapse was the end of the Aztec civilization in the wake of the Spanish conquest of 1521, led by Herman Cortes. The Aztec civilization experienced a loss of ninety percent of its pre-Columbian population, largely as a result of infectious diseases, principally smallpox and measles, which the Spanish brought with them and against which the Aztecs had no resistance. The Aztec kingdom fell from 30 million to just 3 million in a very short time. This was without doubt one of the greatest historical catastrophes in world history, since there was no recovery from such devastation. In less dramatic terms, the defeat of the Incas can also be mentioned in this context, though in this case the Inca culture did not suffer the same degree of devastation as befell the Aztecs. These examples are reminders that major examples of the sudden collapse of civilization can be attributed to European imperialism.

The collapse literature has been inspired by two now classic books: Joseph Tainter's *The Collapse of Complex Societies* (1988) and Jared Diamond's *Collapse:*

How Societies Choose to Fail or Survive (2006). The former has been a basis for more technical studies originally within the field of archaeology and ancient history for the study of collapse, while Diamond's later book was a more popular and widely read book stemming from historical geography.[12] Tainter was concerned with systemic imbalances built into complex systems which he believed were universal tendencies in all societal systems. As societies become more complex, they develop systemic problems arising principally from decreasing returns on inputs, especially in their requirements for energy. Tainter's influential work, which brought a thermodynamic dimension into historical collapse scenarios, was based on archaeological evidence from a range of the major civilizations of the ancient world and from which he tried to develop a theoretical model of a nonapocalyptical nature to account for their demise. Civilizations develop necessarily into complex systems, but a point is reached, essentially a tipping point, where complexity becomes dysfunctional with crises mounting and which eventually leads to the collapse of the system. His main examples on which he elaborated in more detail are the collapse of the western Roman Empire, the Mayan civilization, and the Chacoan, a people who lived in the San Juan Basis of Northern New Mexico. All three in his analysis experienced rapid collapse: the latter by around 1100 AD, the Mayan around 1200 AD, and the Roman Empire around 500 AD. Environmental factors did not play a major role in his analysis, nor did external factors. For Tainter, the problems were endemic structural ones; for example, Rome's collapse was due to excessive costs of running its far-flung empire, while the Mayan collapse was due to the burden of an increasingly costly society and an increasingly weakened population. In all cases 'the costliness of complexity increased over time while benefits to the population decline' (Tainter 1988: 191).

While Tainter's study was based on contested archaeological evidence, there are some interesting applications to contemporary society. His core argument was that complexity arises from the need of societies to solve technical and organizational problems, but once a society reaches a certain level its requirements for energy and other resources are so great that it struggles to maintain the balance between gain and loss. It is not difficult to see a parallel with the problem of environmental sustainability today. However, this application does go beyond Tainter's model in that all the examples he discussed did not concern environmental issues to a significant extent, though other accounts, including Diamond's, relating to the Maya collapse suggest the presence of environmental challenges, such as

---

12 There is a larger literature that can also be noted, for example, Johnson (2017) and Yoffee, N. and Cowgill (1988), McAnany, P. and Yoffee, N. (2010).

drought.[13] The problem of complexity in advanced modern societies is arguably different from complexity in the early civilizations, which had fewer instruments at their disposal to manage social problems, for example, the availability of information and the industrial production of food. The model also does not offer sufficient consideration of the capacity of society for social learning and evolutionary advances. It is an approach that sees all advanced systems caught with the systemic problem of high entropy generating chaos but a return to low entropy is not possible. However, the onset of major crises in complex societies does not necessarily lead to their demise, as is amply illustrated by the history of capitalism, which is inherently crisis prone and yet does not show any signs of coming to a rapid end.

It is also highly questionable that the western Roman Empire collapsed in sense of coming to a rapid end. An alternative view would see it as having undergone a lengthy period of decline lasting two to three centuries. It did of course come to an end, as did other civilizations such as the Celtic one, except where it survived in the western fringes of the British Isles and Brittany. The notion of a civilizational collapse places too much emphasis on a sudden end (see, for example, Eisenstadt 1988). This disguises continuity as in many cases a major rupture does not signal the end of what went before but its transformation into a new form, for example, the October Revolution in 1917 brought about an end to the Russian Empire and the rule of the Tzars. The rise of the USSR with the victory of the Bolsheviks in the subsequent civil war was a major rupture in European and Russian history. However, there was also historical continuity in several respects, for instance, in the absolute system of rule enjoyed by Stalin. In many other examples, there is evidence of the new adopting the old or the old simply surviving, as in for instance the persistence of the *ancien regime*, the survival of Roman Law long after the end of the Roman Empire becoming a template for European law, the adoption of the Catholic Church of the culture of imperial Rome. As the example of the decline of feudalism illustrates, its demise and transition to capitalism took several centuries, making it difficult to speak of collapse. In contrast, the USSR 'collapsed' very rapidly in 1990/91 but it is difficult to see its end as a civilizational collapse, since it quickly and relatively peacefully transformed itself into the Russian Federation and the old elites continued in new guises. Collapse, a term that appears on the titles of many books about the end of the USSR, may be the wrong term to describe something coming to an end, despite the economic chaos that ensued. The Constitution of the USSR allowed for the free exit of its constituent republics from the union. The fact that some fifteen republics invoked this right of exit is in effect a matter of legal dissolution rather than collapse.

---

13 See Kenneth *et al.* 2023.

Jared Diamond's well-known book, *Collapse*, had a different focus and under-standing of collapse. 'By collapse, I mean a drastic decrease in human population size and/or political/economic/social complexity, over a considerable area, for an extended period' (2005: 3). While Tainter was concerned exclusively with the col-lapse of whole empires and civilizations, Diamond examined smaller communities in history that perished, such as the Polynesian culture of Easter Island and the Medieval Norse society in Greenland. He also assigned a greater role to environ-mental degradation as in the depletion of natural resources and generally how so-cieties respond to the natural environment. His story is one of cultural loss, the perishing of a whole society leaving only monumental ruins, as a result of people making mostly the wrong choices when faced with environmental problems or other kinds of social and political challenges. He seeks to overcome the reluctance we have to accept that people in the past may have been responsible for their doom and are not necessarily shining examples of a happy relation with nature. However, his book, despite an enormous wealth of scholarship, has been contro-versial for many reasons, including his assumption that indigenous peoples in the past were responsible for 'ecocide' and that these examples anticipate, or in some way serve as a warning, for the coming of the Anthropocene.

The assumptions of the thesis of civilizational or cultural collapse have been questioned by scholars who argue that Diamond misunderstood the historical re-cord (McAnany and Yoffee, 2010). Hunt and Lip (2010) argue that his analysis of the decline of the Polynesian culture of Easter Island as reckless exploitation of its nat-ural resources was flawed as there was not just one cause but several. The real story, they argue, 'is one of human ingenuity and success that lasted for more than 500 years on one of the world's most remote human outposts' (Hunt and Lip 2010): 41). Berglund (2010) makes a similar argument concerning the Norse Greenlanders, who he claims adapted as well as they could to changing environ-mental conditions, adapting, for example, from an agricultural to a marine econ-omy, and left, when conditions became too harsh, toward the end of the fourteenth century having already outlasted their settlement, where they had lived for 450 years.

Tainter and Diamond in their different ways made very important contribu-tions to how the future of human societies might be imagined. Tainter emphasized rapid decline while Diamond recognized that the collapse of a society takes a long time. But, both identified collapse as a key dynamic in the past with the implica-tion that it will continue in the future. The large critical literature to which this thesis has given rise – including why some societies fail and others succeed or how others cope with upheaval[14] – questions some of the relevance of the specter of collapse for the present day, as well as raising questions about the accuracy of some of the accounts of the decline of previous societies. While Tainter's model was too rigid in its assumption that collapse is the inevitable fate of all complex systems due to the intractable problem of entropy, Diamond offered a broader vision of people in the past making the wrong decisions about the relation of their social and political order to the natural environment. His book, as reflected in its subtitle 'How societies choose to fail or survive', placed too much emphasis on choice. In his analysis, political leaders make choices that may prove to be detrimental to society. This does not take adequate account of the fact that many societal problems cannot be so easily cast in terms of a choice but are deeply embedded in structures that are not easily reduced to choice situations.

One theme that runs through much of the critical literature on the collapse thesis is that in fact the historical record has been one of remarkable resilience and survival, and in the case of societies that eventually perished, their demise was a lengthy one, at least in relation to modern societies, which roughly have been in existence for not more than about 400 years. This is also borne out by Graeber and Wengrow (2021) in their study of the deep-prehistory of humanity. Indeed, many societies that perished did so as a result of the encounter with modern societies. Does it really make sense to see the past in terms of collapse? The fact that major historical change occurred, for instance, in the passage from the medieval world to the modern, does not mean that everything that went before modernity collapsed. If that were the case, the historical condition would be one of endless collapses.

The collapse paradigm has the additional weakness of not allowing for an adequate consideration of agency. While Diamond's book did give a major role to choice, social actors themselves were relatively passive in his account and in Tainter's more or less absent. The danger with this is a lurking Malthusianism whereby situations of catastrophe are rendered depoliticized. Malthusian ideas about civilizational nemesis first arose with the fear of population increase outstripping the supply of food, the famous but highly discredited argument of *An Essay on the Principle of Population* in 1798. Thomas Malthus believed that pressure from population growth will always be greater than the propensity for food supply. The result is a potential threat of mass starvation and decline (in addition to famine, he saw war and disease as also responses to the problem of overpopulation). His position – an expression of his reactionary antirepublican politics – met with fierce opposition from socialists for claiming that inequality was a natural conse-

---

14 Acemoglu and Robinson (2013) and Diamond (2019).

quence of population increase. His book has been seen as a conservative response to socialists, such as William Godwin. The Malthusian predicament is admittedly always lurking in that societies are frequently in danger of destroying the conditions of their own survival when fundamental imbalances occur, though system disequilibrium is unlikely to result from population increase, as famine is more likely to occur as a result of the failure of politics. It is precisely for this reason that we should not lose sight of the political nature of potential catastrophe.

The collapse thesis offers a limited perspective on the challenges facing the world today. Diamond concluded his book with a note of hope that we can 'learn from the mistakes of distant peoples and past peoples' (2005: 525). However, it is not apparent what we can really learn from the collapse of ancient societies. In view of the highly questionable assumptions Diamond made about earlier societies having perished as a result of their failure to live in harmony with their natural environment, many of the lessons do not have much of a foundation. If there are lessons to be learned from the past, it may quite well be the opposite, namely how human resilience is possible in the face of challenging natural environments.

This is a position that Hanusch and Bierman (2020) adopt in an argument that a 'deep time' perspective on the past can offer a guide to the future. In an analysis that addresses long-term institutional survival of various kinds of organizations, there may be a lesson for the kind of organizations we need to find to face the challenges of the future. While the basic argument is unobjectionable, it is not at all clear that because something has survived for long, it is fit for purpose, especially for the very great challenges of climate change and other major problems such as pandemics yet to come.

In their work on human prehistory, Graeber and Wengrow (2021) made a strong case for a new look at the early origins of human society with the proposal that this can reveal something for the future of humanity and how we get out of our current situation in which we are described as 'stuck.' Rejecting the Enlightenment notion of a prior state of nature from which humanity fell, as in Rousseau's notion of an idyllic past that was corrupted by society or the contrary Hobbesian idea of a violent state of nature, they show in an impressive comparative analysis that human prehistory was much more varied than in conventional accounts. Early hunter-gatherer societies should not be understood according to the later model of societies organized around the state and had very different models of social organization, especially about the nature of property that reveals a great deal of creativity. The Upper Paleolithic Period (c. 50,000 to 150,000 BC) was a vast stretch of time in comparison to the relatively short period of the history of civilization, the past about 10,000 to 12,000 years. They reject the conventional story of the absence of social organization prior to the advent of farming and that the agricultural revolution led directly to the first states and thus to civilization. There was no agricultural revolution as such simply because the emergence of farming took around 3,000 years, which is far too long to constitute a revolution, and some 6,000 years stood before its origins and the formation of states (pp. 233–48), during which time there were very many different forms of social life.

This all brings an important fresh perspective to bear on the early history of humanity, but the overall message is not without some problems. The authors, committed to an anarchistic theory of society, reduce modernity and much of civilizational history to the same kind of myths that they debunk on prehistory. Rousseau's theory of the origins of society is just one account, as is Hobbes'. There is no consideration of the dialectical theory of society that posits social struggles as the engine of change. Evolution is reduced to discredited notions of stages and little appreciation of evolutionary leaps in history, including in the period under discussion, for according to Mythen, a major evolutionary shift occurred with the evolution of human intelligence (Mythen 1998). A further problem is the fact of numbers: 10,000 years ago, before the early civilizations had formed, the population of the world was around 5 million and much of it still nomadic (by 1000 CE, it reached 300 million and by 1800 1 billion) while today it is 8 billion. With such vastly different numbers, archaic communities do not offer a model for the future. In sum, it is not entirely clear what a deep view of history can really tell us about our present predicament. It can certainly tell something, such as the recognition that for much of history humanity lived in different forms of social organization and that transitions often take a very long time to an extent that they are not really transitions at all for those living in the period of transition. It is difficult to disagree with the core aim of their book: 'What if instead of telling a story about how our species fell from some idyllic state of equality, we ask how we became trapped in such tight conceptual shackles that we can no longer imagine the possibility of reinventing ourselves?' (p. 9). The problem is that this myth, which clearly needs to be debunked, was already discarded long ago. Something more will be needed to achieve the aim of creating an alternative future.

Catastrophes and History

Theories of the collapse of earlier societies are based on the centrality of catastrophe, generally those human induced. The notion of catastrophe, however, has a wider application beyond the specter of civilizational collapse. The arrival of a catastrophe may not lead to the collapse of a social order. Today, as discussed in the Introduction, there is considerable consciousness of catastrophe as a feature of our time. The Anthropocene is itself a time whose arrow points to a cataclysmic catastrophe, as does the notion of a 'sixth mass extinction.'[15] Revisiting the historical experience of catastrophe may offer a perspective on the current situation, even if to reveal the singularity of the present predicament.

Catastrophes have been a feature of history. It is arguably the case that earlier societies had to cope to a far greater extent with catastrophes than we do today, despite the fact that such cataclysmic events have been very rare. In the geological history of the earth, the five mass extinctions occurred long before the emergence of *Homo sapiens* (Brannen 2018). There is an interesting philosophical question, which we will not explore further, whether these were actually 'catastrophes,' since our notion of catastrophe is anthropogenic, an event that is detrimental to humans. It does not appear to be relevant to prehuman history. While the early history of *Homo sapiens* was turbulent and human survival never guaranteed, as evidenced by the existence of eight now-extinct human species, the Holocene, the geological period in which settled human societies arose, has been a remarkably stable period in climatic terms and when relatively few global-wide cataclysmic catastrophes occurred in the course of its almost 12,000-year history. The Anthropocene, in contrast, portends a catastrophe yet to come, while earlier societies often had to live with the repeated occurrence of catastrophes, both natural catastrophes, resulting from earthquakes and volcanic eruptions, and human-caused ones, such as the effects of war, disease, and famine. Catastrophes yet to come are not only climatic ones, as Smil (2012) outlines in his fifty-year projection of future catastrophes. Nuclear war still remains the most likely global catastrophe, and more probable than an asteroid collision or a supervolcanic eruption destroying most of life. A hydrogen bomb explosion has the capacity to irreparably damage the earth's ozone layer. It is true of course that for many people, especially in the global South, catastrophe is something not yet to come but has arrived.

Catastrophes are distinct from disasters, as Bryan Turner has argued in his theory of catastrophe (Turner 2023). Catastrophes are disasters but not all disasters amount to catastrophes. The distinction is not easy to pin down, since disaster can be culturally constructed as catastrophes. The sinking of the Titanic in 1912 was clearly a disaster but one that led to the rise of the imagination of catastrophe, which was fed by such dramatic and unexpected events.[16] However difficult it is to separate the event from the imaginary, which can have a life of its own, as

---

15 There were five mass extinctions in history, the previous was the Cretaceous mass extinction c. 66 million years when the dinosaurs were wiped out in the aftermath of an asteroid collision (Brannen 2018). We may be amid a sixth mass extinction today as a consequence of anthropogenic activity (Kolberg 2014).

16 See Horn (2018) for a study of the imagination of catastrophe.

we have seen with the notion of 'collapse,' it seems sensible to be able to distinguish between disasters and catastrophes.

Ferguson (2021) in his account of the politics of catastrophe makes no distinction between both, which he uses interchangeably. As a result the notion of 'doom' that he invokes as a feature of catastrophe loses its critical edge in encompassing the notion of disaster, which does not necessarily signal doom. The growth of disaster research in recent times, with the emergence of disaster studies as an interdisciplinary area, has also tended to conflate both. The term catastrophe indicates something greater than a disaster, which suggests something akin to an accident or a natural occurrence. Genocide embodies the sense of catastrophe in a way that disaster, even a megadisaster, does not. We would not normally describe the Holocaust as just a disaster. The Palestinian traumatic event of their dispossession and displacement was called *Nakba*, which means in Arabic 'The Catastrophe.' Hitler, Stalin, Pol Pot, and Mao were more than just disasters, but monumental catastrophes. The notion of catastrophe, itself inadequate for many such occurrences, suggests something of greater significance than what is normally included under the heading of hazards, dangers, disaster. The distinction ultimately refers to the scale of the episode and the extent to which it embodies systemic destruction and large-scale death. The consequences of a catastrophe will be greater than those of a disaster and there may be no adequate solution.

A catastrophe has the character of being an event, a calamity whose significance goes beyond the moment and has implications for the future. It is more than a single discrete episode that can be subject to disaster management. Encompassing the notion of an event, a catastrophe involves a fundamental change in the form or structure of society. In this sense, then, Hurricane Katrina in 2005 was a catastrophe and not simply a disaster in that it brought about major societal upheaval; it was 'a destabilizing event' on a huge scale (Brunsma *et al.* 2007). Similarly, the explosion of the Chernobyl nuclear reactor in 1986 was more than a disaster resulting from an accident. It was one of the events that defined the end of the twentieth century, contributing to the end of the USSR and a new worldwide consciousness of risk. For Ulrich Beck, in the book that offered a new perspective on late modernity, it marked the emergence of the 'risk society' (Beck 1992 [1986]). In this case, the death toll was relatively insignificant in relation to its destructive implications that followed. Critical, too, was the emerging consciousness of major planetary change, following the discovery in the previous year, May 1985, of the ozone hole above Antarctica. As with the Asian Tsunami of 2004, we remember such events for a long time and think about the world in a different way afterward. In such cases, while the event was local, it had a global dimension in terms of its implications. The events of September 11, 2001, in New York encapsulate this sense of a global catastrophe, the significance of which went beyond the death toll. It was a cataclysmic event with long-lasting global dimensions.

Chernobyl and Katrina were very different kinds of catastrophes in that the latter was a natural catastrophe while the former was one of human design. Yet both share the hand of humanity in that while Katrina was a devasting storm, many of the catastrophic consequences were the outcome of a failure of preparation. The devasting implications of earthquakes, for example, in Turkey in 2023, are often due to the poor design of buildings that were not built to withstand turbulence. While nothing can stop an earthquake or a storm, much of the potential damage and loss of life can be avoided. As Tierney has argued within the field of disaster research, disasters involve a mix of different forces, technological, atmospheric, and geological as well as social and political relations. This is especially the case in the context of vulnerable communities. In that sense, catastrophes such as Katrina or Chernobyl are not just external shocks but are endogenous to society (Tierney 2019: 4–19[17]). Smil (2012) sees catastrophes as having long-term effects, which may be brought about by one of two kinds of catastrophes. There are those that bring about a sudden fatal discontinuity that is globally altering and there are those that bring about a persistent but gradual trend. The latter may ultimately achieve the same outcome as a sudden event but the outcome is gradual and is identifiable only in a longer time frame. Both play out in demographic, environmental, political, and economic dimensions. Sudden events are generally of a relatively low frequency, especially events that are global. 9/11 may be such an example or, in theoretical terms, the potential impact of a major asteroid, which so far has not occurred in the history of human civilization. In addition, there is also the phenomenon of slow catastrophes, since not all are sudden-onset events (Jones 2017, Knowles 2020).

History is full of examples of catastrophe. The Lisbon earthquake in 1755 is often mentioned in accounts of catastrophe. It not only led to the destruction of Lisbon but brought about the demise of the Portuguese Empire, with the balance of power shifting from Lisbon to Rio de Janeiro. Above all, it was a European-wide event, with the effects felt in many parts of Europe and the wider Atlantic world as a result of a tsunami that followed. It was a defining event in the making of the European Enlightenment, since it revealed the vulnerability of society to the forces of nature. It marked the end of theodicies – the explanation of catastrophe or evil in the world as divine retribution – and the turn to science for explanations.

Most major wars have been described as catastrophes. The two world wars in the previous century rank as the greatest examples of catastrophe. The First World

---

17 See also Blackie *et al.* (1994); Elliott and Hsu (2016); Killen and Lebovic (2014); and Nancy (2015).

War produced in Europe a profound sense of monumental catastrophe, perhaps in a way that was different from the impact of the Second World War, which despite the horrific deaths and destruction it caused had at least the outcome of a sense of a future that could begin anew. The end of the Great War in contrast in 1918 did not have this sense of a new future, except possibly in Russia, which embarked on a new modernity after the October Revolution in 1917. The war, an apocalyptical event, led to a consciousness of civilizational collapse as a result of the huge number of deaths, which was expressed in a new culture of memorials. The presence of mass death that the war produced had a lasting effect on European societies. There was a profound turning away from the future to the past, despite the fact that the war led to a break from the nineteenth century. The 'roaring 20s' eventually shifted the mood of the time, but not enough to dispel the pervasive feeling of a world in turmoil and the drift toward fascism. Cultural pessimism was reflected in writings of the interwar years on the crisis of civilization and the idea, central to Arnold Toynbee's *Study in History* and Spengler's *Decline of the West*, that ruin is what all civilizations eventually face. Much of this pessimistic literature was also in the vein of conservative responses to the rise of 'the masses' and democracy as well as the peril that communism presented. But all these examples go beyond the category of catastrophe.

Aside from the Great War, which was an avoidable catastrophe, the real catastrophe of the period was the '1918 flu,' which claimed more than 50 million victims worldwide, far more than the number who were killed in the war. The fact that it arrived at the end of the war and continued until 1920 made it all the more devastating. Pandemics and epidemics[18] have been the most significant catastrophes in human history. They have been tipping points in many cases, leading to major societal transformation. Infectious diseases have been the principal cause of death throughout history. Smallpox killed more people than anything else in history. Since 1900 alone more than 300 million died.

From a historical perspective, epidemics had cataclysmic consequences. The decline of Athens and the rise of Sparta was the result of an epidemic. The Antonine Plague, c. 165–262 AD, led to the transformation of the Roman Empire. It played a role in the decline of the Roman Empire in the second half of the 2nd century AD during the reign of Marcus Aurelius when about 10 per cent of the population of the empire died, probably of smallpox. According to Rodney Stark (2020), it led to the rise of Christianity, for Christian communities were more successful than pagan ones in dealing with epidemics due to their ethic of care for the sick. The Plague of Justinian was linked to the final fall of Rome c. 542 AD (it dev-

---

18 I am using both terms interchangeably. Pandemics are epidemics on a global scale.

astated the empire and killed around 25 to 50 % of the population, that is, about 25 to 100 million). The Second Plague or the Bubonic Plague (also known as the Black Death, c. 1346 – 1353, with later waves in the nineteenth century) was arguably the most catastrophic of all epidemics. Apparently it led to decline of feudalism and, according to the Great Leveller thesis, it also led to a drop in inequality in Europe as a result of more than 30 % of population of Europe (about 25 million) having been wiped out. Labor costs consequently rose and the conditions of workers, especially artisans, improved with the beginnings of organized labor and a transformation in social structures that hastened the decline of feudalism (Scheidel 2018). The world by the end of the fifteenth century, c. 1470s, was very different than before (but that does require adding a century to the end of the Black Death). It is hard to say how helpful this perspective really is, since a century almost always makes a difference.

The severity of epidemics was often due to the simple fact that they coincided with another catastrophic event. The 1918 flu coincided with the Great War. The bubonic plague, caused by a deadly bacteria transmitted by fleas that were carried by rats, coincided with adverse weather conditions in the fourteenth century, leading to a major transformation in European societies. The plague interacted with war and climate change and social movements to produce long-term societal transformation. The Little Ice Age in the thirteenth century (when temperatures dropped in Europe by about 2 °C), in combination with the effects of the 1257 Samalas volcanic eruption in Indonesia, led to agricultural failure following a drop in temperature and cattle plague (Cambell 2016). There is a debate about whether the bubonic plague was an exception in terms of long-term consequences and what the time frame might be for a meaningful assessment. It does appear to be the case that we need a very long time frame to discern positive outcomes, perhaps at least half a century.

However, there is no doubt that the human response to the spread of infectious disease had a major impact on the organization of societies. Epidemics led to the consolidation of the medieval state/early modern state. They were key to the formation of the early state, whose main function was security, including protection from disease. Modernity itself was in part a product of the conquest of infectious diseases through vaccination.

One of the striking aspects of these catastrophes was that they occurred without knowledge of the causes. It wasn't until the 1930s that viruses were discovered. Once the cause and equally important the mode of transmission were known, it was easier to control (rats carrying fleas bearing the bacteria – in the case of cholera water-borne bacteria). But, this knowledge came too late for millions of people. Lack of knowledge led to fantasies about infectious diseases, giving rise to stigmatization, mass hysteria, and conspiracy theories. Diseases such as typhoid and cholera became metaphors for death and had a lasting impact on the literary imagination.

As a cause of major societal change, an epidemic or pandemic might be an acceleration of change already underway; it might be a trigger or a catalyst of major structural change (a great leveler) or it might simply be an affirmation of the status quo, that is, it may be a consequence of preexisting change. It may of course entail all three: an acceleration of change in some areas leading to glimpses of an alternative while leaving much unchanged. The Covid-19 Pandemic in 2020/21 reflected many of the historical experiences of infectious diseases, except that in this case it was the first genuinely global pandemic (Delanty 2021). The pandemic in part intensified changes already underway, as in the world of work and technology, in acting as a catalyst for change. However, it also affirmed existing structures as regards patterns of inequality. In the context of the climate crisis, there is the paradox that while humans are destroying the planet, they are also not invincible and in fact vulnerable to the forces of nature. Humans are now beholden to the tiniest particle of life which challenges all possible forms of social and political organization. Yet, societies and especially democracies have been resilient in coping with it.

Conclusion

Catastrophes are events that reveal a great deal about the nature of social life. They reveal the fundamental fact that much of history has been the experience of suffering and that human societies are fragile and highly vulnerable to breakdown. They are also ways to see the future since in many cases there is a rupture with what went before. The outcome can be a transition to something new in the aftermath of a societal collapse or, more likely, a gradual transformation of the present. Catastrophic occurrences may open a space for new thinking, as the example of the Lisbon Earthquake of 1755 indicates, or the Great Fire of London in 1666, which led to the rebuilding of London. Some of the most devasting epidemics in history – the Bubonic Plague, the 1918 flu – created the conditions for a better world, but it is only with a very distant view of the future that this becomes clear. The immediate aftermath of such events was upheaval and immense suffering.

There is one sense in which the current situation is different. It is difficult to find an example in human history of a catastrophe that is genuinely global. The 1918 flu comes close to being such an example in that its effects were felt from North America throughout Europe and India. It is now widely agreed that Covid-19, a pandemic not on the same scale in terms of mass death, has been the first global catastrophe in terms of its worldwide impact on society and the state. However, the planetary crisis is what really marks the novelty of the present in that while the catastrophic consequences are projected to occur in the future, its effects are already present.

A historical example of a different nature of catastrophe that did have quasi-global dimensions was the eruption of Mount Tambora in present-day Indonesia in 1815. It ranks as the greatest volcanic eruption in modern human history (after the far greater Toba eruption 74,000 years ago), with effects right across the northern hemisphere and causing world temperatures to drop perceptively, leading to a decade of global cooling. Byron's poem 'Darkness', written the following year, was one famous response to the apparent darkness that the spread of the volcanic ash led to. In the nineteenth century, the fear was of the world becoming colder, not hotter. In this respect, our situation is not comparable due to the extraordinary advances in science, above all in the past hundred years or so.

Despite the unknown future that we face, we have knowledge that no previous epoch had. That knowledge is not necessarily a source of emancipation, since it leads to greater uncertainty rather than the certainty that we often associate with science. Rather than accept and live with uncertainty, the quest for certainty can be dangerous. The invention of nuclear weapons is one such example. The atom bomb was invented by a group of brilliant physicists led by Robert Oppenheimer, who believed that Nazi Germany was likely to invent the atomic bomb and as a precaution the United States should get there first to protect western civilization. It transpired to be a wrong assumption (Germany did attempt to invent the atomic bomb but did not succeed). Einstein, who was not directly involved in the invention of the bomb, wrote to the US President, Franklin Roosevelt, in 1939 to advise on the development of the bomb. He and Oppenheimer and others believed that the precautionary principle was sufficient to justify such a course. After the war, these influential scientists then unsuccessfully tried to persuade the US government to refrain from further development of nuclear weapons due to their catastrophic consequences, the fact that they cannot be used as military weapons, and the fact that the enemy had been defeated. Despite the defeat of Nazi Germany, a new fear was invented – communism. This was also based on a false assumption that became an orthodoxy in the USA in the 1950s. After 1945, the USSR was militarily not in a position to seek world dominance and was not a direct threat to the USA, which initiated the arms race and the further development of nuclear weapons, including more powerful ones, such as the hydrogen bomb. But the step had been taken and there was no going back. Nuclear war still remains the most likely future cause of global catastrophe. While the short history of nuclear weapons does offer some examples of learning from past error, as the Cuban Missiles Crisis in October 1962 demonstrates, when the world came perilously close to nuclear war, for the current situation with nuclear proliferation, a greater range of more powerful bombs, and a more volatile geopolitical situation, such lessons may be to no avail.

References

Acemoglu, D. and Robinson, J. 2013. *Why Nations Fail.* London: Profile Books.
Alexander, A. 2015. *The Infinitesimal: How a Dangerous Ideas Shaped the Modern World.* London: Macmillan.
Beck, U. 1992. [1986] *Risk Society.* London: Sage.
Berglund, J. 2010. 'Did the Medieval Norse Society in Greenland Really Fail?' In: McAnany, P. and Yoffee, N. (eds). *Questioning Collapse: Human Resilience, Ecological Vulnerability and the Aftermath of Empire.* Cambridge: Cambridge University Press.
Blackie, P., Cannon, T., Davis, I., and Wisner, B. 1994. *At Risk: Natural Hazards, People's Vulnerability.* London: Routledge.
Blumenberg, H. 1985. [1966] *The Legitimacy of the Modern Age.* Cambridge, MASS: MIT Press.
Brannen, P. 2018. *The Ends of the World.* London: OneWorld.
Brunsma, D. Overfelt, D. and Picou, J. (eds) 2007. *Hurricane Katrina: The Sociology of Katrina: Perspectives on a Modern Catastrophe.* New York: Rowman & Littlefield.
Butzer, K. and Endfield, G. 2012. 'Critical Perspectives on Historical Collapse.' Proceedings of the National Academy of the Sciences of the USA.' *PNAS:* 109 (10): 3628–31.
Campbell, B. 2016. *The Great Transition: Climate, Disease and Society in the Medieval World.* Cambridge University Press.
Cohen, N. 1992. (revised edition) *The Pursuit of the Millenium: Revolutionary Millenarians and Mystical Anarchists of the Middle Ages.* Oxford: Oxford University Press.
Danowski, D. and Viveiro de Castro, E. 2017. *The Ends of the World.* Cambridge: Polity Press.
Delanty, G. (ed.) 2021. *Pandemics, Society and Politics: Critical Reflections on the Covid-19 Crisis.* Berlin: De Gruyter.
Diamond, J. 2006. *Collapse: How Societies Choose to Fail or Survive.* London: Penguin Books.
Diamond, J. 2019. *Upheaval: Turning Points for Nations in Crisis.* New York: Little Brown.
Ehrlich P.R. and Ehrlich, A. H. 2013. 'Can a Collapse of Global Civilization be Avoided?' *Proceedings of the Royal Society,* B 280: 20122845. http://dx.doi.org/10.1098/rspb.2012.2845
Eisenstadt, S. N. 1988. 'Beyond Collapse.' In: Yoffee, N. and Cowgill, G. (eds) *The Collapse of Ancient States and Civilizations.* Tuscon, AZ.: Arizona University Press.
Elliott, A. and Hsu, E. 2016. (eds) *The Consequences of Global Disasters.* London: Routledge.
Ferguson, N. 2012. *Doom: The Politics of Catastrophe.* London: Allen Lane.
Freeden, M. 2009. 'Failures of Political Thinking.' *Political Studies,* 75 (1): 141–64.
Fuchs, T. 2018. 'The Cyclical Time of the Body and its Relation to Linear Time.' *Journal of Consciousness Studies,* 25 (7–8): 47–65.
Graeber, D. and Wengrow, D. 2021. *The Dawn of Everything: A New History of Humanity.* London: Penguin.
Habermas, J. 1987. [1985] *The Philosophical Discourse of Modernity.* Cambridge: Polity Press.
Hall, J. R. 2009. *Apocalypse: From Antiquity to the Empire of Modernity.* Cambridge: Polity Press.
Hanusch, H. and Bierman, F. 2020. 'Deep-time Organizations: Learning Institutional Longevity from History.' *The Anthropocene Review,* 7 (1): 19–41.

Hausheer, H. 1929. 'Plato's Conception of the Future as Opposed to Spengler's.' *The Monist,* 39(2): 204 – 24.

Heller, A. 1999. 'Worldtime and Lifetime.' In: *A Theory of Modernity.* Oxford: Blackwell.

Horn, E. 2018. *The Future as Catastrophe: Imagining Disaster in the Modern Age.* New York: Columbia University Press.

Hunt, T. and Lipo, C. 2010. 'Ecological Catastrophe, Collapse, and the Myth of "Ecocide" on Rapa Nui (Easter Island)". In: McAnany, P. and Yoffee, N. (eds). *Questioning Collapse: Human Resilience, Ecological Vulnerability and the Aftermath of Empire.* Cambridge: Cambridge University Press.

Johnson, S. A. J. 2017. *Why did Ancient Civilizations Fail?* London: Routledge.

Jones, L. 2018. *The Big Ones: How Natural Disasters Have Shaped Us.* London: Icon.

Jones, R. 2017. *Slow Catastrophes: Living with Drought in Australia.* Clayton, Viv: Monash University Publishing.

Kennett, D. J., Masson, M., Lope, C.P. *et al.* Drought-Induced Civil Conflict Among the Ancient Maya. *Nature Communications,* 13, 3911 (2022). https://doi.org/10.1038/s41467-022-31522-x

Killen, A. and Lebovic, N. (eds) 2014. *Catastrophes: A History and Theory of an Operative Concept.* Berlin: De Gruyter.

Knowles, S. G. 2020. 'Slow Disaster in the Anthropocene: A Historian Witnessing Climate Change in the Korean Peninsula.' *Daedalus,* 149 (4): 192 – 206.

Kolbert, E. 2014. *The Sixth Extinction: An Unnatural History.* London: Bloomsbury.

Koselleck, R. 2002. 'Time and History.' In: *The Practice of Conceptual History.* Stanford: Stanford University Press.

Knuuttila, S. 2021. 'Medieval Theories of Modality.' *Stanford Encyclopaedia of Philosophy.* https://plato.stanford.edu/entries/modality-medieval/

Luhmann, N. 1998. [1992] *Observations on Modernity.* Stanford: Stanford University Press.

McAnany, P. and Yoffee, N. (eds) 2010. *Questioning Collapse: Human Resilience, Ecological Vulnerability and the Aftermath of Empire.* Cambridge: Cambridge University Press.

Machiavelli, N. 1982. [1532] *The Prince.* London: Penguin.

Mythen, S. 1998. *The Prehistory of the Human Mind.* London: Thames and Hudson.

Nancy, J.-L. 2015. *After Fukushima: The Equivalence of Catastrophes.* Oxford: Oxford University Press.

Pollak, F. 1973. [1961] *The Image of the Future.* Amsterdam: Elsevier.

Posner, R. 2006. *Catastrophe: Risk and Response.* Oxford: Oxford University Press.

Scheidel, W. 2018. *The Great Leveller: Violence and the History of Inequality from the Stone to the Twenty-First Century.* Princeton University Press.

Schutz, A. 1959. 'Tiresias, or our Knowledge of Future Events.' *Social Research,* 26 (1): 71 – 89.

Servigne, P. and Stevens, R. 2020. *How Everything can Collapse.* Cambridge: Polity Press.

Spengler, O. 1926. [1918] *The Decline of the West.* New York: Knopf.

Smil, V. 2012. *Global Catastrophes and Trends: The Next Fifty Years.* Cambridge, MASS.: MIT Press.

Stark, R. 2020. *The Rise of Christianity: A Sociologist Considers History.* New Haven: Princeton University Press.

Strydom, P. 2017. Infinity, infinite processes and limit concepts: Recovering a neglected background of social and critical theory. *Philosophy and Social Criticism,* 43(8), 793 – 811. https://doi.org/10.1177/0191453717692845

Tainter, J. 1988. *The Collapse of Complex Systems.* Cambridge: Cambridge University Press.

Tierney, K. 2019. *Disasters: A Sociological Approach.* Cambridge: Polity Press.

Toynbee, A. 1987. [1934 – 61] *Study in History: Abridgement of Vols 1-VI.* Oxford: Oxford University Press.

Turchin, P. 2023. *End Times: Elites, Counter-Elites and the Path of Political Disintegration.* London: Allen Lane.

Turner, B. S. 2023. *A Theory of Catastrophe.* Berlin: De Gruyter.

Weber, E. 2000. *Apocalypses: Prophecies, Cults, and Millennial Beliefs through the Ages.* Cambridge, MASS.: Harvard University Press.

Yoffee, N. and Cowgill, G. (eds) 1988. *The Collapse of Ancient States and Civilizations.* Tuscon, AZ.: Arizona University Press.

Chapter Four
Modernity and the Concept of the Future: Utopia, Progress, and Prophecy

The idea of the future is closely linked with modernity. In many ways, modernity is defined by a future-oriented time consciousness. In earlier times, as we have seen, the idea of the future was less central to how the present was understood. With modernity, the future provides the present with an orientation that enables the present to transcend itself.

Three major traditions of future thinking emerged with modernity in the eighteenth century: the idea of progress, utopianism, and secular prophecy. These traditions provided fertile ground for nineteenth- and twentieth-century ideas of the future.

Thomas Hobbes already recognized the powerful orientation to the future when he wrote in *The Leviathan* in 1651 'The object of man's desire is not to enjoy once only, and for one instant of time; but to assure for ever, the way of his future desires.'[1] His work established a strong basis for political philosophy to see politics as a future-oriented activity to enable human progress. The appeal to the future was common in eighteenth-century thought. Spinoza articulated a notion of the future based on hope as an affect that is deeply rooted in the human condition.[2] Edmund Burke in his *Abridgement of English History* in 1757 commented: 'Futurity is the great concern of mankind.' Leibniz wrote in 1714, 'The present is big with the future, the future might be read in the past, the distant is expressed in the near.'[3] It was undoubtedly Marquis de Condorcet's *Outline of an Historical View of the Progress of the Human Mind* in 1795 that set the tone for much of the Enlightenment's optimism about the future as a model of progress. In this work, he placed a strong emphasis on future possibility resting on science, the disappearance of equality, and the essential unity of humanity.

Not all were so sanguine about future progress. The appeal to the future was given a famous twist by G. W. F. Hegel in the Preface to the *Philosophy of Right* in 1821 when he invoked the idea of the Owl of Minerva flying at dusk to convey a

---

1 Hobbes (1978 [1651]): Chapter 11: (160–61). In a later passage, he writes 'Anxiety for the future time, disposeth men to enquire into the causes of things: because the knowledge of them, maketh men the better able to order the present to their best advantage.'
2 I am drawing from Gatens *et al.* and their interpretation of Spinoza as a philosopher of hope relevant to our own political present.
3 In the *Monadology and Other Philosophical Writings* (Leibniz 1925: 419).

https://doi.org/10.1515/9783111240602-005

sense of knowledge and foresight always coming too late: 'When philosophy paints its gray on gray, then has a form of life grown old, and with gray on gray it cannot be rejuvenated, but only known; the Owl of Minerva first takes flight with twilight closing in.' This touch of pessimism about the future was also intimated by Emily Dickinson in a poem in 1862, 'The Future Never Spoke,' suggesting that the light of the future does not shine quite so brightly. Yet, an introspective thinker such as Soren Kierkegaard could write in his journals in 1844 that 'It is true what philosophy says that life can only be understood backwards. But then one forgets the other principle: that it must be lived forwards' (Kierkegaard 1996: 161).

The 1790s saw a revival of prophecies which gave the Romantic Age a revolutionary consciousness that was political and cultural and not religious as such. Bundock (2016) has shown how prophecy developed in times of great turbulence, as in the aftermath of the French Revolution, when continuity in history broke down. This is the context to locate the prophetic and visionary writings of William Blake, whose writings are full of references to 'futurity,' which in his work is located as a moment of rupture in the present (Rajan and Faflak 2020). 'I labour upwards into futurity,' he wrote in 1796: 'To the four winds hopeless of future. All futurity seems teeming with endless destruction never to be repelled.'[4] The writings of many of the romantic poets, such as Wordsworth, Byron, and Shelley, make use of prophecy to understand time in terms of futurity. Byron is particularly interesting as a secular prophet of the future. He famously wrote in his diary on 28th January 1821[5] that 'the best prophet of the future is the past' and in *Childe Harold*, there is the melancholic view to the future, 'Still wilt thou dream on future joy and woe?' and 'Smiles form a channel of a future tear.'[6] In *Epistle to Augusta*, he laments:

> 'And for the future – this world's future may
> From me demand little from my care
> I have outlived myself by many a day.'

As mentioned in Chapter Three, one of the most famous writings on the future, also in the prophetic tradition, was Byron's poem 'Darkness,' written in 1816 on the apocalyptical end of the world.

In a similar vein, Shelley in a late essay written in 1815, 'On a Future State,' by which he meant something akin to a state of being, explored the transformation in life, and the human condition beyond mortality. The prophetic tradition also gave

---

4 https://en.wikisource.org/wiki/Vala,_or_The_Four_Zoas/Night_the_Eighth
5 https://lordbyron.org/monograph.php?doc=ThMoore.1830&select=AD1821.23
6 Canto 11, stanzas 4 and 97.

rise to the genre of apocalyptical literature, such as the 'last man' genre, as reflected in Mary Shelley's *Last Man* in 1826 and the book that inspired it *Le Derniere homme* [1805] by Cousin de Grainville.[7]

The term futurity, which emerged at this time, conveys the sense of the future as a condition that is present as opposed to something yet to come – futurity expresses the presence of the future, a notion that lends itself to the idea of the apocalypse. The Romantic Age has been seen as the age of prophecy and a response to the divergence of history and experience. In that sense, prophecy is a modern creation in so far as it was a central to the romantic imagination and its imaginaries of the future, but it is also a story of the failure of prophecies and the prospect of doom. An early intimation of this was in John Milton's allegory, *Paradise Lost*, which conveys a strong sense of a desirable future that was lost.

> 'This horror will grow mild, this darkness light;
> Besides what hope the never-ending flight
> Of future days may bring, what chance, what change
> Worth waiting—since our present lot appears
> For happy though but ill, for ill not worst,
> If we procure not to ourselves more woe.'

Written in 1667, it has been seen as an allegory of the failure of the English Revolution (Hill 1977).

A major influence on the opening of the future in the following century was the worldwide impact of Jeremy Bentham's philosophy of utilitarianism, which, like Hobbes', was a theory that was firmly focused on future outcomes as the measure and guiding principle for law and politics. The future not the past was henceforth the beacon.

Since the eighteenth-century Enlightenment, modernity has been seen as the time of the 'new,' with the implication of a rupture with the immediate past of the medieval age. As Habermas wrote in *The Philosophical Discourse of Modernity*, it 'expresses the conviction that the future has already begun: it is the epoch that lives for the future, that opens itself up to the novelty of the future. In this way the caesura defined by the new beginning has shifted into the past, precisely to the start of modern times' (Habermas 1987: 5). But of course, the past does not vanish. It is redefined by the present, which often sought its legitimation by a past anterior to the recent past that was repudiated. In this way, classical antiquity, already revived by the Renaissance, was given a new relevance by modernity and thus preserved continuity with a lost heroic age. But modernity affirmed the new-

---

7 See Ranson (2014).

ness of the modern age and created a time consciousness that saw the present as containing both the past and the future. This has led to a debate about the legitimacy of the modern age.

One view, which can be characterized as the conservative response, is that modernity lacks legitimacy since it declares a break with tradition. Having cut itself free from the past, the Enlightenment lacks sources of authority of its own. In one version of the conservative thesis, associated with Karl Löwith and, in a different version,[8] by Carl Schmitt, all modern ideas, such as the idea of progress and socialism, are secular versions of religious ideas, products of eschatology, and are therefore inauthentic. Against this position is the argument put forward by one of the most important German philosophers of the mid-twentieth century, Hans Blumenberg. In his major work, *The Legitimacy of the Modern Age*, he advanced the thesis that modernity does not derive its authority from the traditions of thought it repudiated, such as Christianity, but from its own sources (Blumenberg 1985 [1966]). He also asserted that the modern age provides new answers to questions that are not specific to Christianity but are universal. Blumenberg, as Martin Jay has pointed out, also put an end to the claim that Christian eschatology remained a force in history with the startling argument that in fact the world was already secularized at the threshold of the medieval age when the eschatological hopes of the early church were disappointed. Since the apocalypse did not come as anticipated, the world had become secularized with personal salvation as an alternative path to future redemption. In Martin Jay's words: 'It is this anxiety about the future that helps account for the importance of memory in such Christian thinkers as Augustine, who had no optimistic eschatology to secularise' (Jay 1988: 152). Since the future did not arrive, the past remained the main source. Secularization, as a core dynamic in modernity, according to Blumenberg, is not a story of loss but a quest for new answers. Modernity expands possibilities for human self-assertion and rather than diminishing the present, it affirms its legitimacy as opening a space to the future. Instead of seeking refuge in the past, modernity looks to the future.

Blumenberg developed this perspective on a future-directed time consciousness in a later book around two concepts of time, *Lebenszeit und Weltzeit*, 'lifetime' and 'world-time' (Blumenberg, 1986). The first is human time, the temporal horizons of the life-world. The second is the temporal perspective opened up by science, especially astronomy after Galileo, Kepler, and Copernicus.[9] World-time

---

8 Blumenberg, according to Mehring, was closer to Schmitt's argument than to Löwith, against whom both Blumenberg and Schmitt defined themselves (Mehring 2014: 521).
9 See also his earlier book, *The Genesis of the Copernican World* (Blumenberg 1987 [1975]).

encompasses the cosmos and unlike life-time it extends to infinity. The glimpse of infinity that astronomy presented opened up a space for human beings to contemplate what they cannot directly experience, namely infinity. Despite the fundamental difference between human time and the cosmic order of time, modernity foregrounds the orientation to the deep future. The idea of infinity extends the arrow of time beyond the limited horizon of the present.

This chapter looks at how the idea of the future appeared in modern thought. As a point of departure, I am taking Blumenberg's thesis that the modern age opened up a space for the idea of the future in the development of a time consciousness that considerably expanded the scope of human experience. This idea was developed by another major German intellectual historian, Reinhart Koselleck, who argued in a classic essay in 1967 that the modern idea of the future effectively goes back to Kant (Koselleck 2004c). Koselleck concurs with a more general position that sees the idea of the future as a product of modernity, which brought about a time consciousness that affirmed the present. It was certainly very much bound up with the idea of progress, which cannot be reduced to eschatology. Blumenberg, in an essay published a year before Koselleck, had shown the relationship between great advances in astronomy and the idea of progress in that it was in the former that the concept of time was enlarged (Blumenberg 1966). The idea of progress was based on the notion of the future as expectation. I discuss this in what follows in relation to Koselleck and his interpretation of Kant. This leads to another aspect of the idea of the future which the notion of expectation does not fully grasp, namely as an imaginary and is expressed in utopian thought as well as in Marx's sense of the future as a product of political struggle. The third section of the chapter considers the notion of the future in terms of possibility, as associated with the American pragmatist tradition (C. S. Peirce, William James, and George Herbert Mead). The final section looks at the idea of the future that emerged from the phenomenological tradition in philosophy as represented by Martin Heidegger, who gave an important new direction to the idea of the future as a category of experience that was formative of the human condition.

The Future as Expectation

One of the seminal books on the modern idea of the future is Reinhart Koselleck's *Futures Past: On the Semantics of Historical Time*, originally published in 1979 in German (Koselleck 2004a). The essays of which it is comprised, published in the 1960s and 1970s, defined the field of conceptual history. Koselleck, whose reputation was established by an early work based on his doctorate, *Crisis and Critique*,[10] was interested in the formation of historical time, especially in the so-called *Sattelzeit*, c 1750 – 1850, approximately the era of the Enlightenment, when modernity in Europe takes shape around a new consciousness of time and is expressed in 'semantic' change, a change in concepts.

For Koselleck, history is expressed in the language of concepts which make possible consciousness of one's time. His approach was to analyze major shifts in consciousness through an investigation into semantic changes, a method that was very much in the German tradition of interpretative understanding and bore the influence of Heidegger's concern with temporality and experience. The notion of 'Futures Past,' in German *vergangene Zukunft*, encompasses how the present is interpreted in relation to the past and to the future, whereby the future is both an expectation of time to come but also includes past futures, that is the sense of the future that once was. This is so because the present is the product of the past and thus includes previous anticipations of times to come. Every present, 'previous superseded future' is always oriented toward the future, so what is produced in history are various expressions of the future as every future will one day become a past.

Historical time as chronology, the ordering and narrative of events, the subject matter of historical writing, he argued, does not tell us much about historical time, which he said can be grasped in differentiating past and future through the categories of experience and expectation. A key insight, as put forward in the Preface, is that 'the more a particular time is experienced as a new temporality, as "modernity," the more that demands made of the future increase' (2004a: 3). Modernity entails an increase in the weight of the future, since the present is increasingly shortened as a result of the acceleration of time. In the period between 1500 and 1800, there was a major historical transformation in consciousness, leading to the emergence of modernity by the end of the eighteenth century. Prognosis replaced prophecy and gave birth to the idea of progress, which was based on expectations that will be realized in a rapidly approaching future: 'Progress opened up a future that transcended the hitherto predictable, natural space of time and experience and hence – propelled by its own dynamics – provoked new, transnatural long-term processes' (2004b: 22). This was an original and influential formulation of the concept of acceleration, the sense of the present being transformed by the future such that one is always about to enter new times. The view of the past also changed to be something 'other' than the present. 'This in turn led to

---

10 Koselleck (1988 [1959]). This work was heavily influenced by both Karl Löwith and Carl Schmitt, though he did not embrace their strongly antimodernist stance. See also Koselleck (2002 and 2018).

the fact that it was precisely along the plane of progress that the specificity of the epoch had to be expressed' (2005d: 240). Modernity, as the *Neuzeit*, was based on the tension between previous experience and the expectation of what was to come. It was also experienced as a time of transition to a future that beckoned but did not yet exist and was therefore 'other' than the present. It is unclear if Koselleck sees this model of modernity at an end or as still with us. Modernity led to a re-ordering of the past, present, and future in a way that shifted the historical burden from the former to the latter. The future is no longer bound to the past. The only thing that was not clear was the speed and direction of the open future.

The age of ideology followed with movements such as liberalism, socialism, communism, *etc.*, all claiming the future. The concept of revolution lost its older meaning of recurrence and began to be bound up with the delivery of the future through epochal upheaval. In line with Blumenberg, he sees the new historical time consciousness as fundamentally different from earlier ones in that it is now a product of the present and expresses a strong sense of expectation. In effect, the idea of the future was born with modernity.

The major essay "'Spaces of Experience" and "Horizon of Expectation" intro-duces the key notions of experience and expectation in an important conceptual-ization of the future in relation to the past. With this essay, published in 1967, Ko-selleck's legacy goes beyond his interest in historical semantics and conceptual history to making a major contribution to social theory. Experience is defined as 'present past,' that is, events that can be remembered. To experience something is to have memory of past events. Expectation, in contrast, is 'the future made pre-sent'; it concerns what has not yet been experienced but what can be anticipated (2004c: 259). Hope, fear, wishes, and desires all enter into it. Expectation thus dif-fers from experience in that it refers to an experience that is yet to come. For that reason, expectations are forms of projected experience. He entertains the possibil-ity that experience can have a horizon, such that it is possible to speak of a horizon of experience, but he associates it with expectations.[11]

While experiences that one has can be expected to be repeated, the future can also be expected to be different, for the 'horizon of expectation' opens up the pos-sibility of new experiences. There is thus a tension between experience and expect-ation that is intensified with modernity. In this way, the idea of the future goes be-yond what a prognosis normally offers, since a prognosis is a forecast that is derived from current and past conditions. But with modernity, the *Neuzeit*, 'expect-

---

11 G. H. Mead in *The Philosophy of the Present* noted how knowledge can extend 'the horizon of experience' (Mead 1932: 26). See also Chapter Five for more on Mead.

ations have distanced themselves evermore from all previous experience' (2004d 163).

The expansion in the horizon of expectation arises as a result of a transformation in the space of experience, as a result of modern technology and industry (Koselleck is not very specific on the mechanisms by which human experience changes in modernity). According to Koselleck, the idea of progress combines both the changing space of experience and the expansion in the horizon of expectation and thus opens up a new vision of the future as not just different but also better than what has gone before. However, the horizon of expectation exceeds what the space of experience offers, since the former is always ahead, as it were. Modernity, in transforming the space of experience, also establishes a rupture from which the horizon of expectation expands and in fact diverges from the space of experience. This suggests a tension between space and time, for experience is spatial and expectation is what makes possible the consciousness of time. For this reason, it is no longer possible to foretell the future, for example, in the way Cassandra was supposed to have done or as in Christian eschatology. Such visions of the future were based on the fact of things remaining more or less as they are.

For Koselleck, Kant challenged this way of thinking with his notion of *Fortschritt* (progress), of which he claims Kant was probably the originator. He cites Kant's statement in 1784 that 'Reason knows no bounds for its design' (p. 197). He also refers to Kant's notion in his *Anthropology from a Pragmatic Point of View* [1798] of the 'capacity for foresight.' This capacity is linked to the idea of the future. Kant wrote: 'The faculty of visualizing the past intentionally is the faculty of memory; and the faculty of visualizing something as future is the faculty of foreseeing' (1978: 34: 185). While Kant had much that was interesting to say on the idea of the future, both in this work and in others, Koselleck focussed on the idea of progress, which he sees as the quintessence of modernity. The break resided in the idea that a prognosis henceforth could not be based on the anticipation of events that already occurred, for what was to come also had to be better than what went before. For Kant, the future simply had to be better. It is perhaps in this respect that our time is different in that we don't expect the future to be better simply because the present is better than the past. Koselleck was writing about a time shaped by the ideas of the Enlightenment and of the French Revolution when it was almost taken for granted that the future would be different from the past and also better. It somehow followed that if something new emerged, it would be better than what went before. It is true that the French Revolution for many shattered the optimism of the Enlightenment, which preceded the negative impact of the French Revolution, and of course, many intellectuals were conservative critics of the rupture in continuity and these ideas of the promise of a better world.

While the idea of progress is the main example that Koselleck takes, he alludes to a new idea of the republic. The old idea that goes back to the Renaissance and Rome, is now rendered into a concept of movement, from being a condition to a *telos*, a goal to be achieved. This was accompanied by the suffix 'ism,' whereby it became an ideology to achieve a desirable end, serving the purpose of anticipating a future historical movement (2004c: 273).

His analysis was an inspiring and rich account of the transformation in historical time. It was in many ways limited by his main aim, which was to trace shifts in historical time with experience and expectation as registers of such a transformation at the end of the early modern period with the emergence of the *Neuzeit* as something distinct from what had gone before. His concern was not with the future as such but with the writing of history and how the future was seen in the early modern period. But these concepts of experience and expectation are of wider significance beyond the application to this period. An insight toward the end of his essay is of particular interest. He discusses the example of the transformation in constitutional thinking in Germany also in this period whereby the older concepts of constitutions and federal structures gave rise to later ones, which were possible only because of historical experience and 'could be senses as coming possibilities, the concepts contained a prognostic potential which opened out a new horizon of experience' (2004c: 272). The implication here is that expectation encompasses possibility as a potential that is latent in the present. However, this perspective remains undeveloped by Koselleck, for whom the main register of the future is expectation of something not yet manifest. On its own, the notion of expectation is insufficient to grasp the idea of the future, even if it is a key dimension of consciousness of the future. In this respect, he failed to make the link with Heidegger, who in *Being and Time* distinguished expectation from anticipation, associating the latter with a more authentic attitude to the future (see below). Moreover, his account of Kant failed to see other expressions of future time, such as his notion of hope. In the *Critique of Pure Reason*, Kant said the most important question after 'What can I know?' and 'What should I do?' is 'What may I hope? (A805/B833). As discussed in Chapter Six, where I return to Kant in the context of the critical theory, this is one of the most significant expressions of the orientation to the future in modern thought but goes beyond the category of expectation.

Koselleck's theory of the future as a category of historical time that acts on and transforms the space of experience nonetheless remains one of the most important theories of the future, not as facts that need to be discovered but as a way to understand how it can be known. It was ultimately an interpretative account of the future as linguistic in the sense that it required linguistic categories. Perhaps it makes too much of linguistic categories and thus sees historical change in overly semantic terms. There is an absence of historical struggles in his account and the space of experience can be seen in ways that give more prominence to future possibilities, which do not entirely reside in an open future yet to come, but are also contained in part in the achievements of the present, as is suggested by his example of constitutional transformation as a reworking of older forms that contain an excess of potential not fully actualized.

Koselleck, a student of Carl Schmitt, has often been seen by the left as a conservative thinker who did not appreciate the critical currents of modernity. His earlier *Crisis and Critique* in 1959, which bore the strong influence of Carl Schmitt, certainly justified such an evaluation in view of its association of critique as a cause of crisis rather than an outcome. Koselleck, it must be noted, did not share Schmitt's support for the Nazis. His historical semantics, while pathbreaking in many ways, expressed naive belief in modernity, opening up future possibilities. Today, we are more critical of the idea of progress (see for example, Allen 2016). While the idea of progress can be reconstructed in different ways, as Wagner shows, and is not a total trap of Eurocentrism, it does not entirely capture the horizon of expectation today, which is less a matter of anticipating better times than preventing the worst (Wagner 2016). Wagner however does not say that the idea of progress has no relevance for today; it can be reconstructed in a way that can speak to at least certain aspects of our historical present.

The allure of the idea of progress has nonetheless remained an abiding theme in much of contemporary scholarship. Steven Pinker for example has given what is in essence a strong defense of a view of history as progress with the argument that despite the problems of the present, huge progress has been achieved over the past centuries, as evidenced principally by the removal of violence in human affairs. His arguments in *The Better Angels of Our Nature* are meticulously presented with incontrovertible conclusions (Pinker 2011). Across four areas of life, he shows how modern society has evolved new dispositions that have brought about a decline of violence and barbarism, which were normal in premodern societies. We can let aside the objection raised by Graeber and Weingrow (2021: 13–19) that Pinker misunderstood, which he undoubtedly did, prehistoric societies, since his argument is fairly plausible when it comes to societies formed around statehood, essentially the period since antiquity. The four 'better angels of our nature' – a phrase used by Thomas Jefferson – are: the increase in empathy, self-control, the moral sense, and reason. He is not dissuaded by the obvious instances of violence over the past more than one hundred years, for the earlier history of humanity displayed far greater levels of violence. His account of historical progress is based on the view that evolutionary dynamics led to the development of psychological faculties that steer us from violence and which lead people to coexist peacefully. Human subject formation has been irreversibly transformed by the evolution of empathy, which has been significant in cultivating altruism and changes. Another 'angel' is self-control which made possible reductions of violence.' The moral sense is another 'angel' that has come to be increasingly important in regulating social interaction. Finally, the capacity for reason leads people toward nonviolent solutions. The only problem is that on this account, the fact that progress did occur means that all we can say is that the present is better than the past. But it does not follow that the future will be better than the present. These Angels will undoubtedly continue to exist but they may not be enough to deal with the challenges of the present. There is no consideration given to the ecological destruction of the planet. In sum, a perspective on the future that revolves around the idea of progress is not sufficiently robust to prepare us to think about the future. In other words, the fact that progress has occurred does not mean it will continue unbounded or that its course will be much the same as before. It does not, for instance, address the problems that progress indirectly created.

Koselleck drew on authors who were fairly optimistic about modernity and the future. A fuller account would need to incorporate the more ambivalent perspectives, as for example, Jean-Jacques Rousseau, who wrote in *Emile* [1762]: 'Prudence which is ever bidding us to look forward into the future, a future which in many cases we shall never reach; here is the real source of all our troubles! How mad it is for so short-lived a creature as man to look forward into a future to which he rarely attains, while he neglects the present which is his?' (Book 2: 42). In the *Reveries of a Solitary Walker* [1776–1778], this observation reveals his view of the future: 'Everything is in constant flux on this earth. Nothing keeps the same unchanging shape, and our affections, being attached to things outside us, necessarily change and pass away as they do. Always out ahead of us or lagging behind, they recall a past which is gone or anticipate a future which may never come into being; there is nothing solid there for the heart to attach itself to. Thus our earthly joys are almost without exception the creatures of a moment.' (Fifth Walk). In his autobiographical reflections, *Confessions* [1781], Rousseau wrote: 'Imagination, which in my youth always looked forward but now looks back...I no longer see anything in the future to attract me....' (Book VI: p. 216).

The pessimistic legacy of Arthur Schopenhauer was a contrast to the more positive Kantian legacy. In 1818, in his major work, *The World as Will and Representation*, he wrote: 'Life presents itself as a continual deception, in small matters as well as in great. If it has promised, it does not keep its word, unless to show how little desirable the desired object was; hence we are deluded now by hope, now by what was hoped for. If it has given, it did so in order to take. The enchantment of distance shows us paradises that vanish like optical illusions, when we have allowed ourselves to be fooled by them. Accordingly, happiness lies always in the future, or else in the past, and the present may be compared to a small dark cloud driven by the wind over the sunny plain; in front of and behind the cloud, everything is bright, only it itself always casts a shadow. Consequently, the present is always inadequate, but the future is uncertain, and the past irrecoverable' (Chapter XLVI). Schopenhauer saw the world in terms of suffering and entertained the thought it might be better if humanity did not exist in order to reduce the quantity of suffering. 'It would be better if there were nothing. Since there is more pain than pleasure on earth, every satisfaction is only transitory, creating new desires and new distresses, and the agony of the devoured animal is always far greater than the pleasure of the devourer.' He developed these ideas in a late essay in 1850, 'On the Suffering of the World.'

The Future as an Imaginary and the Emergence of Utopianism

Less an alternative to the notion of the future as expectation than an additional dimension is the idea of the future as an imaginary. Arjun Appadurai in an insightful essay, 'The Future as a Cultural Fact,' has made the case for looking at the imagination as 'a vital resource in all special processes and projects, and needs to be seen as a quotidian energy, not visible only in dreams, fantasies and sequestered moment of euphoria and creativity' (Appadurai 2013: 287). Writing from the perspective of anthropology, he notes the power of the imagination in small-scale societies in ritual and in festivities, but argues for its wider relevance in the anthropology of the future. The imagination, along with anticipation and aspiration are three human preoccupations that shape the future as a cultural fact. His thesis has a sharp critical edge in linking the notion of the future as a cultural fact with an 'ethics of possibility,' which is a contrast to the 'ethics of probability,' the latter arises in the context of the growth of casino capitalism which benefits from the growth of catastrophe. The ethics of possibility refers to 'those ways of thinking, feeling, and acting that increase the horizon of hope, that expand the field of the imagination, that produce greater equity in…capacity to aspire, and that widen the field of informed, creative, and critical citizenship' (2013: 295).

The concept of the imagination that he invokes remains undeveloped. This concept and the more or less indistinguishable concept of the imaginary has figured in the writings of C. S. Peirce and goes back at least to Kant (Kaag 2005). The concept of the imaginary also has a strong Freudian legacy and was pivotal to the work of Jacques Lacan and has also been used by Paul Ricoeur. Sartre's 1940 essay on the imaginary opened a phenomenological perspective to it (Sartre 2004). However, it was Cornelius Castoriadis's use of the term that has the widest influence as a philosophical concept (Castoriadis 1987). Johann Arnason (1989) has done much to clarify the relevance of Castoriadis for social theory. Charles Taylor's

Modern Social Imaginaries has been highly influential in sociological and historical applications (Taylor 2004). Benedict Anderson's notion of 'imagined communities' is undoubtedly one of the most well-known historically grounded applications of the concept of 'imagined' realities (Anderson 1983).

Castoriadis, who is clearly the principal influence today on the notion of the imaginary, developed a theory of the radical imaginary, which is very different from the more general notion of a social imaginary. As the term suggests, it is a radical projection and as used by Castoriadis, it refers to something more than the social construction of reality, as in Durkheim's notion of social representations or the idea of social imaginaries. Unlike Lacan, who contrasted the imaginary and the symbolic to the radical force of the real, Castoriadis asserts its radical nature. This is also present in Sartre's account in which the capacity to imagine is the basis of the possibility of freedom. There is then a basic difference between Castoriadis's future-directed conception and the somewhat domesticated notion of social imaginaries, as in Anderson and Taylor. The widespread use of the notion of an imaginary in social science today is often vague (Levy and Spicer 2013). This vague and catch-all use of the term seems to me to be at the cost of clarity if everything is an imaginary.[12]

However, the main problem is that while many collective realities can be described as imaginaries, it is not at all clear that these are radical imaginaries, as in Castoriadis's famous use of the term in the final pages of *The Imaginary Institution of Society* (pp. 369 – 73). Castoriadis clearly had in mind a specific sense of the radical imaginary to capture the striving or creation of something new: 'The radical imaginary emerges as otherness and as the perpetual orientation of otherness.' This conception thus has a more specific meaning than the general notion of social imaginaries, which generally refer to collective representations of social phenomena, not all of which have a radical dimension to them. In fact, many are decidedly affirmative. As I see it, the imaginary is centrally about creativity, consciousness of the future, and the emergence of the new.

In my view, Castoriadis's notion of a radical imaginary needs to be reserved for specific expressions of social imaginaries as future-oriented projections. Nonetheless, the notion of social imaginaries in general is in need of more scrutiny. It is not only a question of deciding which lineage of the term is to be adhered to. I believe Adams *et al.*, following Arnason, make too strong a claim when they suggest the notion of social imaginaries is becoming an overall field of inquiry itself (Adams *et al.* 2017: 16). If this were the case, almost every major concept would be a field of inquiry. The now vast literature on imaginaries never makes clear ex-

---

12 A more specific rendering can be found in Beckert (2016) and Beckert and Bronk (2018).

actly what an imaginary (whether social or radical) is other than that it is not reducible to the imagination and that it is the source of the new. The fact that it is in widespread use does not in itself mean it is theoretically coherent. However, there is no doubt that the concept is important and captures a crucial dimension of culture. This, I think, is the key point. The imaginary is a dimension of culture. It can hardly be considered to be something independent, even if the imaginary is linked to the imagination, as Castoriadis (following Lacan) and Sartre claimed, as had earlier Peirce (following Kant). Cultural phenomena entail imaginary elements in that many things, whether tangible or intangible, have to be imagined. They cannot be directly experienced. This is especially the case with future-oriented realities. The ability to think of the new requires an imaginary signification and this is made possible by the imagination.

There is insufficient attention to how the imagination relates to other human faculties, for example, reason and emotion. Traditionally, philosophy has paid more attention to reason and sociology to emotion. There have been useful attempts to link emotion and the imagination (as in Morton 2013). The literature on emotions has partially addressed the problem of reason but in the more limited sense of rationality, not reason, as in the Kantian legacy (Elster 1999; Williams 2000). Attempts to mediate reason and the imagination are yet more sparse. Gilbert Durand was an exception, as is Morag's *Emotion, Imagination, and the Limits of Reason* (2016), though this is clearly primarily a case for the centrality of emotion. Reason does not fare well in this account. To be sure, Kant sought to mediate reason and the imagination, but it is generally accepted that this was unsatisfactory. Perhaps this is why the idea of the imagination was taken up in a different tradition, since Freud with the work of Lacan and Castoriadis, but in accounts that were more or less irreconcilable with reason. Then, there is the other trajectory on the imagination that goes via Sartre and Ricoeur. The proliferation of the concept of 'imaginaries' today reveals a state of conceptual confusion.

The problem here is the bifurcation of reason and the imagination. The imagination is the faculty that creates images (Lennon 2015). The imaginary makes the new possible, but it must be mediated by other concepts in order to emerge. Images give form to diverse elements, but images on their own are not enough to create new realities. Form is a concept of structure and thus requires more than an image to sustain it. It requires other elements, not all of which are imaginary. Habermas has identified a core problem with Castoriadis's concept and which continues in the eclectic Castoriadis-inspired literature. In a short, and by no means entirely satisfactory, critique of Castoriadis in the *Philosophical Discourse of Modernity*, he writes: 'Castoriadis cannot provide us with a figure for the mediation between the individual and society' (Habermas 1987: 334). The imaginary is one source of mediation but it is not the only one.

The solution to some of these problems with the status of the notion of the social imaginary is to see it as an integral part of the cultural model of societies rather than seeing it as an overall synthetizing force or as a separate entity. The creation of something new is not only a matter of the power of the imagination, even if it is the source. It is also not only a matter of something that is not yet existent. The future is produced as a result of possibility contained within the actual. In my view, this relation between actuality, that which exists, and potentiality as the 'not yet,' needs to be given greater prominence. I am not convinced that the notion of the imaginary alone is able to capture all elements in the configuration. However, it does provide an important way of understanding the future as a projection of the present.

This conception of the future as an imaginary projection offers a perspective on the future that goes beyond the notion of an expectation, as in Koselleck's analysis. An imaginary can give form to a vision of a desirable future. It may lead to the projection of an ideal, such as a specific desirable future, leading in turn to a goal to be pursued. It thus reaches beyond the present. It captures the utopian idea, a dream, a hope or vision of a better world. For it to be realized, it needs to connect with agency/politics, i.e. a goal to be pursued. Viewed in such terms, the notion of an imaginary can be related to the utopian tradition, which expresses a future imaginary that is very different from the idea of progress. While the notion of progress suggests only a trajectory of improvement, the idea that the future will be different and better, the utopian imagination projects an alternative order that was not necessarily an ideal to be realized.

Utopianism was very much a product of the modern political imagination. The earlier Renaissance notions of utopia were purely imaginary visions of alternative societies that either existed beyond the known world or might exist in the future, as in Thomas Moore's *Utopia* [1516], a work that set the trend. At a time when much of the world was unexplored, yet known to exist, it was undoubtedly more interesting to look for alternatives in such uncharted places than in a future time beyond the present. Literally meaning 'a good place' that is nowhere, the notion of utopia underwent transformation with modernity from a largely spatial concept to a temporal one: it became an ideal that could be realized. However, it also incorporated a perspective on dystopia, since aspects of the 'ideal' society could be seen as oppressive and invoking it a veiled critique of the existing society.

The seventeenth century was a period in which utopia flourished. In many cases, it was a product of new political philosophies, as in the case of Tommaso Campanelli's *City of Sun* in 1623, which depicted a utopian society based on equality. Francis Bacon's *New Atlantis* in 1627 envisaged the real possibility of utopia. James Harrington wrote *The Commonwealth of Oceana* in 1656 to describe a utopian constitutional republic.[13] Authors such as Jonathan Swift and Daniel Defoe used the genre of the travelogue to write works that contained utopian elements but also, as in Swift's *Gulliver's Travels* [1726], political satire. Defoe's *Robinson Crusoe* [1719] hinted at the downside of utopia. Voltaire's *Candide* [1759] was one of the first to depict the negative aspects of alternatives to the status quo. By the end of the eighteenth century, utopian thought became part of liberal and socialist political philosophy. Elements of it informed Kant's thinking, as in his vision of a cosmopolitan order in *Perpetual Peace* [1795]. Intimations of dystopia emerged, already contained in *Candide*, as in Samuel Butler's *Erewhom* in 1872, which was a critical look at the harshness of Victorian society, and in Edmund Bulwer-Lytton's *The Coming Race* in 1871.

In Karl Mannheim's *Ideology and Utopia*, the concept of utopia expresses the radical dimension of ideology (Mannheim 1991 [1929]). Utopias transcend the present and are future oriented, while ideologies are past oriented. Once realized, they tend to revert to the form of ideology or may take the form of dystopia, an antiutopia. Utopias are comprehensive visions of a future order that is fundamentally different from what previously existed. Early Christianity has often been seen as a utopia. But with the formation of a church, the utopian impulse declined or was carried forward by rebellious millenarian sects. However, it was with modernity that the utopian imagination flourished as a secular idea. Modernity gave rise to the idea that human will can transform the world. It expressed itself in the idea of reason and, as we have seen, in the idea of progress. In seventeenth-century England, the forerunners of radical utopianism were the Diggers.

By this time, utopia ceased to be a purely imaginary world or a fantasy that did not or could not exist. The Enlightenment gave rise to the movement of utopian socialism, which was a major inspiration for Karl Marx. Marx was a proponent of utopianism but different from the mainstream movement of utopian socialism, which was particularly influential in France, with Saint-Simon and Fourier as famous proponents. In Britain, representatives include Robert Owen in the early nineteenth century and later William Morris, who in *News from Nowhere* in 1890 imagined a future socialist Britain. Such visions were commonplace in the nineteenth century but lost their zeal by the twentieth century. H. G. Wells' *A Modern Utopia* in 1905 was in this tradition of speculative imagining of an alternative future (see Chapter Five).

Marx was critical of such expressions of utopianism, since they were not connected with an analysis of how they might become realized. His vision of communism – as opposed to socialism, which was a stepping stone to the promised land –

---

13 See Claeys (2020) and Kumar (1987) for historical reconstructions of the idea of utopia.

in contrast was based on a theory of social struggles that would realize the utopian ideal of a society without alienation and exploitation. His philosophy of dialectics, derived from the philosophy of Hegel, showed how the future is created by the struggles of the present rather than being only an ideal. The force of the idea is not sufficient to bring about its realization without a political project. However, a political project that is not animated by an imaginary ideal will be devoid of transformative potential. Marx avoided the tendency in Hegel's conception of dialectics to defuse politics of transformative power, seeing instead dialectics to be largely an achievement of the mind. The result was that he was not able to show a clear path to the future.[14] In the Introduction to the *Philosophy of History* in 1831, he had a somewhat limited view of America as the future: 'America is therefore the land of the future, where, in the ages that lie before us, the burden of the World's History shall reveal itself perhaps in a contest between North and South America, it is the land of desire for all those who are weary of the historical lumber-room of old Europe.' With Hegel, the future had arrived.

For Marx, in contrast, the future was yet to come. The realization of utopia was thus postponed to a more distant future than the immediate one. So, in the end, Marx despite his critique of the French utopianists, retained a view of communism as a utopia. As Karl Mannheim noted: 'Socialism is one with the liberal utopia in the sense that both believe that the realm of freedom and equality will come into existence only in the remote future' (Mannheim 1991: 215–6). With the prospect of a socialist utopia, Mannheim observes, a distinction arose between the 'near' and the 'remote.' Conservatism had already made similar and more complex distinctions about past time, but had an undifferentiated vision of the future. Radical utopias changed that with a historical-time sense of more than one dimension and 'the future is always testing itself in the present' (pp. 220–1).

The utopian ideal remained an abiding inspiration in Marxist thought, especially in the critical theory tradition, which was premised on the preservation of hope in a world that appeared to have lost hope. Desroche in a classic work on hope wrote that 'utopia and hope are twin sisters. In utopia there is the hope of a different society. In hope there is the utopia of a different world. In both there is the strategy of alterity' (1979 [1973]: 23). I return to the question of hope in Chapter Six.

The mainstream Marxist tradition remained firmly within the scope of utopianism coupled with a political project to realize one interpretation of what communism could be. Russia, and in particular Saint Petersburg in the first two decades of the twentieth century, was the surprising receptacle for radical utopian

---

14 An alternative reading of Hegel would see this as less of a problem. See Malabou (2004).

ideas, which were taken to an extreme level by Leon Trotsky and above all by V. I. Lenin, who set forth the basic ideas in 1902 in *What Is to Be Done?* Lenin's vision of a communist Russia as the vanguard for a communist Europe, which he believed would follow Russia's lead, was realized in a political program that was the ultimate example of a radical utopian ideology. After 1917, it led to the creation of a new social and political order that endured for more than 70 years. In 1917, the Bolshevik Revolution sought nothing less than overcoming of the present in the name of an imaginary future. Until his death in 1924, Lenin pursued this vision of a future order with a zeal and ruthlessness that had no comparisons in world history. Lenin was driven by the belief that everything could be sacrificed for the goal of a communist future. It was eventually an imaginary of a future that was to fail (Arnason 1993). However, it was also an example of a future imaginary that was turned into a present. It was also clear that the utopian ideal had lost its critical edge by the early 1920s and had become, in Mannheim's terms, an ideology of total state power. Susan Buck-Morss's study of the decline of 'mass utopia' in Russia sees the utopian dreamworld as having had a longer existence. However, her narrative is one of its decline, perishing with the end of the USSR, but also undermined by the wider transformation of mass utopia in the western world. In her account, 'the historical experiment of socialism was so deeply rooted in the Western modernizing tradition that its defeat cannot but place the whole Western narrative into question' (Buck-Morss 2002: xii). It is certainly true that the collapse of the USSR unleashed a Pandora's Box of furies, for it marked the end of a long period of relative stability presided over by the two world powers.

The Future as Possibility

The notion of the future as possibility was implicit in Koselleck's concept of expectation and is also suggested by the idea of the imaginary. It was developed more explicitly in the American pragmatist tradition. Pragmatism emphasizes a view of the world and human action as oriented to the future. Against the established currents in philosophy, such as rationalism and neo-positivism, the present time is not fully the product of the past governed by laws but is always open to the future. Everything is in a process of emergence or making and is incomplete in itself. The future is what provides completion. The future is not a telos but an outcome of choices people make. Temporality was built into the pragmatist philosophy, since time is the ultimate test of whether something is worth pursuing or not. Pragmatists opposed the view that there is an objective or ultimate truth or that there is certainty. Pragmatist thinkers placed the emphasis on finding practical solutions to social problems, encouraging skepticism and learning from experience.

One of the major figures in pragmatism, William James, wrote about the 'specious present' in 1890 in his *Principles of Psychology*, a term originally used by E. R. Clay in 1880. The specious present refers to the illusion that the present moment is the essence of time. By specious present, he meant the immediate present, the short duration of a few seconds to a few minutes. This is how we experience the present moment and it is the basic intuition of time, sometimes called 'chronoception' (meaning time perception). What is always experienced is the present, even when we are thinking of the past. The memory of past events or past experiences is always necessarily from the present, so what is really being experienced is the present moment in the way it defines the past.

For James, time is also a continuous flow, with the present just a moment in it. This does not mean that the present will be superseded by a future, such that we step from a past to a present to a future; rather the present moment is superseded by another present moment and so on with a continuous series of present moments. Along with A. N. Whitehead and Henri Bergson, discussed in Chapter Two, he was an important figure in advancing the concept of process and the related idea of a stream of consciousness, a term he invented, and which gave a new meaning to temporality, as well as influencing the literary trend in modernism represented by Marcel Proust, James Joyce, and Virginia Woolf. Reality is a constant flow or process that unfolds in space and in time and we experience, as different kinds of duration, as in the specious present, the memory of past events. Consciousness is a constant process of interpretation, of making sense of what the mind perceives. In essence, it was a view of time as sensation. James's conception of time is based on the fact that we experience change as the duration of specific events or experiences. The passage of time occurs through different states of consciousness. For James, we are constantly processing time by an ever-changing present which reworks the past and moves toward the future. The future is something we are oriented toward. It has a stronger pull than the past, simply because action is always future oriented.

James' theory of action is composed of three elements: choice, emotion, and futurity, which constitute rationality (Barbalet 1997). According to Barbalet, William James, in an influential essay, 'The Sentiment of Rationality,' makes the point that the 'relation of a thing to its future consequences' is of the greatest practical importance. It accounts for the ever-present sense of expectancy that the social actor experiences. James 'notes the "permanent presence of the sense of futurity" and that the future is qualitatively different from and in a significant sense discontinuous with the present. This is because the future comprises multiple possibilities whereas the present is determined and therefore not a possibility but an accomplished reality. It is action which makes the continuity of a possible future with the realized present, as James demonstrates, leaving unrealized other possible futures' (Barbalet 1997: 107). The real significance of James's is that he brought into central focus the idea of possible futures as something that is implicit in social action. This was an original contribution since it offered a different perspective from the mainstream view that the present is defined by the past. For James, action, which is based on an emotional disposition, is always seeking an end and to that extent, it implies a relation to the future. With this idea, James made temporality central to action.

James's arguments about 'futurity' defined the pragmatist movement as taken up by John Dewey. It placed a strong emphasis on knowledge as based on action and guided by a concern for the future. It also greatly influenced the social interaction tradition in sociology, with the idea that action is always creative and realizing possible futures.

Charles Sanders Peirce was also a major figure in the movement and generally credited with being the founder of pragmatism. His particular version of pragmatism, which he preferred to call 'pragmaticism,' was more concerned with the metaphysical laws of logic. Part of his large corpus of papers, which were never organized systematically into books and much remained unpublished, concerned what he once called 'The Logic of the Future.'[15] This body of thought is abstract and not directly relevant to social analysis, but it is noteworthy in advancing modal logic, in essence a mode of thought that is not based on facts but on possibility and probability. Modal logic resolves around three modalities – possibility, actuality, and necessity. It shows that the future frames the present, not in the way that the present is framed by the past but by containing possibilities for the future. The past cannot be changed, except in our interpretation of it, but the future can be influenced by the choices made in the present. There is thus a tension between experience and possibility. Strydom, in his interpretation of Pierce, suggests that what Peirce offered was a view of society and human subjectivity not as given or complete but made up of relations that are not fully realized and are open-ended. Such relations are guided by universal concepts, such as truth, justice, beauty, etc. which allow the human subject to transcend the present. 'As universal, they are necessary meta-cultural structures that fulfil a transcendental role by operating in the structuring manner of 'laws or principles'...Although universal, these concepts have a contingent origin, having been generated historically and stabilized evolutionarily, and therefore remain subject to time – albeit, not historical but evolutionary temporality' (Strydom 2023:170). Peirce thus identifies sources of possibilities in human action and consciousness and which are 'indeterminate'

---

15 See Bellucci and Pietarinen (2019).

marked by 'indefiniteness.' The implication is that such concepts harbor an inexhaustible store of possibilities that could be realized.

Peirce's conception of the future was then essentially one of possibility built into the structure of thought and consciousness. His writings on the future were not always lucid and were embedded in his work on modal logic. Writing on time, he clarified that the future always has a bearing upon the present. Past, present, and future have a 'bearing upon conduct' (by conduct he means the 'conduct of life'). Posing the question, 'How does the future bear upon conduct?', he wrote in 1913: '...according to pragmatism the conclusion of a reasoning proper must refer to the future' and 'the only controllable conduct is the Future conduct' (Peirce 1998: 359). The value of all action is ultimately on the effects it has on future conduct.

He made a similar statement in an earlier paper in 1902 in which he grounded the idea of the future in a notion of potentiality: 'A man [sic] may become aware of any habit, and may describe to himself the general way in which it will act. For every habit has, or is, a general law. Whatever is truly general refers to the indefinite future; for the past contains only a certain collection of such cases that have occurred. The past is actual fact. But a general (fact) cannot be fully realized. It is a potentiality; and its mode of being is *esse in futuro*.'[16] (Peirce 1931–1958: CP 2.148). Later, he wrote: 'The rational meaning of every proposition lies in the future' (CP5: 427).

The strong orientation to the future is also reflected in his conception of reality. The real is always incomplete and extends into the future. Unlike teleological reasoning, we can reason from knowing the future, which is also indefinite. The real must include what is expected from the future, not just a matter of being content with what has happened or what the present has to offer. Reality is also to include what will be, what will result from what is done in the present and therefore the meaning of what we do resides in the future (see also Rossela 2023).

In sum, in line with pragmatist thinking in general, Peirce offers a conception of the social world and political possibility. His theoretical framework shows that the future derives from two main sources: what is potentially possible in the present – what is possible now – and what might be possible in the future. While Peirce's work did not have much if any direct relevance for social and political applications, he was a major influence on John Dewey, who was one of the most important political theorists in the United States in the twentieth century. His writings on education have been particularly important in transmitting pragmatist thought. Against the mainstream conservative and liberal view about education as the transmission of the wisdom of the past to the present, he advocated a prag-

---

16 Bold in original version.

matist philosophy for educators to see the purpose of education to prepare people for the future.

James and Peirce were also major sources of inspiration for George Herbert Mead, who laid the foundations of an important tradition in sociological theory, later known as symbolic interaction. He stood firmly in the pragmatist tradition, while incorporating the philosophy of phenomenology and the work of Henri Bergson, who was another major influence on his thought. In regard to temporality, his work offers a more sociologically relevant interpretation of the metaphysical work of Peirce. He also wrote a book on time, *The Philosophy of the Present* (Mead 1934). Less well known than his major work, based on lectures, *Mind, Self and Society,* it is an important work in concretizing the pragmatist conception of time within an intersubjectivist framework and in demonstrating that the self is a temporal process (Adam 1990: 38–42; Joas 1997). The social nature of time arises out of the way the subject responds to events, which are interpreted in the context of interaction and thus the response will depend on the social context. While, as in James, the present is the main experience of temporality, it is always more than the present since there is the anticipation of the future. The future is structured by the present as is the past, which is also subordinated to the present. Mead's perspective highlights that 'what is going to happen can actually affect what has just happened.' He wrote: 'the future is continually qualifying the past in the present' (Mead 1932: 38). What he describes is an actor reflecting on a path of action and in so doing constructing the future: 'We are at any moment surrounded by an indefinite number of possible sensations. Which of these will be picked out is decided in terms of the response that is already being made. There you have the future, the conclusion of the act, implied in what is now going on but which is not yet achieved, coming in to set up the conditions in terms of which stimuli shall arise' (Cited in Flaherty and Fine, 2001: 156).

Mead brought time consciousness into sociological theory and made an important contribution in bringing the rather abstract work of Peirce into sociological analysis. However, his work remained undeveloped and the central concept of possibility in Peirce with its emphasis on the transcendent possibilities of the present lacks the critical force that was also not developed by Peirce in terms of concrete applications. Adam is correct in saying that Mead reduced time too much to experience and thus lost sight of non-temporal time in the sense of time that is not directly experienced (Adam 1990: 41). While he saw the present unbounded, the past and the future were a domain of possibilities. Yet, his work lacked a critical edge and was absorbed by a conservative sociology that did not pay attention to the structures of power and domination in the present.

The concept of possibility, originally developed within pragmatist thought, was a very important contribution to an adequate understanding of the future as the domain of the emergence of the new. It remained undeveloped and unclear how it relates to the notion of the imaginary. Mead made a crucial step in bringing the idea of the future as part of a temporal concept of the social self into sociology, but in doing so, it lost its connection with the idea of possibility in Peirce. Mead's legacy in the end, despite his engagement with the natural sciences, was as in a conservative sociological theory.

The Future as Experience

One of the great works of twentieth-century philosophy was on time, Martin Heidegger's *Being and Time*, published in 1927. The book is rich in insights on the idea of the future and was one of the first systematic attempts to understand the future as part of what he called 'the horizon of temporality' (p. 365).[17] One of the key ideas in this book was that human existence was defined by the relation with time. Time is both existential and ontological – it is what makes reality possible. Human existence, referred to as *Dasein*, literally 'to be there', is temporal in that one of the fundamental features of the human condition is awareness of finitude. There may be a sense in which time is eternal, as in the Christian interpretation, often associated with Augustine. There is the infinitude of time in cosmic terms. But the human experience of time is marked by death.

Death is one of the preoccupations of Heidegger in this work, which is a product of the phenomenological tradition and bears the influence of Husserl, to whom *Being and Time* was dedicated. Heidegger was also influenced by William James and C. S. Peirce, whose ideas were influential in early twentieth-century European circles. Heidegger's concern with the problem of existence made *Being and Time* a signal work in what was to become existentialism. Unlike the French existentialists, such as Sartre, Heidegger's concern was less with freedom than with the problem of the meaning of human existence.

The meaning of human condition, a term that effectively equates *Dasein*, is mortality, the fact that life ends with death. The awareness of our mortality gives us a sense of time. It follows then that this awareness of time is also an anticipation of death, which is an aspect of the orientation to the future. The human being is a 'being toward death,' which is the sense he understands the future (p. 325). The anticipation of death is integral to the human condition. In fact, it is this feature of the human condition that arises from the future (see

---

17 Page references are to those in the outer margins. Italics and bold in the following citations are as in the text, as translated by John Macquarrie and Edward Robinson.

pp. 329–30). He writes that 'The present is rooted in the future' (p. 326). By this, he means the human condition is shaped by its orientation to the future, which therefore is not something beyond the present but deeply integral to it. In a key passage, he writes: *'Only an entity which, in its Being, is essentially futural so that it is free for its death and can let itself be thrown back upon factical "there" by shattering itself against death'* (p. 385). The category of the future is needed in order to make sense of the present, which is an important insight that Heidegger developed. 'Even historiological disclosure temporalizes itself in terms of the future.' (p. 395).

Heidegger's concern with death is one of the main foundations of philosophical writings on death, along with Kierkegaard. The distinctive feature of his work is the relation of death to temporality. Death does not mark entry to eternal life; there is no future after the finality of death. It is the point at which time ends for the human being. This view of time led Heidegger to a phenomenological position of time, that is, time is something experienced and related to the category of 'care.' Some of his most interesting remarks concern the temporality of care (p. 325 ff). The phenomenological turn in European philosophy, inaugurated by Edmund Husserl, marked a new interest with understanding reality, i.e. phenomena, as it is experienced by the human mind. The category of human experience was central to this movement. While Husserl aimed to make phenomenology a rigorous method, Heidegger brought it in a different direction that only became clear in his later work, whereby experience is essentially linguistic. *Being and Time* brought phenomenology away from the concern with consciousness that was a feature of Husserl and made the problem of existence more fundamental to it. Human existence, the problem of being, is revealed in the experience of time.

Time, for Heidegger, is not a series of moments or episodes that can be organized into past, present, and future such that one moves from one to the other and that at one point, the past ends and the present begins and ends with entry to the future. While in many ways time is a flow, as in Bergson or Whitehead, the notion of process also does not quite capture Heidegger's notion of temporality, since it is a going backward and forward. Time is often reduced to the present, since this is how it is generally experienced, but for Heidegger that was an 'inauthentic' response to temporality. The human being is in the present but is also going back to the past and anticipating the future. The future as such does not arrive but is only an anticipation of an ending, not a new beginning. Presence is not only in the present but it also includes the presence of the past and, in the form of anticipation, the future. While death, in the sense of the experience of finitude, is the essence of the future, it is not the only dimension of the future, but it is the dimension that defines the future as an ending and not as in Koselleck (who was almost certainly also influenced by Heidegger) the promise of a better world. The future dimension of temporality is also related to the category of 'care.' So, what Heidegger offers is a conception of temporality that incorporates past, present, and future through the categories of human experience. In this respect, it is not fundamentally different from William James's except in his preoccupation with the problem of the meaning of existence. It is not clear what Heidegger's position was on Einstein's discovery of the nature of time. We know he was familiar with his ideas and was almost certainly influenced by the new conception of time as relative to the perceiver of events. However, we do not know how he positioned the phenomenological account of time in relation to the cosmological space-time framework.

While Heidegger's main aim was to situate Being within temporality, there is also an argument that Being is spatial. The notion of Being-in-the-world expresses the spatial dimension of human existence, as embodied in space and in time, and reflected in his reflections on dwelling and space as lived space, the 'life-world' (a term first used by Husserl). Space is constitutive of the world and spatiality is essential to the basic state of Being-in-the-world (p. 113).

In the section on 'The Temporality of Understanding' (pp. 336–340), Heidegger offers a perspective on the future as a projection: 'The future makes ontologically possible an entity which is in such a way that it exists understandingly in its potentiality-for-Being. Projection is basically futural; it does not primarily grasp the projected possibility thematically just by having it in view, but it throws itself into it as a possibility' (1980: 336–7). He distinguishes between the authentic and the inauthentic future. The former is a condition of 'waiting' characterized by expectation, while the latter is a condition of 'anticipation':

'To designate the authentic future terminologically we have reserved the expression "anticipation." This indicates that Dasein, existing authentically, lets itself come towards itself as its ownmost potentiality-for-Being that the future itself must first win itself, not from a Present, but from the inauthentic future. If we are to provide a formally undifferentiated term for the future, we may use the one with which we have designated the first structural item of care-the "ahead-of-itself." Factically, Dasein is constantly ahead of itself, but inconstantly anticipatory with regard to its existential possibility.' (p. 337). The distinction that Heidegger made between the condition of expecting and anticipation was an original insight: 'Expecting is founded upon awaiting, and is a mode of that future which temporalizes itself authentically as anticipation' (p. 338). For Heidegger, anticipation is more authentic than expectation since it relates to something deeper in the human condition in the experience of temporality as finitude. Unlike expecting, it is not about the arrival of an external event but something more existential that is intrinsic to human existence in anticipation of death (Bowring 2022: 354).

Heidegger's conception of time has been influential. He showed how the human condition is deeply embedded in temporality. His notion of the future offered an alternative to the conventional views, as in Kant, who associated it with the idea of progress, or the older traditions coming from Aristotle that saw the future as simply that which comes after the present or the Christian eschatological notion of an eternal time to come. However, any account of Heidegger cannot avoid confronting the unpalatable fact that he was not simply politically naïve or just opportunistic, but he was a Nazi sympathizer and, as the Nazi Rector of the University of Freiburg, an ardent supporter of Nazism. *Being and Time* might be excused as written prior to the rise of Nazism and was not a political work, but the arguments set forth in it on the human condition were somehow compatible with a frame of mind that could easily be adapted to serve totalitarianism. In any case, it is now clear since the publication of the *Black Notebooks* that his political inclinations were well established long before Hitler's rise to power in 1933 and almost certainly go back to the mid-1920s when he was writing *Being and Time*.[18] Aside from Heidegger's dark political legacy, the question can be asked how helpful this perspective is when it comes to how the future should be viewed today. In a late essay in 1969 on the 'task for thinking' in relation to possibility of modern technological civilization being overcome, he wrote: 'The preparatory thinking in question does not wish and is not able to predict the future. It only attempts to say something to the present which was already said a long time ago precisely at the beginning of philosophy and for that beginning, but has not been explicitly thought' (1978: 379). This would appear to suggest that everything that could be said about the future was once said a long time ago.

His existential ontology ultimately was one which saw the human condition as devoid of a capacity for self-transcendence with only the comforting thought of death, not of life that lies ahead. *Being and Time* explicitly claims that the human being is facing death from the moment of birth and there is no redemption possible.

The sense of temporality that was behind Heidegger's work was very much that of the individual as an abstract being. Whatever the merits of this approach, it does not work well when transposed to the societal level or applied to any kind of collective subject, except his support for the futurist vision of the 'Thousand-year Reich.' While Heidegger did conceive of *Dasein* in intersubjective terms and led the way to sociological phenomenology, it failed to grasp the political predicament that marks the approach to the future. His preoccupation with death presents problems in responding to the mass deaths of the totalitarian political systems

---

18 Mitchell and Trawny (2017).

of the twentieth century with which he was implicated. Death may not have been a political project in his work, but mass death was a fact of the age in which he lived and wrote. His work was dismissive of modernity and cultivated an intellectual ethos of mystification and obscurantism.

Heidegger, along with Ludwig Wittgenstein and Sigmund Freud, was one of the most influential thinkers of the twentieth century. Despite his complicity with the Nazi regime, he had many famous Jewish students, including Hannah Arendt, Karl Löwith, Hans Jonas, and Herbert Marcuse, all of whom distanced themselves from his politics and took various positions in relation to his work, including a 'left-Heideggerianism,' as represented by the young Herbert Marcuse (see Wolin 2015). Arendt famously broke from Heidegger. However, she remained a critic of modernity, seeing the modern age in terms of a story of decline. Her major work, *The Human Condition* in 1958, offered a pessimistic view of the future and a lament for a lost past, though not one that had given up hope for the future, which remained a vital orientation for the present. In the Preface to the essays collected in *Between Past and Present*, she sees the present as a small moment in time, a gap, between remembrance and anticipation, but one in which all that can be done is to create a space for thinking in order to have hope for a meaningful future. 'This small non-time-space in the very heart of time, unlike the world and the culture into which we are born, can only be indicated, but cannot be inherited and handed down from the past; each new generation, indeed every new human being as he inserts himself between an infinite past and an infinite future, must discover and ploddingly pave it anew' (Arendt 1961: 13).

Another of Heidegger's famous students was Hans-Georg Gadamer, who wrote the book that brought Heideggerian thought into a wider field of hermeneutics and opened up the phenomenological tradition to hermeneutical interpretation. In *Truth and Method*, published in 1960,[19] Gadamer developed the hermeneutical approach implicit in *Being and Time*. Hermeneutics, as the method of interpretation, shows how the present is always a reinterpretation of the past. We are always in dialogue with tradition, which can never be surmounted but only renewed. The hermeneutical turn, which was important in the social and human sciences, suffered from a lack of critical thinking, as in the arguments of Jürgen Habermas, who in bringing Freud into the picture, developed, along with Paul Ricoeur, a critical hermeneutics that was more in tune with the need for evaluation as well as interpretation.

---

19 Second edition in 1965 (Gadamer 1975).

The Heideggerian position represented by Gadamer ultimately was unable to address the future despite his efforts to broaden the 'fusion of horizons,'[20] to use the most famous term in *Truth and Method*, a term that was very likely an inspiration for Koselleck in his 1967 essay on the 'horizon of expectation.' The difference, however, was that the latter was interested in the horizon of the future, while Gadamer's hermeneutical philosophy was concerned with the past. This is not to suggest the future did not matter to him. In an essay in 1966, he offered his somewhat uncertain thoughts on the future and the role of philosophy in view of the movement toward a 'world order' and what he regarded as purely 'scientific civilization' (Gadamer 1966). In a later and more critically relevant essay on the European heritage in 1984, he highlighted the importance of the legacy of unity and diversity, arguing for a hermeneutical relation to the other: 'To participate with the other and to be part of the other is the most and the best that we can strive to accomplish' (Gadamer 1992: 235).

The concept of the horizon that he had made so central to the hermeneutical process of understanding and interpretation in *Truth and Method* is highly pertinent to the idea of the future: 'A horizon is not a rigid frontier, but something that moves with one and invites one to advance further' (Gadamer 1979: 217). To expand one's horizon is to see further, beyond the present: 'to have a horizon means not to be limited to what is nearest, but to see beyond it' (p 269). However, on its own, the notion of the horizon, as in Gadamer and Koselleck, lacks critical force.

Conclusion

In this chapter, I discussed some of the most important ideas of the future in modern thought, especially in the line from Kant to Heidegger. I argued that the idea of the future is essentially a product of modernity and bears the imprint of the Enlightenment. The authors discussed here are all essential interlocutors for thinking about the future, even if the accounts they offered suffer from deficiencies. Koselleck' s writings provided a crucial conception of the future in terms of an expectation. I have also tried to show that another strand in modern thought gave the idea of the future a strong sense of an imaginary that is realized in a political project. The pragmatist tradition drew attention to the key concept of possibility as a way to approach the future. Finally, the phenomenological tradition conceived of the future in terms of the category of experience, but with Heidegger, the notion

---

20 Gadamer (1975: 273).

of expectation is contrasted with the idea of anticipation as the basis of an alternative conception of the future.

One outcome of all these philosophies of the future was an interpretive approach. The category of the future is a product of interpretation; it is not positively given or something that can be objectively known. What is significant is not the factual substance of the future but the form by which it is known, which can be as discussed in this chapter an expectation, an imaginary, or a possibility. The future is disordered and incoherent until we impose a pattern on it to make sense of it. So, the idea of the future is related to how societies make sense of themselves through their cultural models, to their self-interpretation and self-understanding. This put the category of experience at the core of the idea of the future. It concerns how time is felt, as Wittman has discussed in relation to how time itself is experienced (Wittman 2016). But as we will see in Chapter Six, the future also exerts itself through the potentials that compel the human subject to go beyond the present. In that sense, the future is more than a form of sensemaking; it concerns potentiality and possibility. Historical and philosophical hermeneutics of the future must be broad enough to encompass its many dimensions. The future is an open-ended idea that in itself goes beyond attempts to actualize. Indeed, the very idea of the future makes possible the many different interpretations that there are of it.

References

Adam, B. 1990. *Time and Social Theory*. Cambridge: Polity Press.
Adams, S., Blokker, P., Doyle, N., Krummel, J., Smith, J. 2017. 'Social Imaginaries in Debate.' *Social Imaginaries*, 1 (1): 15–52.
Anderson, B. 1983. *Imagined Communities: Reflections on the Origin and Spread of Nationalism*. London: Verso.
Arendt, H. 1958. *The Human Condition*. Chicago: University of Chicago Press.
Arnason, J. 1989. 'The Imaginary Constitution of Modernity.' *Revue européenne des sciences sociales*, 27(86): 327–337.
Arnason, A. 1993. *The Future that Failed: Origins and Destinies of the Soviet Model*. London: Routledge.
Allen, A. 2016. *The End of Progress: Decolonizing the Normative Foundations of Critical Theory*. New York: Columbia University Press.
Appadurai, A. 2013. 'The Future as a Cultural Fact.' In: *The Future as a Cultural Fact: Essay on the Global Condition*. London: Verso.
Arendt, H. 1961. 'The Gap Between Past and Future.' In: *Between Past and Future*. New York: Viking Press.
Barbalet, J. 1997. 'The Jamesonian Theory of Action.' *The Sociological Review*, 45 (1): 102–21.
Beckert, J. 2016. *Imagined Futures: Fictional Expectations and Capitalist Dynamics*. Cambridge, MASS.: Harvard University Press.

Beckert, J. and Bronk, R. (eds) 2018. *Uncertain Futures: Imaginaries, Narratives, and Calculation in the Economy.* Oxford: Oxford University Press.

Bellucci, F. and Pietarinen, A.-V. (eds) 2019. *Logic of the Future: Writings on Existential Graph. Vol. 1 History and Applications.* Berlin: De Gruyter.

Bergson, H. 1910. [1889] *Time and Free Will: An Essay on the Immediate Data of Consciousness.* London: Allen and Unwin.

Blumenberg, H. 1966. 'On a Lineage of the Idea of Progress.' *Social Research*, 41 (1): 5–27.

Blumenberg, H. 1987. [1975] *The Genesis of the Copernican World.* Cambridge, MASS: MIT Press.

Blumenberg, H. 1985. [1966] *The Legitimacy of the Modern Age.* Cambridge, MASS: MIT Press.

Blumenberg, H. 1986. *Lebenszeit und Weltzeit.* Frankfurt: Suhrkamp.

Bowring, F. 2022. 'Death and the Form of Life.' *European Journal of Social Theory*, 25 (3): 349–65.

Buck-Morss, S. 2000. *Dreamworld and Catastrophe: The Passing of Mass Utopia in East and West.* Cambridge, MASS: MIT Press.

Bundock, C. 2016. *Romantic Prophecy and Resistance to Historicism.* Toronto: Toronto University Press.

Castoriadis, C. 1987. [1975] *The Imaginary Institution of Society.* Cambridge: Polity Press.

Claeys, G. 2020. *Utopia: The History of an Idea.* London: Thames and Hudson.

Desroche, H. 1979. [1973] *The Sociology of Hope.* London: Routledge & Kegan Paul.

Elster, J. 1999. *Alchemies of the Mind: Rationality and the Emotions.* Cambridge University Press.

Flaherty, M. G. and Fine, G. A. '2001. 'Present, Past and Future: Conjugating Georg Herbert Mead's Perspective on Time.' *Time and Society*, 102/3: 147–61.

Gadamer, H.-G. 1966. 'Notes on Planning for the Future.' *Daedalus*, 95 (2): 572–89.

Gadamer, H.-G. 1979. [1960/1965]. *Truth and Method.* London: Sheed and Ward.

Gadamer, H.-G. 1992. 'The Diversity of Europe: Inheritance and Future.' In: Misgeld, D. and Nicholson, G. (eds) *Applied Hermeneutics.* New York: SUNY.

Gatans, M. *et al.* 2021. 'Critical Exchange: Spinoza: Thoughts on Hope in Our Political Present.' *Contemporary Political Theory*, 20, 200–231. https://doi.org/10.1057/s41296- 020-00406-4

Graeber, D. and Wengrow, D. 2021. *The Dawn of Everything: A New History of Humanity.* London: Penguin.

Habermas, J. 1987. [1985] *The Philosophical Discourse of Modernity: Twelve Lectures.* Cambridge: Polity Press.

Heidegger, M. 1977. [1969] 'The End of Philosophy and The Task of Thinking.' In: *Martin Heidegger: Basic Writings.* London: Routledge & Kegan Paul.

Heidegger, M. 1980. [1927] *Being and Time.* Oxford: Blackwell.

Hobbes, T. 1978. [1651] *Leviathan.* London: Penguin.

Husserl, E. 1964. [1928] *The Phenomenology of Internal Time-Consciousness.* Bloomington: Indiana University Press.

James, W. 1890. 'The Perception of Time.' In: *The Principles of Psychology*, Vol. 1. New York: Henry Holt.

Jay, M. 1980. 'A Reflection on *The Legitimacy of the Modern Age*.' In: *Fin-De-Siècle Socialism and Other Essays.* London: Routledge.

Joas, H. 1997. *G.H. Mead: A Contemporary Re-Examination of his Thought.* Cambridge, MASS.: MIT Press.

Hill, C. 1977. *Milton and the English Revolution.* London: Faber and Faber.

Kaag, J. 2004. *Thinking through the Imagination: The Aesthetics in Modern Cognition.* New York: Fordham University Press.

Kant, I. 1978. [1798] *Anthropology from a Pragmatic Point of View*. Translated by V. L. Dowell. Carbondale: Southern Illinois University Press.

Kierkegaard, S. 1996. *Soren Kierkegaard Papers and Journals: A Selection*. A. Hannay (ed.). London: Penguin.

Koselleck, R. 1988. [1959] *Crisis and Critique: Enlightenment and the Pathogenesis of Society*. Cambridge, MASS: MIT Press.

Koselleck, R. 2002. *The Practice of Conceptual History*. Stanford: Stanford University Press.

Koselleck, R. 2004a. [1979] *Futures Past: On the Semantics of Historical Time*. New York: Columbia University Press.

Koselleck, R. 2004b. [1965/1979] 'Modernity and the Planes of Historicity.' In: *Futures Past: On the Semantics of Historical Time*. New York: Columbia University Press.

Koselleck, R. 2004c. [1967/1979] '"Spaces of Experience" and "Horizon of Expectation": Two Historical Concepts.' In: *Futures Past: On the Semantics of Historical Time*. New York: Columbia University Press.

Koselleck, 2004d. [1977/1979] '"Neuzeit": Remarks on the Semantics of Modern Concepts of Movement.' In: *Futures Past: On the Semantics of Historical Time*. New York: Columbia University Press.

Koselleck, R. 2018. [2000] *Sediment of Time: On Possible Histories*. Stanford: Stanford University Press.

Kumar, K. 1987. *Utopia and Anti-Utopia in Modern Times*. Oxford: Blackwell.

Leibniz, G. W. 1925 [1898/1714] *The Monadology and Other Philosophical Writings*. Oxford: Oxford University Press.

Lennon, K. 2015. *The Imaginary and the Imagination*. London: Routledge.

Malabou, C. 2004. *The Future of Hegel: Plasticity, Temporality and Dialectics*. London: Routledge.

Mannheim, K. 1991. [1929] *Ideology and Utopia*. London: Routledge.

Mead, G. H. 1932. *The Philosophy of the Present*. London: The Open Court Company.

Mehring, R. 2014. *Carl Schmitt: A Biography*. Cambridge: Polity Press.

Morton, A. 2013. *Emotion and the Imagination*. Cambridge: Polity Press.

Morag, T. 2016. *Emotion, Imagination and the Limits of Reason*. London: Routledge.

Mitchell, A. and Trawny, P. (eds) 2017. *Heidegger's Black Notebooks: Responses to Anti-Semitism*. New York: Columbia University Press.

Peirce, C. S. 1931–1958. *Collected Papers of Charles S. Peirce*. Edited by C. Hartshorne & P. Weiss (Vols. 1–6). Cambridge, MA: Harvard University Press.

Peirce, C. S. 1998. *The Essential Peirce: Selected Philosophical Writings, 1893–1913*. Vol. 2 Bloomington: Indiana University Press.

Pinker, S. 2011. *The Better Angels of Our Nature: A History of Violence and Humanity*. London: Penguin.

Rajan, T. and Falak, J. (eds) 2020. *William Blake: Modernity and Disaster*. Toronto: Toronto University Press.

Ranson, A. 2014. 'The First Last Man: Cousin de Graineville's *Le Dernier homme*.' *Science Fiction Studies*, 41 (2): 314–40.

Rossela, F. 2023. 'An Apology for a Dynamic Ontology: Peirce's Analysis of Futurity in a Nietzschean Perspective.' *Philosophies*, 8 (35).

Rousseau, J.-J. 1985. [1781] *The Confessions*. London: Penguin.

Sartre, J.-P. 2004. [1940] *The Imaginary: A Phenomenological Psychology of the Imagination*. London: Routledge.

Strydom, P. 2023. 'The Critical Theory of Society: From its Young Hegelian Core to the Key Concept of Possibility.' *European Journal of Social Theory*, 26 (2): 153–79.

Taylor, C. 2004. *Modern Social Imaginaries.* Durham, NC: Duke University Press.

United Nations. 1987. *Report of the World Commission on Environment and Development: Our Common Future.* Oxford: Oxford University Press.

Wagner, P. 2016. *Progress: A Reconstruction.* Cambridge: Polity Press.

Williams, S. 2000. *Emotions and Social Theory.* Sage.

Wittman, M. 2016. *Felt Time: The Science of How We Experience Time.* Cambridge, MASS.: MIT Press.

Wolin, R. 2015. *Heidegger's Children: Hannah Arendt, Karl Löwith, Hans Jonas, Herbert Marcuse.* Princeton: Princeton University Press.

Chapter Five
Ideas of the Future in the Twentieth Century: Futurism, Modernism, Sociology, and Political Theory

The previous chapter looked at some of the main philosophical conceptions of the future that were produced by modernity. In this chapter I shift the focus to the idea of the future in social and political science from the middle of the twentieth century, looking in particular at sociological approaches to the future. The major narratives of the future of the eighteenth and nineteenth centuries crystalized in the course of the twentieth century into a variety of different ideas and counternarratives. Some of these, especially in the early to mid-twentieth century, were antimodernist and viewed the future with foreboding, but others were far more visionary and provided a foundation for post-1945 ideas of the future.

In the period after the Second World War, the future became a concern for the social sciences, economics, and political theory. This was a contrast to the prewar period. Many of the ideas of the future prior to the middle of the twentieth century in western societies were anchored in the past, which was seen as coming to an end but with uncertain implications. The future that loomed on the horizon was an uncertain one, and for many intellectuals it instilled fear and foreboding about the future course of civilization. The first half of the twentieth century was dominated by the two World Wars and the chaos that followed in the wake of the collapse of the central European empires and the rise of communism, first in Russia and then in China. The theme of the crisis of civilization pervaded much of the thought of the period. The era, the first half of the twentieth century, was also conscious of the transformation of the world by technology, which tended to be seen as a threat to the individual. A profound pessimism about the future was much in evidence, especially in European thought since 1914 (some of this literature will be discussed in this chapter).

The political mood in the United States was more optimistic, as reflected in American pragmatism and the phrase attributed to Abraham Lincoln, that 'the best way to predict the future is to create it.' Despite the influence of American philosophers, such as C. S. Peirce and especially William James, in European intellectual circles, their more optimistic political outlook was not what was central to the reception of their work. For Weber, as earlier for Hegel, America was the future, not Europe. Spengler's *The Decline of the West* in 1918 was one of the most widely read books of the period, and in many ways it was, as Spengler wrote, 'a philosophy of the future' (1934: 23). The period was also marked by a retreat

https://doi.org/10.1515/9783111240602-006

from cosmopolitanism and a turn to national protectionism in economic policy in an era that saw the rise of fascism and totalitarianism. It was also a period that saw a new interest in the occult, which was connected to modernism, and offered spiritual prophecies and predictions that provided a certain degree of reenchantment (Bramble 2015).

After 1945 a new confidence about the future arose, especially in the western world. The postwar economic recovery in Europe was rapid once it started and the United States emerged from the war as the beacon of western civilization. It was inevitable that the new ideas of the future would be ones that were taking shape there. In the context of the Cold War, a much diminished and dependent Europe looked westward. Thus was born the new ideas of the future that appeared to give a new meaning to the older notion of progress, now reborn as modernization. The western world from the end of the 1940s to the early 1970s, the so-called 'Thirty Golden Years,' was a period of tremendous optimism and relative prosperity; it was the age of the middle class, suburbia, the Apollo missions, and the baby-boomers. It was the era too that saw the advancement of science and technological supremacy, much of it dependent on the United States. In the late 1960s in the heyday of the Apollo missions, the US government spent 4% of the Federal Reserve on NASA missions, which were also tied to the race for global dominance. These developments gave a new meaning to the 'American Dream,' a vision of the future that was also invoked by Martin Luther King in his 'I have a Dream' speech in 1963 in Washington.

In Europe the project of European integration – with the vision of never again war – brought about a fundamental transformation in the continent, leading to a more future-oriented politics than one rooted in the past. The foundation of UNESCO in 1945 was a product of the new turn to the future. Under the visionary leadership of Julian Huxley – who was an early proponent of transhumanism[1] – it fostered the conservation of the natural and cultural heritage of world cultures for the future, giving a new direction for archaeology (Meskell 2010). We should not lose sight of the fact that behind the rosy self-caricature of 'the Thirty Golden Years' of western prosperity and peace was a world divided into four blocs: the West and the USSR, as two nuclear superpowers; the so-called 'Third World', which the two superpowers were competing to control; and China, which, under the brutal regime of Mao in this period, was undergoing horrific transformation with the disastrous collectivization of farms and then the cultural revolution that along with state terror claimed the lives of around 70 million people. Then, within the category of the West was the fact that many of the western powers

---

1 See Chapter Seven.

New Political Ideas of the Future after 1945 ━━ **125**

were still colonial powers and the peace that emerged in 1945 was peace only for those western countries that had previously been at war with each other. France was at war with Algeria from 1954 to 1962, despite *les trente glorieuses.*

Against this background of technological and economic advancement, the consolidation of the welfare state, and a qualified peace in western societies, new ideas of the future emerged. The new opening to the future was not entirely oblivious to the new threat of nuclear annihilation, since the Second World War ended with the prospect of an even worse war to come based on the military doctrine of Mutual Annihilation Destruction (MAD), as philosophers such as Bertrand Russell warned in an essay 'The Future of Man' in 1951 and Karl Jaspers in *The Future of Mankind* in 1961. Jaspers argued for a new kind of anticipatory thinking: 'The significance of anticipatory thinking lies in illumination of possibilities, not in prediction, and much less in knowledge of the future' (1961: 283). Despite the call for a new global ethics, as in Hans Jonas' (1984) *Imperative of Responsibility* in 1979, the absence of war gave rise to the comforting illusion of peace, which was only the postponement of a war of 'exterminism,' and the cultivation of new ideas of the future around science and technology (Thompson *et al.* 1987).

These ideas will be considered in this chapter under the following headings. First, in political theory we look at two influential and very different conceptions of the future, those of F. A. Hayek and Bertrand de Jouvenel. Second, a feature of the first three decades of the postwar era was the rise of futurology, but with its origins in the rise of futurism from the end of the nineteenth century. Third, we look at the developments in sociological theory that were explicitly focused on new thinking about the future. In the 1970s the prominent American sociologist Daniel Bell was a leading figure in the social forecasting movement. Niklas Luhmann in Germany wrote important work on the idea of the future. I also look at later figures, such as Ulrich Beck, John Urry, and other theorists of globalization who advanced important ideas about the future. Finally, I look at a specific and relatively recent strand within sociological theory that built on the phenomenological tradition, as revived by Alfred Schutz, to produce important theories of the future (Schutz 1959, 1967).

New Political Ideas of the Future after 1945

Two major political theorists of the post-1945 period were the Austrian economist and political philosopher F. A. Hayek and Bertrand de Jouvenel, a French political philosopher. Their concerns were very different but they had a common interest in how an alternative future might be possible. They both saw the problem of the future as in part a problem of knowledge in the sense that while we cannot know what is going to happen in the future, we need an appropriate approach to the unknowability of the future. They also shared a common dislike of the dominance of planning, though in the case of Hayek, this was a stronger belief. They were also prominent figures of the right, in the case of Hayek, what was to become neoliberalism, and de Jouvenel, conservative liberalism. The background that shaped their visions of the future was a time in which science had become the principal lens through which the future could be not only discerned but made possible. Neither opposed the apparent triumph of science and the scientific worldview but were aware of its limits.

Hayek's most famous book, not necessarily his greatest, was *The Road to Serfdom*, published in 1944 and generally regarded as the foundation of what was to become neoliberalism. It was an attack on central planning at a time when this was seen as the primary purpose of government. The ideas of J. M. Keynes, whose influential *The General Theory of Employment, Interest and Money* was published in 1936, established the orthodoxy that was accepted by the right as well as the left that governments should intervene in the economy. Since the New Deal in the United States and the circumstances of the Second World War, which favored central government to manage the war economy, Hayek perceived a threat to freedom. The context of the book was also a rebuttal of William Beveridge's 1942 publication *Social Insurance and Allied Services*, which led to the National Health Service, spearheaded by the Labour Party after 1945. His main target was the political and economic ideas of the left, including the New Deal, but it encompassed all forms of government planning. Hayek, who was living in London at the time of writing the book, associated planning with totalitarianism in an argument that differentiated little between the various kinds of socialism and national socialism. While he was a figure of the political right, his work was a revision of neoclassical economics, which he held was based on the wrong assumptions about the nature of knowledge and what government can reasonably do.

Neoclassical economics, he claimed, assumed incorrectly that people act on the basis of full and relevant information on the means to attain their desired ends.[2] Economic policy needs to take into account the fact of uncertainty. He argued that while people act on the basis of self-interest in their pursuit of means to achieve their ends, they do so on the basis of incomplete knowledge. The knowledge that actors have is also incomplete as far as market conditions are concerned. The market, he held, is a complex system that can never be fully known. If the market,

---

2 The account offered here is necessarily brief and confined to what is relevant regarding the conception of the future that was at work in his writings. For a more detailed discussion, see Chapter Five in Delanty and Harris (2023).

which is future oriented, cannot be fully known, it cannot be planned for. Underlying Hayek's economic and political philosophy was this simple epistemological thesis about the nature of market complexity, which is believed to have implications for knowledge, which is necessarily limited. This meant that government policy should also be limited. In making this claim, he was setting forth the basic axiom of neoliberalism, which was a revision of neoclassical economics to accommodate the problem of the unpredictability of the market, which cannot be fully mastered by technocratic government.

Underlying his epistemological claim about the nature and limits of knowledge was an ontological claim concerning the nature of order, which is not fixed and immutable but subject to change and is unpredictable. He saw this in positive terms and thought that a political system that seeks to establish order will necessarily result in tyranny. Governments should not try to prevent a spontaneous order from emerging from market forces, which can make the necessary adjustments to produce an optimal equilibrium between supply and demand. So, market forces constitute a form of order which is unpredictable and consequently unknowable. He was awarded the Nobel Prize for Economics in 1974 for applying these ideas to the price system.

The idea at work in Hayek's economic and political theory was very much bound up with his view that a desirable future cannot be planned for and that any attempt to do so will result in a loss of freedom. This idea was in many ways in contradiction to the utopia of a free society that the neoliberal moment sought to realize against the status quo of the planned society. As became later all too clear, neoliberalism required the state to implement its vision of a free market. This glaring contradiction was encapsulated in Hayek's own controversial support for the Pinochet regime in Chile, which was the first country to implement neoliberal reform.

For Hayek in *The Road to Serfdom*, there were two visions of the future: one based on the goal of security and one based on freedom. He believed western societies in choosing the goal of security – the welfare state, full employment, democracy, etc. – as the primary aim was doing so at the cost of freedom, which was not in his view compatible with security, since it would require the strong hand of the state. The centrally planned state would, he held, require dictatorial measures, as was the case in the USSR and China. Hayek's arguments did not differentiate between different kinds of planning and equated democracy with planning. The questions he posed about how society should be coordinated and what kind of knowledge is needed for such coordination were never satisfactorily answered. The future requires intervention in the present, but what kind of intervention is required? For Hayek, it cannot be governmental planning; it can only be the market left to its own devices through the pricing system. The extreme nature of this argument met with the disapproval of many thinkers who were broadly supportive of this general position, including Karl Popper, Raymond Aron, and Bertrand de Jouvenel. Then, there is the paradox for this future to emerge; it needs the strong hand of the state to create it, as in Chile. Once created, the neoliberal order, as it gradually consolidated in the 1980s, especially in the USA and UK, no longer needs a future, since it is the future. Thus was born the 'end of history' argument, the claim announced by Fukuyama in an essay in 1989 and in a book in 1992, that ideological struggle to shape the future is over, since democracy and capitalism have supposedly won over rival systems (Fukuyama 2020). Aside from the fact that no sooner was the end of history announced that a new era of ideological and cultural struggle commenced, the reality of the neoliberal era was the rise of authoritarianism within democratic systems, since the neoliberal order needed the state apparatus, including military backup, to maintain its grip over society. It was, in short, a continuous project of societal transformation.

The political theory of Bertrand de Jouvenel had much in common with Hayek's. He was in general agreement with his ideas on the market economy and was a member of the Mont Pelerin Society that Hayek had founded to advance his political project of what was to become neoliberalism. However, he had a more nuanced conception of future thinking as well as the role of the state and wrote one of the most important books on the idea of the future. *The Art of Conjecture* was published in French in 1964 (in English in 1967) by a conservative French political philosopher with an ambivalent political background during the fascist period. By the time he came to write this book he embraced a particular variant of liberalism that was largely compatible with Hayek and could be stretched to accommodate monarchy. Nonetheless, his 1964 book is without doubt one of the major works on the idea of the future and his undoubted legacy within and beyond the futurology moment that was prominent in this period, having emerged in 1949 as a term. In this influential and lucidly written book he set forth the case for the need for the present to have 'foresight' in order to realize a desirable future. He explored the meaning of 'possible futures,' which are not to be seen in terms of utopianism but of a practical political philosophy. Early in the book he notes that the old ideas of the future associated with the Enlightenment thinkers have now become our past. However, his main preoccupation was in offering an alternative to the dominance of forecasting and prediction.

His book is a nondoctrinaire work in arguing for the importance of a practical philosophy of the future rather than a utopian attitude or one that sees the future as the extension of the present or something in the hands of experts. Jouvenel was writing at a time when the mainstream trend was one that saw the future revealed by scientist forecasts, especially in economic trends (see Anderson 2018). In line with Hayek's thinking, he argued that 'the future is a field of uncertainty' (Jouvenel, 1967: 5). In the book, he explores the logical problems of whether it is or not possible to have knowledge of the future and offered a compelling analysis of the science of prediction in a variety of fields, as in demography and economic growth trends. We can't know that which has not yet happened; yet, the only useful knowledge is knowledge of the future. He rejects the possibility of certain knowledge of the future. He is also critical of the prevailing movement of futurology, which he notes emerged in 1949 (p. 17–8). Prediction and forecasting is not necessarily scientific but gives the illusion of certainty. Against this culture of scientific positivism, he makes the case for conjecture.

It is interesting to note that Karl Popper had published a book with a similar title in 1963, *Conjectures and Refutations*, in which he revised the famous thesis of falsification in his major 1934 work, *The Logic of Scientific Discovery*. In his book, Popper made the case for conjectures as statements that can make a reasonable claim to truth but are not objectively valid or can claim certainty, thus modifying his earlier strong argument for the principle of falsification as the hallmark of the method of science (Popper 1963). Jouvenel, who did not refer to Popper with whom he was acquainted, embraced this notion of conjecture, which, as the title of his book indicates, was more of an art than a science. As an art, it is supposedly different from the rigor of a prediction or forecast. He cannot, as he admits, entirely get rid of these concepts, which have become so much a part of our language and integral to science. Rather like Popper, in the end he makes the case for a less rigorous use of such approaches when it comes to the future in order to accommodate the view of the unknowability of the future. So, the art of conjecture is an art but one tied to a practical purpose. The need for this arises because of the undoubted fact that progress in society – much of which comes from technological change – does not mean that progress in knowledge has been attained.

He put forward the notion of 'futuribles' as a concept and founded a journal of that name to describe the object of thought when the mind is directed toward the future (p. 18). He stressed the importance of this consisting of images, which we can say encompasses the domain of the imagination, as a way of thinking about desirable futures, as opposed to a future that is simply going to happen and can be revealed through forecasts. This brings in the question of the possible (p. 45). On the one side, we want change – in the sense that we want the future to be different and better than the present – but on the other side we want certainty so that we can know that our desired future will arrive. This amounts not necessarily to a contradiction, but to a problem that is not easy to resolve, since the certainty that is sought is not possible and thus change may not happen, or happen in a way that is not desired. This is the Cassandra problem; or as he puts it, the problem is that 'the myth of Oedipus seems specially designed to show that Man is powerless to change a future of which he has foreknowledge' (p. 52).

The notion of a conjecture goes some way to overcoming some of these problems as well as problems of logic in thinking about the future, including the prevalent view of the future as somehow preexisting, settled before it arrives and only needing to be discovered. This positivistic view of the future is perhaps a caricature, since the social forecasting movement, as represented by Daniel Bell, for example, aimed to make interventions in social trends, which they believed could be influenced (see below). Nonetheless, the dominant social forecasting movement would have seen such interventions as relatively limited in political scope. Forecasts, Jouvenel writes, 'have a limited horizon' (p. 128). Such models of forecasting, as in economics, demography, and voting behavior, are based on figures and quantitative data. The nature of such models, which he agrees have their practical uses, do not offer much help with finding a balance between the demands of freedom and foreknowledge. 'In between the unachievable and the unchanging stands the ample zone of feasible futures. It is the social strategists' concern to recommend plausible procedures for favouring change and procuring some sufficient degree of foreknowledge' (p. 248).

The position that emerges from this book is in the end not fundamentally different from the positions he is opposed to. While opposed to a regime of experts, the art of conjecture is in the end in the hands of experts. To be sure, it is a position that gives great scope for political visions of desirable futures over purely technocratic ones. In that respect his position differed from Hayek's. But practically it is based on the method of social forecasting with greater scope for the arts of political projections. As with social forecasting, the timespan is relatively short to refer to the medium term. Writing in 1964, he posed the question of what the world might look like in 2003. For those in search of a broader and more long-term vision of the future, the book is limited in scope. He offers no insight into what a desirable future would look like other than the need to keep open its possibility.

Responses to the Future: From Fear of the Future to Futurology

The futurist movement including the diverse field of futurology was a product of the post-1945 period which led to a new belief in science as the way to know and master the future. However, it had precursors in the early twentieth century. While these currents of thought expressed a different view of the future from the dominant post-1945 narratives, they also helped to constitute the future as a focus for interpretations of the human condition.

The Italian futurist movement of the early twentieth century celebrated speed, technology, and modernity. Filippo Tommaso Martinetti published a famous *Futu-*

rist Manifesto in 1909 that helped to define the movement (Berardi 2011: 19–21). An offshoot of the avant-garde movement, it stood for the future unfettered by the past. It was primarily an artistic movement in painting, as was the Russian futurist movement but extended across the cultural sphere. Politically, it tended to be right-wing with profascist tendencies due to close association of politics and art, but it was also bound up with anarchism (Wittman 2021). Gramsci was initially interested in it but concluded it was reactionary. He realized it was converging with fascism.[3]

The allure of fascism for many intellectuals was that it promoted an aestheticization of politics that celebrated violence as a way to bring about a rebirth of the nation and even civilization. Despite its opposition to the politics of the left around equality and democracy, fascism was very much a product of modernity and stood for a conception of modernity that was in the name of a very different future. Many European intellectuals – Carl Schmitt, Martin Heidegger, Ernst Jünger, Charles Maurras, Andre Gide, W.B. Yeats, Ezra Pound, Gabriele D'Annunzio – embraced or flirted with fascism (Herf 1986). They were variously attracted to aspects of fascism, which was linked with futurism in its strong orientation to a notion of the future as a radical break from the present and its promise of future redemption.

Not all the early futurists were so easily seduced by the temptations of fascism. One prominent example of the early futurist movement was the English writer H. G. Wells, who went against the grain in making the future central to his writings, thus challenging the tendency to see in the future only the destruction of the past. In many ways, he prepared the way for radical thinking about the future that was shorn of the baggage of the past. He was a social critic, a Fabian, and a socialist, whose most important works were written in the period before the First World War. Wells was enormously productive; the author of numerous works of science fiction and writings on history and current affairs, he was influential in liberal and left political and intellectual circles in Britain. His science fiction, a genre that he helped to shape along with Jules Verne, included the famous *The Time Machine* [1895], *The First Men on the Moon* [1901], *The Invisible Man* [1897], and *The War of the Worlds* [1898]. According to what was probably in part a myth, a radio performance in 1938 in the USA of *The War of the Worlds* by the US broadcaster and film director Orson Welles led to a public panic, due to people believing the broadcast was describing a real Martian invasion. His writings had a utopian touch in exploring alternative social possibilities but also embraced dystopia, as in *When the Sleeper Awakes* [1899]. He saw his work in a tradition that went

---

3 Gramsci (1971: 93).

back to the first works of science fiction, Mary Shelley's *Frankenstein; or, The Modern Prometheus* [1818] and *The Last Man* [1826], the latter set in a desolate plague-ridden England in the year 2073. However, he later abandoned science fiction for social satire and nonfiction.[4] *The Time Machine* is one of his most important works. Published in 1895, it is set in the year AD 802,701 when a Time Traveller recounts from a voyage he had made and returned by a time machine that he devised. Wells was ahead of his time in imagining the possibility of a journey to and back from the future as a consequence of the four dimensions of space, with the fourth being time: 'any real body must have extension in *four* directions; it must have length, Breadth, Thickness and – Duration ... There are really four dimensions, three which we call the three planes of Space, and a fourth, Time' 2005: 4). His book was a reflection of 'humanity upon the wane' in a very distant future when humanity did not remain one species but differentiated into two, one subterranean and the other living in the 'Upperworld.' 'A second species of Man' had ominously evolved, the tyrannical Morelocks, who ruled over those in the Upperworld, the Elio, who represented the more positive aspects of humanity but were subdued and weak in intellect and in the capacity for resistance. The book was both a reflection on time and on evolution and incorporated utopian and dystopian elements.

Wells was also the author of future-oriented nonfiction, important examples being *Anticipation of the Reaction of Mechanical and Scientific Progress upon Human Life and Thought* [1901], in which he speculated what the world would be like in 2000, and *A Modern Utopia* [1905]. Another work, anticipating Nazism, was *The Shape of Things to Come* [1933]. In 1902, in a landmark lecture in London at the Royal Institution, entitled 'The Discovery of the Future,' he put forward a notion of the future as unknowable (Wells 1913). 'It is our ignorance of the future and our persuasion that that ignorance is absolutely incurable that alone gives the past its enormous predominance in our thoughts.' But he says that we are also deluded in thinking that our knowledge of the past is as certain as we often think it is, since much of it is based on memory or has been invalidated by science. The essay is perhaps the first statement of the need for future studies. In it he makes a compelling case for the need for the study of the future, which opens up an alternative to the dominance of the past on science and intellectual inquiry: 'an inductive knowledge of a great number of things in the future is becoming a human possibility. I believe that the time is drawing near when it will be possible to suggest a systematic exploration of the future.' He argued that the older visions of the future before Darwin have lost their relevance, for example, Auguste Comte, who he endorses as a future-oriented thinker; but, as a product of the first half of the nineteenth century, he ac-

---

4 On science fiction and ideas of the future, see Jameson (2007) and Bowler (2017).

knowledges that his vision of the future of humanity was limited in that he had no conception of the fact that, since Darwin, humanity has not yet reached its final stage. As we look to the future, the prospect of finality vanishes.

With a background in biology, he believed in the basic message of Darwin that life evolves progressively and wrote with Julian Huxley, an evolutionary biologist and first director of UNESCO, *The Science of Life*, in 1930. However, one of his last works in 1945, *The Mind at the End of its Tether*, depicted a grotesque world in which the human race becomes extinct. His work was an expression of radical liberalism and a strong belief in future possibility but also gave a warning that catastrophe was always lurking in the background. Wells was not a communist, but he had hopes for Russia, as made evident by the fact that he visited and met Lenin and Stalin, to open a path to a different future (Smith 1986: 271 and 310). However, his analysis of developments under Stalin was somber and his conclusion was that no progress would be achieved. H. G. Wells, who died in 1946, was one of the most important British writers of the first half of the twentieth century.[5]

Another famous work of the period was *Brave New World*, published in 1932 by Aldous Huxley, brother of the biologist Julian Huxley. Along with Orwell's *Nineteen Eighty-Four*, which was inspired by it, the novel has remained one of the most compelling accounts of the future under the conditions of advanced Fordism. Huxley departed from Wells' view of the future in that he was more critical of the uses of technology and less inclined to strike a balance between utopianism and anti-utopianism (Hilligan 1967: 113). The turn from utopianism to dystopia and antiutopianism was in many ways a reflection of the turbulent political situation in the 1930s. In the Foreword to the second edition in 1946, Huxley commented that it was a book about the future and one of its main themes was how social stability can be created (Huxley 1932/1946). The opening words of the novel are 'Community, Identity, Stability' which invoked the specter of a society in the year AF 632 under more or less total control by a technological apparatus (AF signified post-Ford). 'Every change is a menace to stability' (p. 180). In the much-cited Chapter 17, the central character, the Savage, submits to order and authority, saying, 'I'm claiming the right to be unhappy' (p. 192). Revisiting the novel in a 1958 essay, Huxley developed the theme he explored of submission to power: 'Under a scientific dictator education will really work – with the result that most men and women will grow up to love their servitude and will never dream of revolution.'[6]

---

5 See Roberts (2019).
6 This sentence with the key phrase that people 'will grow up to love their servitude and will never dream of revolution' is often thought to be in *Brave New World* but is in *Brave New World Revisited* at the end of Chapter 12.

Brave New World and Yevgeny Zamyatin's *We* in 1924 were the literary inspirations for one of the leading British figures of the era who articulated one of the most famous specters of the future. For George Orwell the future was distinctively dystopian as in *Animal Farm* [1945] and *Nineteen Eighty-Four* [1949]. While Huxley's projection was over 600 years into the future and Wells, over 8000 years, Orwell's projection was 36 years, from 1948 when he completed it. The novel contained the most famous evocation of a totalitarian future: 'If you want a picture of the future, imagine a boot stamping on a human face – forever' (p. 302). Bernard Crick, in his biography of Orwell, commented: '*Nineteen Eighty-Four* is to the twentieth century what Thomas Hobbes' *Leviathan* was to the seventeenth. He had characterized and shown the plausibility of, but had also parodied, totalitarian power, just as Hobbes had characterized and tried to justify autocratic power' (Crick 198: 570).[7] A feature of the society he was characterizing was the control over the past in order to control the future. '"Who controls the past," ran the Party slogan, "controls the future: who controls the present controls the past"' (p. 40).

Wells, but above all, Huxley and Orwell set the tone for dystopian visions of the future in the first half of the twentieth century.

Another trend in this period was the vision of catastrophe. The Irish poet W. B. Yeats captured the mood of catastrophe and impending doom in his 1919 poem, *The Second Coming*[8]:

> Turning and turning in the widening gyre
> The falcon cannot hear the falconer;
> Things fall apart; the centre cannot hold;
> Mere anarchy is loosed upon the world,
> The blood-dimmed tide is loosed, and everywhere
> The ceremony of innocence is drowned;
> The best lack all conviction, while the worst
> Are full of passionate intensity.
>
> Surely some revelation is at hand;
> Surely the Second Coming is at hand.
> The Second Coming! Hardly are those words out
> When a vast image out of *Spiritus Mundi*
> Troubles my sight: somewhere in sands of the desert
> A shape with lion body and the head of a man,
> A gaze blank and pitiless as the sun,
> Is moving its slow thighs, while all about it

---

7 See Gleason *et al.* (2005) on the significance of the novel for our time.
8 In Yeats (1974).

Reel shadows of the indignant desert birds.
The darkness drops again; but now I know
That twenty centuries of stony sleep
Were vexed to nightmare by a rocking cradle,
And what rough beast, its hour come round at last,
Slouches towards Bethlehem to be born?

In the second stanza, the biblical theme of revelation and the apocalypse convey the sense of the end of civilization. In Yeats's poem, the future is not bright but pervaded by a sense of fear and disruption. Yet, the future is there and has arrived. A supporter of the Irish nationalist movement, he was intrigued by the possibility of a new beginning in Ireland with the coming of a republican revolution that would realize the romantic dream of Irish rebirth. However, the revolution when it came was, as in another famous poem, a 'terrible beauty' and betrayed its sense of future mission. The suggestion is that the future is a powerful image and desire but, when realized, it can be a catastrophe. With its realization also comes a profound sense of lost, namely the loss of the future, which once realized is no longer a future. This leaves only a sense of nostalgia in its wake.

The vision of the future in the writings of intellectuals in the first half of the twentieth century reflected different attitudes, ranging from the more optimistic faith that progress will triumph and that the future must be imagined in ways radically different from the past, as in the writings of H.G. Wells, to the sense of foreboding and nostalgia, as in Yeats.

T.S. Eliot's 1925 poem 'The Hollow Men' explored the theme of the end of the world: 'This is the way the world ends not with a bang but with a whimper.' His major work, the *Four Quartets*, published between 1936 and 1941, was an enigmatic reflection on humanity's relation to time. It is regarded, along with his 1922 poem, *The Wasteland*, as one of the great poems in the English language and led to the award of the Nobel Prize for Literature in 1948. In the first poem of the quartet, 'Burnt Norton,' written in 1936, we find what is often regarded as the most famous evocation of the human experience of time in the opening stanza.

Time present and time past
Are both perhaps present in time future
And time future contained in time past.
If all time is eternally present
All time is unredeemable.
What might have been is an abstraction
Remaining a perpetual possibility
Only in a world of speculation.
What might have been and what has been
Point to one end, which is always present.

Footfalls echo in the memory
Down the passage we did not take
Towards the door we never opened
Into the rose-garden. My words echo
Thus, in your mind,
But to what purpose
Disturbing the dust on a bowl of rose-leaves
I do not know.[9]

The message appears to be that in the passage of time there is loss and that the human condition can only contemplate the possibility of another temporal order. The idea that 'All time is unredeemable' but 'eternally present' points to a spiritual temporality different from the human one. Human experience is located in time but there is also an eternal time always present mostly beyond reach due to the fragmentation of human consciousness except in moments where it is encountered. Whatever it meant, it is clear it was not a message of hope for better times but only offering the comforting thought of an eternal time running parallel to human existence. Eliot was a deeply conservative figure, who converted in 1927 to Anglicanism from his Unitarian upbringing in Boston. It is possible that his interest in time and the human condition was influenced by Henri Bergson, as Eliot had attended his seminars in 1910–11 in Paris. However, Eliot's political views were antithetical to progressive politics and reflected an English Christian conservatism that included antisemitism.

Other and more radical ideas of the future can also be found in the interwar period, which was a time of intense political struggle. For many intellectuals, the future is in the hands of those who struggle for it. The Spanish Civil War (1936–1939) was a major arena for a struggle for the future, with widespread support from the left and from writers in Europe and North America for the Second Republic. The famous authors do not need introduction: George Orwell, Laurie Lee, Ernst Hemingway, Stephen Spender, W. H. Auden. Sarah Watling has shown how the cause of the Republican movement in Spain was also defining episode for many female authors who came to Spain to respond to their deeply felt need to take up a side and find common cause with others fighting for justice and freedom (Watling 2023). The intensity of the experience was such that the present moment was strongest, but it was also a struggle for the future. However, it was also a story of defeat for the progressive values of the Second Spanish Republic and the loss of the future until its reemergence 40 years later.

---

9 In Eliot (1963).

After 1945, ideas of the future took on a different character. The futurology movement emerged by the end of the 1940s and, as reflected in Jouvenel's *The Art of Conjecture*, the future was not constituted as a proper object of consciousness and not as something to be feared. Jenny Andersson, in her authoritative study of the futurist movement during the Cold War period, especially between around 1964 and 1973, has characterized it as a field of struggle between different conceptions of how the world should be controlled (Andersson 2018; also 2012). Different positions competed, ones that emphasized imagination and creativity and more technocratic ones that stood for science and scenario building (Staley 2002). The future was the long-term future; however, this was in fact seen as relatively close to the present in that it could be controlled or influenced by the present. 'Future research gave rise over time to the emergence of a very particular form of expertise, a kind of meta expertise in world futures, equipped with forecasts and scenarios of world development' (Andersson 2018: 4). She emphasizes that the period saw a variety of approaches to the future, despite the undoubted dominance of the scientific forecasting one (also Williams 2016). In this period, before the onset of the capitalist crisis from 1973, the future was a domain of possibility; it was not simply an outcome of progress but needed to be mastered by reason, technology, and imagination. The utopian imagination had a new lease of life, but in this case it was a practical possibility. Andersson emphasizes the Congress for Cultural Freedom, created in 1955, as a key institution for research into the future and a forum for intellectuals – such as John Dewey, Bertrand de Jouvenel, and Daniel Bell – to engage with future research. The futurist movement – in western societies – attracted liberals, not radicals; it was closely allied with major US organizations, such as the RAND Corporation, founded in 1945, and was inclined in the direction of social engineering, which was a natural outcome of the emphasis on planning and technology. One influential book was Denis Gabor's *Inventing the Future* in 1964, which expressed great confidence in technological mastery (see Gabor 1964, Anderson 2021). Through John Dewey, the pragmatist tradition was transmitted to a wider public policy community.

Karl Popper was not a member of the futurist movement, but his ideas resonated with the new thinking about the future in the post-1945 period. His vision of the 'open society' as in *The Open Society and its Enemies* [1945] was itself a future-oriented concept. In a later work, *The Myth of the Framework*, he wrote: 'The future is open. It is not predetermined and thus cannot be predicted – except by accident. The possibilities that lie in the future are infinite. When I say "it is our duty to remain optimists, they include not only the openness of the future but also that which all of us contribute to it by everything we do: we are responsible for what the holds in store' (1994: xiii). His final writings included a theory of propensities, which he saw as an objective theory of probability: 'Quite apart from the fact that we do not know the future, the future is objectively not fixed. The future is open: objectively open. Only the past is fixed; it has been actualized and so is gone' (1995 [1990]: 18).

With the declining appeal of the idea of modernization and the related notion of progress, from the late 1960s, along with the beginning of radical politics in the latter years of the decade, the futurist movement broadened to include more radical perspectives and the new voices from the left that were not part of the earlier institutional technocratic orientation in the future movement in the USA. This perspective could be broadened to include the rise of critical theory and especially the writings of Herbert Marcuse, who questioned the culture of expertise (to be discussed in the next chapter). It certainly included new radical voices such as Johann Galtung, for whom the idea of the future was a normative notion and needed to be attached to the radical imagination, and not just reason. The influential report of the Club of Rome's *Limits to Growth* of 1972 marked the arrival of a new notion of the future, which did not fit easily into the post-1945 future movement (Meadows *et al.* 1972). By the 1970s, it is clear that at least two broad conceptions of the future crystallized: a technocratic one based on control and increasingly sustainability, and a counter or antisystemic one inspired by radical politics (see also Adam and Groves 2007). In her account of futurology, Jennifer Gidley draws on aspects of the social theory of Habermas to bring a more critical dimension into the movement (Gidley 2017). However, her discussion of Habermas (2015) is confined to his critique of positivism in his 1968 book *Knowledge and Human Interests* and fails to address the more important ideas of the future in his work (see next chapter for a wider discussion of critical theory).

Once the futurist movement goes beyond the dominant technocratic and liberal paradigm, it loses its specificity and it becomes difficult to apply the notion of futurology to the post-1970s currents that have a more radical view of the future. The engagement of sociological theory with the idea of the future from the later 1970s also gives it less of an ideological and utopian quality. The publication in 1970 of *Future Shock* by Alvin Toffler marked the arrival of more critical and sociological approaches to the future. Not a work of critique as such, his book, written for a middlebrow readership on current affairs, painted a picture of a dysfunctional kind of future that had already arrived (Toffler 1970). He was responding to the sense of shock that comes from rapid change that comes from information overload and technological advancement within a relatively short time. It was a view of the future in terms of fear of the future. However, it was not a particularly theoretical work and, despite its enormous success, it offered only a superficial description of the psychological effects of social change in a period that saw the transformation of industrial society in the western world into postindustrial society. In a similar vein, Paul Ehrlich's book in 1968 presaged the trend toward pessimistic views of the future in a widely read but much-criticized book, *The Population Bomb* (Ehrlich 1968).

Toffler developed his ideas in a later book, *The Third Wave*, in 1980 with an argument largely based on examples from the USA in the 1970s that there is now a new wave of social transformation forming, a 'third wave.' The first wave was the formation of civilization from about 800 BC to the period 1650–1750 when modernity emerged. The second wave broke down the first with industrialization, which is today confronted by a new wave (Toffler 1980: 28–30). His analysis effectively reduces the future to the contemporary situation of postindustrial society and its impact on industrial society.

Before concluding the present discussion on futurist thought in the twentieth century before the 1970s, when new perspectives opened, a few brief remarks on developments beyond western societies are in order. Two major examples of the modernist penchant for a future-oriented utopia can be mentioned. As noted in the previous chapter, one of the striking examples of the pursuit of utopia was the Marxist-Leninist movement in Russia. Despite Marx's own reservations about proletarian revolution having a real possibility since the failure of the Paris Commune in 1871, the Bolshevist pursuit of communism under Lenin can be seen as a modernist movement that created a powerful vision of the future, a 'dreamworld,' to refer to Buck-Morss (2002), that lasted for some seventy years. Even if it lost its utopian character in the Stalinist era, when it was downgraded to Five Year plans, the notion of a future remained a legitimating myth. In contrast, the Chinese project lacked the modernist pursuit of a future. The shocking reality of Maoist China was that it was a political project based on destruction without any vision of the future.

According to Chang and Halliday in their chilling biography of Mao Tse-tung, Mao was interested only in presiding over a military power rather than in a future legacy. In a revealing episode, during a visit to Moscow he was skeptical of the purpose of Lenin's mausoleum, which he remarked was of no use to Lenin since he was dead. Mao left no heir and also, unlike the Chinese emperors, was not interested in a successor or what would happen after his death, for which no preparations were made (Chang and Halliday 2006: 464). Up to 48 million people died of starvation and overwork in the four-year Great Leap Forward (1958–1960) alone – overall some 70 million died as a result of Mao's directives – making it the greatest famine in world history. Mao had actually allowed for even more deaths (p. 534). The Great Leap Forward on the one level was a dystopian project to remake Chinese society according to a faulty blueprint borrowed from Stalin, for whom it also produced catastrophic results, but on the other, it was the antithesis of a future, since it was a failure and sustained by state terror. In this case, there was no mass utopia to decline, just mass death and terror.

Maoist China is a complex example of the modernist zeal in that it seemed to be devoid of an orientation to the future. It is rivaled only by the even more extreme project that it had inspired, the ultra-Maoist movement of the Kymer Rouge led by Pol Pot to create a rural utopia in Cambodia from 1975 to 1979. The horror of agrarian collectivization in the making of Kampuchea, which abolished city life and money, entailed the killing of between 20 and 25 per cent of the population (Short 2004). The other example that can be noted was Brazil in the post-1945 period when the modernist imagination took hold in a major project of nationalist development, culminating in the foundation of a new national capital in 1958. The creation of Brasilia is one of the greatest examples of modernist urban planning in the twentieth century. The design of the 'Plano Piloto,' the futuristic center designed in the shape of an airplane, by Lucio Costa and the monumental architectural designs of the architect Oscar Niemeyer were a blueprint for the perfect city (Niemeyer, a communist, was influenced by Soviet architecture, as well as more directly the French modernist Le Corbusier). It was an example of what Holston referred to in the study of the early history of the city as an imagined future (Holston 1989). However, it was also an example of a largely failed project in that the intended functionality did not play out in the way it was intended, as urban life even in the perfectly designed city does not follow fixed rules. The visitor to Brasilia today is struck by the presence of what was once a future but is now a receding past.

Sociological Theory and the Future

Sociological theory offers important insights into the future. It is true that the concept of the future has not been at the forefront of classical sociological theory, concerned as it was largely with the past. The classical sociological theory of Max Weber and Emile Durkheim was not primarily concerned with the future. The major concern of Weber's sociology was historical, with its characteristic focus on the comparative history of civilizations and the relationship between economy and cultural value systems, such as religion. The classical sociologists were products of the late nineteenth century, when the tremendous transformation of modernity was becoming visible in the transition from 'tradition' to the uncertain prospects of 'modernity.'

Despite the historical direction of their work, it is of course the case that the classical sociologists were deeply concerned about the future of modern society. Weber's work reflected a concern with the dominance of instrumental rationality and the loss of freedom and meaning that has come with the 'iron cage' of modern rationalism as embodied in capitalism and bureaucracy. The basic problem in

Durkheim's sociology concerned the future possibility of an appropriate form of solidarity to develop in modern society. The 'division of labour' and the general movement toward modernity eroded the old forms of solidarity, which he referred to as 'mechanical solidarity,' but did not bring into play new forms of solidarity compatible with the reality of modern society, which requires 'organic solidarity,' a confusing term which meant a form of solidarity that was not based on direct social relations. The result was that modernity was suspended between the past and the future. It can also be noted that Durkheim in *The Elementary Structures of the Religious Life* [1912] had some important insights about the time more generally as a social phenomenon. Both thinkers died prematurely: Durkheim died disillusioned in 1917 at the age of 59 in the middle of the Great War, and Weber in 1920 at the age of 56 after contracting the 1918 Flu. The future for both looked bleak and a certain pessimism pervaded their work about the future.[10] However, neither were by nature pessimistic. Their work, despite its canonical influence, remained undeveloped.

A new generation of sociologists – undoubtedly conscious of new conceptions of time in the natural sciences and in philosophy – gave greater emphasis to the future. As noted in the previous chapter, George Herbert Mead (1932) wrote an important but somewhat short book on time, *The Philosophy of the Present*. In this book, influenced by the American pragmatist tradition and the natural sciences, especially physics, he offered a theory of social time for social science, highlighting the intersubjectivist framework that his sociological theory advanced. Although he was very well informed about the discoveries of Einstein and other physicists and mathematicians such as Herman Minkowski, as well as the theory of time in natural philosophy as in A. N. Whitehead, he appeared to be advancing a theory of social and historical time that did not extend beyond the immediate future. The future is not entirely free from the present and only makes sense as seen from the present. 'The past is there conditioning the present and its passage into the future' (p. 17). The future is conditioned by the present: 'We live always in a present whose past and future are the extension of the field within which its undertakings may be carried out' (p. 90). While Mead's conception of the future was somewhat limited, he had made an important contribution to the study of time and society. However, his attempt to bring the new conceptions of time in physics into social and historical time was never pursued.

From Mead onward, time consciousness in sociological analysis became increasingly important, especially since the phenomenological turn in philosophy

---

10 In 1917 Durkheim wrote a short piece on the future, but confined to the question of postwar economic recovery.

brought about by Husserl entered sociology, with the work of Alfred Schutz, whose major contribution was *The Phenomenology of the Social World*, published in German in 1934 and translated into English in 1967 (Schutz 1967).[11] Other figures in the classical tradition who wrote important works on social time were Pitrim Sorokin (1943), George Gurvitch (1964) and, in a later work, Norbert Elias (1992 [1984]). Nonetheless, while these works were significant on social time, they did not have a great deal to say on the idea of the future.

It was the notable achievement of the American sociologist Daniel Bell to put the concept of the future on the sociological agenda. His concern was not specifically with the theory of time, which he did not address, but with the more practical question of how the future can be rendered an object of sociological analysis. Bell was one of the major figures in sociology in the USA and author of influential works, including *The End of Ideology* in 1960 and in 1973 *The Coming of Post-Industrial Society: A Venture in Social Forecasting* (Bell 1960 and 1999 [1973]). *The End of Ideology* was an account of the end of the utopian impulse in western societies in the postwar era, when ideological exhaustion set in. This was of course itself a very ideological claim and reflected a particularly conservative ethos in the USA at this time. While Bell was proclaiming the end of the future in one sense of the term – the distant future and the prospect of a very different future to the present term – he soon discovered the immediate future, the topic of this 1973 work, *The Coming of Post-Industrial Society*, and the social forecasting approach. Many of the theoretical ideas were set out in an essay in 1967 on 'The Year 2000' (Bell 1967). As he notes in the essay, the year 2000 exerted a certain fascination, being sufficiently far but imaginable within the life time of people of Bell's generation. In fact, thirty-three years from the time of writing approximates to a generation, a period of time into the future that is not too far away to consider from the vantage point of the present. It is clear that Bell had in mind the immediate future, not the distant future that was the time horizon of the utopian imagination.

The context of the essay was the Commission on the Year 2000, set up in 1964 by the American Academy of Arts and Sciences. Like de Jouvenel's *Futuribles* project in Paris, it was designed to explore long-range thinking of different aspects of the future of the United States as well as the wider world. There were other similar organizations founded in this period, along similar lines, such as The Committee on the Next Thirty Years in the UK.[12] The mystical allure of the end of the millennium and the beginning of a new one was a symbolic marker of change to come. Bell was appointed President of the Commission on the Year 2000, which he de-

---

11 See Muzzetto (2006) on the concept of time in his work.
12 Michael Young (1968) wrote a book on the background and the need for social forecasting.

scribes as 'an effort now to indicate the future consequences of present public policy decisions, to anticipate future problems, and to begin the design of alternative solutions so that our society has more options and can make a moral choice, rather than be constrained' (Bell 1967: 639). In this description, we can attest to the influence of pragmatism, as mediated by John Dewey, and the Great Society vision of the Lyndon Johnson presidency. The future he was anticipating was one that would be shaped by technology, which spearheaded the arrival of the 'post-industrial society,' a term that can be attributed to Bell and first used in his 1967 essay (p. 643). As a sociologist, he was acutely aware that major societal change, even that which can be anticipated by the year 2000, does not happen in total; 'a complex society is not changed by the flick of the wrist.' It is unlikely that society, in three decades from now, he reasons, will be fundamentally different, regardless of changes in technology (pp. 641–2). Predicting social change for the immediate future is possible. The tone of the essay is optimistic about forecasting future trends, but also that they can be mastered while acknowledging the increase in social problems: 'the society of the year 2000, so quickly and schematically outlined, will be more fragile, more susceptible to hostilities and to polarization along many different lines. Yet to say this is not to surrender to despair, for the power to deal with these problems is also present' (Bell 1967: 646). Daniel Bell died in 2011 at the age of 91. Most sociologists writing in 2011 would not write with the same optimism about the future. For example, in one of his last books, *Towards 2000*, the British sociologist and cultural theorist Raymond Williams saw only 'the sense of the loss of the future' in contemporary culture, the loss of a capacity to create something new (Williams 1983).

Yet, in 1999 in the lengthy Foreword to the 1999 edition of his *The Coming of the Post-Industrial Society*, Bell remained upbeat that the postindustrial society, which he acknowledges is now entering the 'information age,' unlike all previous societies, comes with the promise for people to have greater control over their lives. As the title indicates, he opens the over-500-page book, by describing it 'as an essay in social forecasting.' The future is a relational term and cannot be predicted as such. His preference is for forecasting over prediction. Predictions deal with events, which, due to the interaction of many factors, are mostly very difficult to predict. Then there is the problem discussed by Robert Merton in 1949 of self-fulfilling prophecies (Merton 1968). Forecasting is different and possible only where there are regularities and recurrences of phenomena, and it also rests on the fundamental rationality of social actors. Bell was interested in three kinds of social forecasting that could be empirically analyzed by social indicators: 'the extrapolation of social trends, the identification of historical "keys" that turn new levels of social change, and projected changes in major social frameworks' (Bell 1999: 7). His model of a social forecast was not, then, a prediction, but about understanding change in the 'social frameworks' of western societies. Bell's belief in the pragmatic possibilities of social forecasting belongs to an era now long gone when it was possible to believe in a collective future and one that could be enabled by social science. Unlike today, this was a period of stability when it was possible to think of the future as a continuation of the present.

Bell's concept of the future was not much different from the present, of which it was an extension. It lacked any real connection with a deeper sense of the future. In 1973, the same year as Bell's book was published, the unorthodox British economist E. F. Schumacher published *Small is Beautiful: Economics as if People Mattered*. This classic work has rarely been mentioned in the sociological or historical literature, yet it is an example of a major critique of mainstream economic thinking as well as the futurist movement by an economist (Schumacher 1973). Schumacher's book is particularly insightful in its critique of planning, forecasting, and prediction, which he claims are all based on muddled semantics and a failure to appreciate the unpredictability of life.[13]

Another namesake of Daniel Bell, Wendell Bell, writing in the 1970s, opened the sociology of the future to a wider sense of the future, seeing it as part of a new social science of 'Future Studies' (Bell 1997). The work of Wendell Bell was more connected with the futurist movement in a wider sense than Daniel Bell's social forecasting. He saw the future as open and introduced the idea of dispositions as real but unrealized possibilities that are latent or dormant.[14] His collection, edited with Mau in 1971, *Sociology of the Future*, was a landmark work in opening up the idea of the future to sociological analysis (Bell and Mau 1971).[15] Their remarkable Introduction, which acknowledges the influence of H. G. Wells and Georges Gurvitch, emphasizes the importance of viewing the future both through speculation and through the creative imagination. They argue against the attempt to describe what the future will look like. Their aim is to replace the concern with the past with the perspective of the future, which they speculate will soon lead to a revolution in sociology. The future cannot be known; it is real, they argue: 'the future is real to the extent to which present alternatives or possibilities are real; and a purely deterministic model is inappropriate to deal with this reality because until the future has become the present, some alternative possibilities remain open' (p.9). In the end the revolution in sociology did not come. What came instead was postmodernism, which as argued earlier in this book did not embrace the idea of the future.

---

13 See in particular Chapter 15, 'A Machine to Foretell the Future.'
14 See Adam (2011).
15 See his later reflections on his early work (Bell 1996).

The approach to the future in the futurist literature of the era was indebted to Fred Pollak's *Image of the Future* (1973 [1961]). Pollak claimed the rise and fall of images of the future preceded or accompanied the rise and fall of cultures throughout history. 'An image of the future is an expectation about the state of things to come at some future time. We may think usefully of such expectations as a range of differentially probable possibilities rather than as a single point on a continuum,' according to Bell and Mau (p. 23). Drawing on this idea, Bell and Mau see the image of the future as real. They stress 'initiative, novelty, spontaneity, self-modification, creativity, goal-seeking, and self-determination by thinking of social change as a complex cybernetic system.' (p.19).

One of the most important contributions to the theory of the future was Niklas Luhmann's 1976 essay, 'The Future Cannot Begin: Temporal Structures in Modern Society.' He begins by noting the fact the immediate future has always been a concern of human beings. His topic is the distant future; however it is characterized, it is beyond the immediate future. It was only with the emergence of modern societies from the eighteenth century that the future became a problem since it could be conceived as an open limit, 'a store house of possibilities,' because the past was no longer seen as commencing from a fixed point and the future begins to be seen as different from the past, which loses its hold over the present. The future can be conceived of as an 'open future' of 'not-yet realized possibilities' (Luhmann 1976: 131). His essay was influenced by the early work of Koselleck in locating the birth of the future in the eighteenth century and the emergence of a 'present time' consciousness at a time when the structure of time changed in the direction of a higher temporal complexity. In this period, the older conception of historical time as chronology gives way to a new conception of time. In his essay, Luhmann goes beyond the emerging notion of the social construction of time as social time by placing the emphasis on the future. He defines time 'as the interpretation of reality with regard to the difference between past and future' (p.135). This requires sundering the relation of time to chronology in order to bring the future into focus. In the chronological framework there is only a series of past events leading to the present with the future beginning where the presents ends. In this respect, he draws on G. H. Mead's work on time, *The Philosophy of the Present*, which as mentioned above shows that the relevance of time depends on the capacity to mediate past and future within a present (Mead 1932). In complex societies, beginning with modernity, the problem of time changes and also because of socio-cultural evolution. According to Luhmann, there are two ways to theorize time in nonchronological terms: the theory of modalities and phenomenological analysis. The notion of modalities – such as necessity, possibility, and actuality –

as in Kant's philosophy[16] suggests that the possible can only remain unfulfilled, rather like the notion of a horizon that cannot be reached, since as one approaches it, it recedes further.

This brings us to the key insight that Luhmann offers, namely that a phenomenological approach to the future, in building on the notion of modalities, can be conceived as a time horizon of the present. 'The future as a temporal horizon of the present' means that 'it cannot begin' (p.140). Luhmann makes much of the notion of the future as a horizon, a concept that he attributes to Husserl and to Mead, who used the notion of 'the horizon of experience' and not as in Koselleck the 'horizon of expectation.' Husserl himself wrote in 1917: 'Remembering, although it is not expectation, does have a horizon directed towards the future of the remembered.'[17] A feature of a horizon is not only that it cannot be reached or surpassed but also that it is located in the present. This is the key point for Luhmann, who wants to develop a theory of time as 'temporal modalities' with an iterative use of modal forms for all possible modes of past and future temporalities. With respect to the future, this suggests at least two notions of future time: 'future presents' and 'the present future.' These terms are convoluted and not entirely clear, but what Luhmann means is that the *present future* refers to the open future which allows for new presents, *future presents*, to emerge and become a present in the future. In other words, there is always the possibility of the future to become present. But the anticipation of the future always opens up the possibility of a yet new future. So, in contrast to ancient societies which thought of the future in terms of coming events, 'we experience our future as a generalized horizon of surplus possibilities that have to be reduced as we approach them' (p.141). So, the open future involves degrees of 'futurization' and also 'de-futurization,' by which he means the way societies constantly battle with time, which needs to be 'negated.' Societies, like people in their everyday life, are constantly battling with time, trying to negate it yet while always waiting more time (like academics writing papers for deadlines). In yet other words, as societies become more complex, the problem of time becomes more critical in order to solve problems of coordination.

Luhmann sought to combine phenomenological analysis with a theory of modalities. His essay makes a further argument in claiming that time under conditions of high complexity is scarce, in the sense that the present future offers possibilities that cannot be easily fulfilled, except by technology, which is a way in which the future is actualized. Luhmann's brilliant essay with its perspective on

---

16 See Abaci (2019). Kant did not apply this to the future as such and confined its application to metaphysics, but it is relevant to the theory of time.

17 See Mensch (1999); Brough 1975).

'iterative modalizations' (present future, future presents, future of past presents *etc.*) broke new ground but ultimately does not answer the question of how we respond to the future, to the question of 'how to begin the future.' His answer is that it cannot begin. The conclusion that follows from this approach is that we are caught up in an unending present, since this is the locus from which the future is viewed. The future never arrives because the horizon constantly shifts and because time disappears into the operations of systems, rather like in astronomical time, time comes to an end as the speed of light is approached. His theory of the future in the end became a theory of risk. In *Observations on Modernity*, he wrote: 'Modern society experiences its future in the form of the risk of deciding' (Luhmann 1998 [1992]: 70 – 1). In *Risk: A Sociological Analysis* he developed this perspective: 'the entire future as future must be seen to fall under the dichotomy of risk and danger' (2002: 27). The problem in many ways is due to the powerful but inadequate metaphor of the horizon that is at work here. A horizon disappears as one approaches it, as does the future. This is one of the most compelling metaphors of future time, but the phenomenon of the disappearing future does not capture other aspects, such as the needs of the present to secure the conditions of their future.

Luhmann aimed to bring together systems theory, with its focus on complexity, with phenomenological analysis through a notion of modalities, i.e. concepts of possibilities. In the final analysis, we do not get a satisfactory solution to the important questions he posed and end up with a high level of abstraction on paradoxes. In the more advanced systems theory, as in *Social Systems*, that he went on to develop, the social actor disappears altogether in a conception of time reduced to the 'temporalization of complexity' and stabilization of complex systems (1995 [1984]).[18] As he put it in his book on risk, not only is it the case that 'we cannot know the future' but we cannot change it: '... no one is in a position to claim knowledge of the future nor the capacity to change it' (p. 48). In the next chapter, I argue that there is a more productive purpose in combining phenomenological analysis with critical theory. The concept of the future in terms of expanding and disappearing horizons ultimately limits the future of its normative possibility.

Conclusion: The New Sociology of the Future

In the 1970s, the theory of time entered sociological theory. As we have seen, major contributions were made by Daniel Bell, Wendell Bell, and Niklas Luhmann. In

---

18 See also Luhmann (1998).

other traditions of sociology, various theorists incorporated a perspective on time into their work. In many cases, time effectively amounted to a theory of social change, as in Giddens (1987), or a notion of the compression of space and time. Rational choice theory, not normally discussed in relation to time, is also significant, especially in relation to future time, since it is primarily about calculating strategies of future possibilities. However, it is limited by a very narrow time range, more or less the very immediate future.

The notion of social time became the focus of sociological analysis following from G. H. Mead and Alfred Schutz, who brought phenomenological theory into sociological analysis. Zerubavel (1981, 1922), Young (1988), and Martins (1974) are examples of the approaches to time in sociological theory that show how social life is temporally constructed. Many of these accounts see time as a way in which social relationships are constituted, a perspective developed by Elias (1984). Barbara Adam (1990) and Helga Nowotny (1992, 1994) have written about the major developments in time in relation to social theory.[19] Adam's book brought several traditions together in a far-reaching analysis of time and social theory, albeit one that strangely excluded the critical theory tradition while giving more centrality unnecessarily to the limits of Giddens's structuration theory insofar as this concerns a theory of time. The insightful claim that '[h]uman time is characterised by transcendence' (p. 127) consequently remained undeveloped. Nowotny's book, published originally in German in 1989, advanced the important argument that 'the temporal category of the future is being abolished and replaced by that of the extended present' (1994: 51).

In this large literature on time in sociology and social theory, which consolidated in the 1980s, there was little reflection specifically on the idea of the future. The emphasis in these writings was on the present in relation to the past, and often with a concern with the diversity of experiences of time against the general movement in modernity toward the standardization of time.[20] It was almost as if the future followed from the present.

In very recent years, the absence of a perspective on the future has changed for the better. John Urry wrote his last work on the future in sociology (Urry 2016). In this work, he sought to advance a theory of the future in terms of complexity and contrasted this approach to two competing ones: (1) the individualist model of human action, which as in rational choice or any theoretical approach that emphasizes the rationality of social actors includes the futures people generate as a result of their action in the present, and (2) structural approaches that see

---

19 See also Baert (1992), Bergman (1992).
20 A major historical work being Landes (1983).

the future the outcome of relatively fixed structures. Complexity theory offers an alternative to any account of the future that reduces it to action or to structures. It emphasizes how systems are dynamic, processual, and unpredictable; they are open systems with energy flowing in and out of them (Urry 2016: 57–9). Systems evolve, adapt, and self-organize. This is a view of the future emerging from the operations of complex systems. 'Time is not viewed as a dimension along which systems move. Rather, systems are constituted through their becoming, through process' (p.60). Unpredictability and uncertainty are thus key aspects of the future. 'The future is never a simple prediction or smooth extrapolation from what is happening in the present. There is no empty future just waiting to happen' (p. 190). However, beyond that insight, nothing further was demonstrated.

Since the early 1990s, the theory of the risk society and theories of globalization brought about a new conception of the future as risk. Since the Brundtland Report, *Our Common Future*,[21] in 1987, and the Chernobyl catastrophe in 1986, consciousness of environmental came increasingly to the fore. The outcome was a notion of the future as risk. Ulrich Beck's book, *The Risk Society*, in 1986 provided an influential theory of the future of the world as a global risk society (Beck 1992). 'The centre of risk consciousness lies not in the present, but in the future. In the risk society, the past loses the power to determine the present. Its place is taken by the future' (1992: 34). Risk is about anticipating the direct and indirect consequences of human action, both in the present and in the past, in order to manage the potentially catastrophic outcomes both for the present and for future generations. It encompasses both the immediate and the long-term future. Risk derives from human action rather than from nature as such. The risk society is a product of modernity when human action generated a range of problems that put the future at risk; it is ultimately a global society since the risks are not local or national. The politics of the risk society must become cosmopolitan. Luhmann, as discussed earlier, adopted a similar perspective on the future as risk, but in this case, without the normative critique that Beck advanced for a cosmopolitical response. However, Luhmann shares the view of society now as a global society or 'world society'.

Theories of globalization led to new insights about the future as an intensification of the compression of time and space, in the work of leading sociologists writing in the 1990s, such as Anthony Giddens, Manuel Castells, Ulrich Beck. The impact of electronic communication led to a view of the globalization as an information society in which the future is, in a sense, eliminated, reduced to speed and

---

21 UN 1987. The report was chaired by the former Norwegian Prime Minister, Gro Harlem Brundtland.

a virtual present. According to Hartmut Rosa, the primary feature of the information age is acceleration, the fact that increased speed brings about a reorganization
of the temporal structures of society (Rosa 2013). One outcome is the paradoxical
effect of eliminating time in a shrinking present and thus wiping out the future,
which is arrived at in almost every aspect of life quickly. While this is an important
insight into the temporal structures of contemporary society, it gives too much
weight to the phenomenon of acceleration, which as Byung-Chul Han comments
is a problematical concept because 'in the proper sense of the word presupposes
a course which directs the flow' (2017: 5 and 23). Time continues to flow but is
often directionless. The internet is a directionless space and thus not necessarily
characterized by acceleration, which is often accompanied by deacceleration.
And, not everything that moves accelerates – light does not. As Zygmunt Bauman
(1998) argued, time is also for many people stationary, as not everywhere is transformed by globalization.

In recent years, there has been a surge of interest in theories of the future in
sociology that draw on the phenomenological tradition broadly defined to include
social imaginaries and the legacy of G. H. Mead.[22] Mische (2009) in a phenomeno-
logically influenced approach to sociological analysis seeks an alternative to basing
future possibilities on objective structures. She shows how hope and other future-
oriented ideas are constitutive of the future as well as being socially constituted.
Such ideas provide projections, which can be based on the creative imagination
or on willful foresight. Tavory (2018) argues for an interactionist approach that
sees social situations shaped not only by past-induced habits but also by future situations anticipated in interaction. In an earlier article, Tavory and Eliasoph (2013)
developed an approach to the analysis of the coordination of futures as anticipated
in action by highlighting three 'modalities of the future orientations' that social actors need to coordinate: 'protention,' as the movement from the present to the immediate future, trajectories that are imagined, and plans and temporal landscaped
that provide basic cognitive structures for the organization of time. Oomen *et al.*
(2022) apply the notion of social performances to future imaginaries as particular
kinds of social practices. Performativity shows how images and expectations of the
future structure decision-making and social organization. In such approaches to
the future, which generally operate in the micro- and mesoorder of society,
there is a strong emphasis on affective relations, which give rise to different responses (anticipation, expectation, hope, potentiality, etc.).[23] Phenomenological ap-

---

22 See Suckert (2022) for a survey.
23 In anthropology, see for example Bryan and Knight (2019), Collins (2008), and Salzar (2017), and
in STS, see Adam and Groves (2011) and Oomen (2021). Also Altstaedt (2024), Cantó-Milà and Seebach (2015, 2024), Hanusch and Bierman (2020), and Selin (2008).

proaches to the future in general draw attention to the idea of 'lived futures' that contain latent possibilities resisting closure. As Adam and Groves (2007) showed, the future is always being made in the present.

The future is no longer marginalized in sociology today, as is clear from the trends discussed in this chapter. However, due to the emphasis on how social actors in the present construct the future, the prospect of an open future is reduced to what social practices generate. The result is that the sources of transcendence are domesticated by the pull of the past over the present. In systems theory, which, in contrast to phenomenological approaches, operates at the macrolevel order of society, societies no longer have the capacity for self-transcendence. In essence, the future in all these accounts is seen by how it is perceived or produced by the present. Luhmann was onto something important with his notion of iterative modalities, but it remained undeveloped. The legacy of phenomenology was a conception of time as social time and was past oriented, while the notion of modalities was future oriented. However, the conception of modality did not make a satisfactory connection with a normative position, still less a critical one. Phenomenological-inspired approaches to the future have been the basis of valuable research in recent times but need to be complemented by an approach to time that goes beyond the category of social time, which is just one dimension of temporality.

References

Abaci, U. 2019. *Kant's Revolutionary Theory of Modality.* Oxford: Oxford University Press.

Adam, B. 1990. *Time and Social Theory.* Cambridge: Polity Press.

Adam, B. and Groves, C. 2007. *Future Matters: Action, Knowledge, Ethics.* Leiden, Boston: Brill.

Adam, B. 2011. 'Wendell Bell and the Sociology of the Future: Challenges, Past and Present.' *Futures*, 43: 590–95.

Adam, B. and Grove, C. 2011. 'Futures Tended: Care and Future-Oriented Responsibility.' *Bulletin of Science. Technology and Society*, 31 (1) 17–27.

Altstaedt, S. 2024. 'Future-Cultures: How Future Imaginations Disseminate Through the Social.' *European Journal of Social Theory*, 27 (2).

Andersson, J. 2012. 'The Great Future Debate and the Struggle for the World.' *American Historical Review*, 117 (5): 1411–1430

Anderson, J. 2018. *The Future of the World: Futurology, Futurists and the Struggle for the Post-Cold War Imagination.* Oxford: Oxford University Press.

Andersson, J. 2021. 'The Future BoardGame: Prediction and Power over Time.' In: Andersson, J. and Kemp, S. (eds). *Futures.* Oxford: Oxford University Press.

Baert, P. 1992. 'Time Reflexivity and Social Action.' *International Sociology*, 7 (3): 317–27.

Bauman, Z. 1998. *Globalization: The Human Consequences.* Cambridge: Polity Press.

Bazzani, G. 2022. 'Futures in Action: Expectations, Imaginaries and Narratives of the Future'. *Sociology*, 57 (2): 382–97.

Beck, U. 1992. [1986] *The Risk Society.* London: Sage.

Beckert, J. 2016. *Imagined Futures: Fictional Expectations and Capitalist Dynamics.* Cambridge, MASS.: Harvard University Press.

Beckert, J. and Bronk, R. (eds) 2018. *Uncertain Futures: Imaginaries, Narratives, and Calculation in the Economy.* Oxford: Oxford University Press.

Beckert, J. and Suckert, L. 2021. 'The Future as a Social Fact: The Analysis of the Perception of the Future in Sociology.' *Poetics*, 84: 101499.

Bell, D. 1960. *The End of Ideology: On the Exhaustion of Political Ideas in the Fifties.* Cambridge, MASS.: Harvard University Press.

Bell, D. 1967. 'The Year 2000: The Trajectory of an Idea.' *Daedalus*, 96 (3): 639–65.

Bell, D. 1999 [1973] *The Coming of Post-Industrial Society: A Venture in Social Forecasting.* New York: Basic Books.

Bell, W. 1996. 'The Sociology of the Future and the Future of Sociology.' *Sociological Perspectives*, 39 (1): 39–57.

Bell, W. 1997. *Foundations of Future Studies: Vol. 1. History, Purposes and Knowledge.* London: Routledge.

Bell, W. and Mau, J. 1971. *Sociology of the Future.* New York: Russell Sage Foundation.

Berardi, F. 2011. *After the Future.* Edinburgh: AK Press.

Bergman, W. 1992. 'The Problem of Time in Sociology.' *Time and Society*, 1 (1): 81–134.

Bowler, P. 2017. *A History of the Future: Prophets of Progress from H. G. Wells to Issac Asimov.* Cambridge: Cambridge University Press.

Bramble, J. 2015. *Modernism and the Occult.* London: Palgrave.

Brough, J. 1975. 'Husserl on Memory.' *The Monist*, 59 (1): 40–62.

Bryant, R. and Knight, D. 2019. *The Anthropology of the Future.* Cambridge: Cambridge University Press.

Buck-Morss, S. 2002. *Dreamworld and Catastrophe: The Passing of Mass Utopia in East and West.* Cambridge, MASS: MIT Press.

Byung-Chul, H. 2017. *The Scent of Time.* Cambridge: Polity Press.

Cantó-Milà, N. and Seebach, S. 2015. 'Desired Images, Regulating Figures, Constructed Imaginaries: The Future as an Apriority for Society to be Possible.' *Current Sociology*, 63 (2): 198–215.

Cantó-Milà, N. and Seebach, S. 2024. 'Between Temporalities, Imaginaries and Imagination: A Framework for Analysing Futures.' *European Journal of Social Theory*. 27 (2).

Chang, J. and Halliday, J. 2006. *Mao: The Unknown Story.* London: Verso.

Collins, S. G. 2008. *All Tomorrow's Cultures: Anthropological Engagements with the Future.* Oxford: Berghahn.

Crick, B. 1980. *George Orwell: A Life.* London: Seeker and Warburg.

Delanty, G. and Harris. 2023. *Capitalism and its Critics: Capitalism in Social and Political Theory.* London: Routledge.

Durkheim, E. 2009. [1917] 'The Politics of the Future.' *Durkheimian Studies*, 15: 3–6.

Ehrlich, P. 1968. *The Population Bomb.* Ballantine Books: New York.

Elias, N. 1992. [1984] *Time: An Essay.* Oxford: Blackwell.

Eliot, T. S. 1963. *T. S. Elliot: Collected Poems, 1909–1962.* London: Faber and Faber.

Fukuyama, F. 2020. [1992] *The End of History and the Last Man.* London: Penguin.

Gabor, D. 1964. *Inventing the Future.* London: Seeker and Warburg.

Gidley, J. 2017. *The Future: A Very Short Introduction.* Oxford: Oxford University Press.

Giddens, A. 1987. 'Time and Social Organization.' In: *Social Theory and Modern Sociology.* Cambridge: Polity Press.

Gleason, A., Goldstone, J. and Nussbaum, M. (eds). 2005. *On Nineteen Eight-Four: Orwell and Our Future.* Princeton: Princeton University Press.

Gramsci, A. 1971. 'Notes on Italian History.' In: *Selections from Prison Notebooks.* London: Lawrence and Wishart.

Gurvitch, G. 1964. *The Spectrum of Social Time.* Dordrecht: Reidel.

Habermas, J. 2015. [1968] *Knowledge and Human Interests.* Cambridge: Polity Press.

Hanusch, H. and Bierman, F. 2020. 'Deep-time Organizations: Learning Institutional Longevity from History.' *The Anthropocene Review.* 7 (1): 19 – 41.

Hayek, F. A. 2007. [1944] *The Road to Serfdom.* Chicago: Chicago University Press.

Herf, J. 1986. *Reactionary Modernism: Technology, Culture and Politics in Weimar and the Third Reich.* Cambridge: Cambridge University Press.

Hilligan, M. 1967. *The Future as Nightmare: Wells and the Anti-Utopians.* Oxford: Oxford University Press.

Holston, J. 1989. *The Modernist City: An Anthropological Critique of Brasilia.* Chicago: University of Chicago Press.

Huxley, A. 1932/1946. *Brave New World.* New York: Harper & Row.

Huxley, J. 1958. *Brave New World Revisited.* https://www.huxley.net/bnw-revisited/

Jameson, F. 2007. *Archaeologies of the Future: The Desire called Utopia and Other Science Fiction.* London: Verso.

Jasanoff, S.; Kim, S.-H. (eds). 2015. *Dreamscapes of Modernity. Sociotechnical Imaginaries and the Fabrication of Power.* Chicago: University of Chicago Press.

Jaspers, K. 1961. *The Future of Mankind.* Chicago: University of Chicago Press.

de Jouvenel, B. 2017. [1964/1967]. *The Art of Conjecture.* London: Routledge.

Jonas, H. 1984. [1979] *The Imperative of Responsibility: In Search of an Ethics for the Technological Age.* Chicago: University of Chicago Press.

Landes, D. 1983. *Revolution in Time: Clocks and the Making of the Modern World.* Cambridge, MASS.: Harvard University Press.

Luhmann, N. 1976. 'The Future Cannot Begin: Temporal Structures in Modern Society.' *Social Research,* 43 (1): 130 – 52. 12

Luhmann, N. 2002. *Risk: A Sociological Analysis.* New Brunswick, NJ.: Transaction Publishers.

Luhmann, N. 1995. [1984] *Social Systems.* Stanford: Stanford University Press.

Luhmann, N. 1998. *Observations on Modernity.* Stanford: Stanford University Press.

Martins. H. 1974. 'Time and Theory in Sociology.' In: Rex, J. (ed.) *Approaches to Sociology.* London: Routledge & Kegan Paul.

Mead, G. H. 1932. *The Philosophy of the Present.* London: The Open Court Company.

Meadows, D., Meadows, D., Randers, W., and Behrends III, W. 1972. *The Limits to Growth: A Report for the Club of Rome's Project on the Predicament of Mankind.* New York: Universe Books.

Mensch, J. 1999. 'Husserl on the Future.' *Husserl Studies,* 16 (1): 41 – 64.

Merton, R. 1968. (1949) 'The Self-fulfilling Prophesy'. In: *Social Theory and Social Structure.* New York: Free Press.

Meskell, L. 2010. *A Future in Ruins: UNESCO, World Heritage, and the Dream of Europe.* Oxford: Oxford University Press.

Mische, A. 2007. 'Projects and Possibilities: Researching Futures in Action.' *Sociological Forum,* 24 (3): 694 – 704.

Muzzetto, L. 2006. 'Time and Meaning in Schutz.' *Time and Society,* 15 (1): 5 – 31.

Nowotny, H. 1992. 'Time and Social Theory: Towards a Social Theory of Time.' *Time and Society*, 1 (3): 421–54.

Nowotny, H. 1994. [1989] *Time: The Modern and Postmodern Experience.* Cambridge: Polity.

Oomen, J. 2021. *Imagining Climate Engineering: Dreaming of the Designer Climate.* London: Routledge.

Oomen, J., Hoffman, J., and Hajer, M. 2022. 'Techniques of Futuring: On how Imagined Futures Become Socially Performative.' *European Journal of Social Theory*, 25 (2): 252–70.

Orwell, G. 2000. [1949] *Nineteen Eighty-Four.* London: Penguin.

Pollak, F. 1973. [1961] *The Image of the Future.* Amsterdam: Elsevier.

Popper, K. 1963. *Conjectures and Refutations: The Growth of Scientific Knowledge.* London: Routledge.

Popper, K. 1994. *The Myth of the Framework: In Defence of Science and Rationality.* London: Routledge.

Popper, K. 1995. [1990] *A World of Propensities.* Bristol: Thoemmes Press.

Rosa, H. 2013. *Social Acceleration: A New Theory of Modernity.* New York: Columbia University Press.

Roberts, A. 2019. *H. G. Wells: A Literary Life.* London: Palgrave.

Russell, B. 1951. 'The Future of Man.' *The Atlantic*, March. https://www.theatlantic.com/magazine/archive/1951/03/the-future-of-man/305193/

Salzar, J. F., Pink, S., Irving, A., and Sjöberg, J. (eds) 2017. *Anthropologies and Futures: Researching Emerging and Uncertain World.* London: Bloomsbury.

Schutz, A. 1959. 'Tiresias, or our Knowledge of Future Events.' *Social Research*, 26 (1): 71–89.

Schutz, A. 1967. *The Phenomenology of the Social World.* Evanston: Northwestern Univ. Press.

Schumacher, E. F. 1973. *Small is Beautiful: Economics as if People Mattered.* London: Blond and Briggs.

Selin, C. 2008. 'The Sociology of the Future: Tracing Stories of Technologies and Time.' *Sociological Compass*, 2/6: 1878–95.

Shelley, M. 2008. [1826] *The Last Man.* London: Penguin.

Short, P. 2004. *Pol Pot: The History of a Nightmare.* London: John Murray.

Smith, D. 1986. *H. G. Wells: A Biography.* New Haven: Yale University Press.

Sorokin, P. 1943. *Sociocultural Causality, Space and Time.* Durham: Duke University Press.

Spengler, O. 1932. [1918]. *The Decline of the West.* London: Allen and Unwin.

Staley, D. 2002. 'A History of the Future.' *History and Theory*, 41 (4): 72–89.

Suckert, L. 2022. 'Back to the Future. Sociological Perspectives on Expectations, Aspirations and Imagined Futures'. In: *European Journal of Sociology*, 63 (3): 393–428.

Tavory, I. 2018. 'Between Situations: Anticipation, Rhythms, and the Theory of Integration.' *Sociological Theory*, 36 (2): 117–37.

Tavory, I. and Eliasoph, N. 2013. 'Coordinating Futures: Towards a Theory of Anticipation'. *American Journal of Sociology*, 118 (4): 908–42.

Thompson, E. P. *et al.* 1987. *Exterminism and Cold War.* London: Verso.

Toffler, A. 1970. *Future Shock.* New York: Random House.

Toffler, A. 1980. *The Third Wave.* London: Collins.

UN 1987. *Our Common Future: World Commission on Environment and Development.* Oxford: Oxford University Press.

Urry, J. 2003. *Global Complexity.* Cambridge: Polity Press.

Urry, J. 2016. *What is the Future?* Cambridge: Polity Press.

Watling, S. 2023. *Tomorrow Perhaps the Future: Following Writers and Rebels in the Spanish Civil War.* London: Jonathan Cape.

Wells, H.G. 1913. *The Discovery of the Future.* New York: B. W. Huebsch. https://www.gutenberg.org/cache/epub/44447/pg44867-images.html

Wells, H. G. 2005. [1895] *The Time Machine.* London: Penguin.

Williams, R. 1983. *Towards 2000*. London: Chatto and Windus.

Williams, R. J. 2016. 'World Futures.' *Critical Inquiry*, 42 (3): 473–546.

Wittman, L. 2021. 'Italian Futurism ad the Explosive "NOW".' In: Andersson, J. and Kemp, S. (eds). *Futures*. Oxford: Oxford University Press.

Yeats, W. B. 1974. [1919] *W. B. Yeats Selected Poetry*. London: Pan.

Young, M. 1968. *Forecasting and the Social Sciences*. London: Heinemann.

Young, M. 1988. *Hidden Rhythms: Schedules and Calendars in Social Life*. London: Thames & Hudson.

Zerubavel, E. 1981. *Hidden Rhythms: Schedules and Calendars in Social Life*. Chicago: University of Chicago Press.

Zerubavel, E. 1982. 'The Standardization of Time: A Sociohistorical Perspective.' *American Journal of Sociology*, 88 (1): 1–23.

Chapter Six
Critical Theory and the Future: The Sources of Transcendence

The previous chapters explored a wide variety of conceptions of the future in modern thought. These differ in many respects. One difference we can see lies in the temporal view of the future as something that has already happened to something that will happen in either the near future or the very distant future. Some of these differences revolve around a positive or a negative view of the future. Another issue is the question of the knowability of the future, with positions varying from those that see it as something that can be known and mastered and the position that it cannot be unknown due to its unpredictability.

Within contemporary social science, as discussed at the end of the previous chapter, the orthodox approach to the future that emanated from positivistic science has been challenged by phenomenological conceptions. Against a view of the future that prevailed since the middle of the twentieth century that emphasized prediction, forecasting, and control, we have seen in recent years a revival of phenomenological approaches, especially in sociology but also in anthropology. In these developments there is a new emphasis on the future as a product of imaginaries and practices. The future is thus seen as emanating from social action and is produced by the present in ways that reflect creativity, performativity, expectations, the striving for transcendence, *etc.* Such theories, in line with phenomenological thought in general, draw on social constructionism and offer a good basis for thinking beyond seeing the future in terms of catastrophe or as simply unknowable or a category that can be reduced to risks that may or may not be managed. While these sociological approaches have opened up productive and promising lines of research they are also limited in scope.

A central problem with the phenomenological approach to the future and generally with social constructionist theories is that they do not offer an adequate normative view of the future. They have little to say on the question of desirable futures as opposed to undesirable ones and they lack critical depth. Aside from the normative problem, there is a more fundamental problem concerning the theorization of the future in all its dimensions which cannot be reduced to social practices or social imaginaries or problem solving activities. Where the orthodox positivist approaches with their characteristic faith in prediction, forecasting, modeling, *etc.* lead to too strong a view of the future as something that can be known and controlled, phenomenological approaches provide an antidote that is simply too weak in its critical reach and analytical depth. Generally, such ap-

https://doi.org/10.1515/9783111240602-007

proaches accept too much of the subject's own self-understanding and operate only in the meso or micro order of society. Both lack a sense of future as a product of forces that cannot be reduced to the present and which are in part historical and evolutionary but also reside in higher-level structures of consciousness and in the nature of reality, which includes systems of reference that have a transcendental function, i.e. reason and general cultural models that are the carriers of the main components of the idea of the future. They fail to address the challenges of something that is not, or only, partly actual and multileveled. Potentiality, a key aspect of conceptualizing the future, is not something that can be understood in terms of experience alone. The future is contingent on events to come; it is open but it is also limited by events that cannot be imagined.

The argument I am putting forward in this chapter is that an adequate conception of the future must account for the fundamental reality of transcendence. Without such a notion we cannot deal with the problem of how societies undergo transformation such that temporal realities as the past, present, and future are possible. To speak of the future is unavoidably to ask questions about what is possible. Such questions cannot be answered by talking about the present disconnected from structures developed in the course of history and emerging ones taking shape in our present. Now, while this points in the direction of a philosophical and historical hermeneutics of the future in terms of its trajectories and emergent forms, it is also a critical endeavor in that it is about examining the potentialities of the present and the legacies of the past. Present potentialities open up future possibilities.

In light of this perspective on present potentialities and future possibilities, which I argue is the only adequate approach to the future, a consideration of critical theory is warranted. While I am not claiming that critical theory offers a definitive solution to the inadequacies of other theories of the future, it does offer an essential perspective that is otherwise missing. An adequate theory of the future will benefit from the insights of both the phenomenological and critical approaches. Indeed, it is remarkable that most, if not all, theories of the future do not consider the critical theory tradition. Accordingly, this chapter seeks to reconstruct the concept of the future in critical theory. I also try to show that the key concepts of critical theory are in fact temporal concepts and are especially pertinent to the idea of the future even where this is not specifically discussed. Indeed, as I will try to show, critical theory was precisely about future possibility and how transcendence enters into the social world on the macro and micro levels from ideas that evolved in the course of human evolution.

The Intellectual Origins of Critical Theory: A Brief Outline

Critical theory is a variant of Hegelian-Marxism but incorporates theoretical ideas in the writings of Immanuel Kant and Sigmund Freud, as well as to a lesser extent C. S. Peirce and Max Weber.[1]

Critical theory is guided by the basic principle that society is not given and settled but comprised of potential sources of transcendence. The Hegelian notion of dialectics as taken up by Marx gave to critical theory a way to see the present in terms of future possibilities, since the present is incomplete. Marcuse, referring to Hegel's *Science of Logic* [1812 – 16], summed up this core insight in Hegel as follows: 'The concept of reality has thus turned into the concept of possibility. The real is not yet "actual," but it is at first only the possibility. Mere possibility belongs to the very character of reality; it is not imposed by an arbitrary speculative act.' He sums up Hegel's concept of real possibility as a 'concrete tendency and force': 'The existing state of affairs is a mere condition for another constellation of facts which bring to fruition the inherent potentialities of the given' (Marcuse 1971 [1941]: 150 – 3). In this way, the future is a product of possibilities emerging out of 'real potentialities.' Dialectics is the driving force.

While positivism was concerned with the positivity of the given, critical theory drew from Hegel a concern with negation in order to resist affirmation, facticity, and immediacy. It was through such attempts at negation that transcendence is possible. The mechanism that makes this possible is dialectics. The notion of dialectics can be understood in different ways, but it is essentially a way to make sense of reality in all its forms as a constant struggle between subject and object, between subjective aspiration and objective reality, a struggle that takes place through a third category, which serves a mediation between the first and second categories.

In Marx's reappropriation of Hegel's philosophy, the present is incomplete due to the nature of capitalism, which constantly transforms and revolutionizes everything. Thus, the working class, the basis of capitalism, potentially becomes a revolutionary subject once it develops the appropriate level of consciousness.

While normative in its concern with emancipation from domination, critical theory was primarily an intellectual movement that was concerned with the identification of alternatives with the present. Future possibilities by which the present can transcend itself are immanent in society, as opposed to emanating from exter-

---

1 C. H. Peirce was incorporated into critical theory by Habermas, following K.-O. Apel's lead in the 1970s. Weber's sociology entered critical theory in the 1920s via Georg Lukacs, who directly influenced Adorno and Horkheimer.

nal forces. According to Strydom, following Honneth and Habermas, the key concept of critical theory is immanent transcendence, i.e. the internal transformation of society by ideas that while being immanent in society entail its transcendence (Strydom 2020). This works in several ways, for instance, the discrepancy between ideas and reality, as in the ideal of modernity around justice and equality and the reality of systemic social justice and oppression deriving from capitalism. Another aspect of critique was the Marxist emphasis on class struggle, though this became somewhat diluted in the early Frankfurt School. Marcuse, for a time, saw the revolutionary subject to be the student movement. Letting aside the question of who are the agents of progressive change, a key insight is that an agent of change is always latent if not embroiled in social struggles.

The Hegelian roots of critical theory were also reflected in the concept of mediation, which has played a key role in critical theory. This concept refers to the ways in which everything is interconnected. The existence of one phenomenon is dependent on another. But more than this, it is the medium through which the dialectical movement unfolds. Since Hegel, critical theory has been particularly concerned with the mediation of ideas, that is, the process by which ideas diffuse through society, as in for example the ways by which democracy as an idea increasingly came to diffuse throughout the world since the eighteenth century. However, after Marx it is clear that such forms of mediation only happen as a result of struggle, not as gifts from the state. The notion of mediation also draws attention to the way ideas are not just external or above society and social struggles but are integral to society. An idea that at first is marginal, for example, until recently, the idea of a green economy or the need for a planetary politics to reduce global warming, becomes increasingly adopted and thus takes on a new significance as a form of mediation.

Mediation is also illustrated in the concept of recognition, another key Hegelian concept. For Hegel, a self exists as a self only in relation to another self who recognizes the other. As developed later by Axel Honneth, such relations of recognition are not simply given but unfold through social struggles since recognition has to be fought for (Honneth 1996 [1992]).

The dialectical conception of society remained fundamental to critical theory, giving to it a concern with social contradictions and the need for an immanent analysis of future possibilities in light of potentials opened up as a result of social struggles or new interpretations of older ideas.

In the course of its history, critical theorists became increasingly doubtful as to where the sources of transcendence might lie. Max Weber's pessimistic diagnosis of modernity as a process of irreversible rationalization leading to bureaucratization and the dominance of capitalism appeared to eradicate any possibility for major transformation (though this needs to be considered alongside Weber's preference for liberal democracy and his hope that it would be possible in Germany). The experience with fascism and above all the Holocaust led to the incorporation of Sigmund Freud's work on the unconsciousness into the analysis of modernity in order to account for the emergence of new kinds of domination and the pathological nature of mass politics with the rise of authoritarianism, even within democracies. Herbert Marcuse sought to combine Marx and Freud in order to understand the nature of both domination and resistance in post–Second World War America. A later turn in critical theory with Jürgen Habermas developed a critical hermeneutics drawing on Freud's psychoanalytical model of interpretation.[2]

The critical theory of Habermas and the work of Karl-Otto Apel also drew on the writings of Charles Sanders Peirce and other figures in American pragmatism to broaden the scope of critical theory to take into account developments in the nature of interpretation and language, which included the logic of reason. While pragmatist political theory was limited to largely problem solving and, with John Dewey, political education, the American pragmatists developed advanced theories of language and logic. This move was important in bringing critical theory in the direction of a theory of communication and a broader notion of rationality than the notion of instrumental rationality encompassing aspects of reason. It led to a view of communication as the source of transcendence since the subject is constantly interpreting in communicative contexts various registers of reference that are themselves of a semiotic nature (Strydom 2011).

Critical theory obviously is centrally about critique, as opposed to just description or value-neutral interpretation. In the German philosophical tradition since Kant, critique is a form of self-reflexive thought and is concerned with the relation between subjectivity and objectivity, self-knowledge, and the conditions and possibility of knowledge. In this tradition of thought, critique has a diagnostic role in identifying problems and guiding society toward their solution. As Kant wrote in the Preface of the *Critique of Pure Reason:* 'Our Age is, in especial degree, the age of criticism, and to criticism everything must submit.'[3] Critique aims to change our view of the world, such that we will see things differently; it is concerned with potentials within the present and the exercise of judgment. An interpretation is always an evaluation entailing judgment. In Kant's critical philosophy, critique was principally confined to demonstrating the limits of reason, as in the monumental *Critique of Pure Reason* [1781/1787]. As he wrote, its purpose was 'not to extend knowledge, but only to correct it' (B26). It was thus a relatively confined endeavor to critique traditional metaphysics in claiming knowledge on things that are not

---

2 For a fuller account, see my book *Critical Theory and Social Transformation* (Delanty 2021).
3 Kant (1970: A xi. footnote).

admissible objects of knowledge. While Kant's critical philosophy had no direct social or political application, it did establish a lasting basis for critique that was later given a wider and more relevant application in the social world, first with Hegel and then with Marx, and was taken up in different ways and at different times by critical theory.

Kant merits some special consideration for our focus on the future due to his conception of reason embodying transcendence and his appropriation by later critical theory. The following is a brief but necessary discussion of his critical philosophy which provided an account of reason that remained influential long after Kant and was an important way to understand the nature of transcendence.

Undoubtedly the most influential legacy of Kant for modern thought was a conception of reason concerned with the conditions of the possibility of knowledge. For Kant, our knowledge is confined by the structures of our minds, which limit direct knowledge of the external world. Space and time are such structures of human sensibility that allow us to perceive the external world. On that basis, Kant developed a complex theory of 'categories of the understanding' that enable us to have knowledge. Knowledge has a transcendental logic in that it transcends sensory experience but also provides the conditions to have knowledge of the things that we perceive or experience. For Kant, reason – a complex edifice of systems of reference comprised of ideas, principles, concepts, categories – is the origin of such concepts or structures. Kant distinguished *transcendence* from the *transcendental*. The latter pertains to what is immanent in our cognitive makeup and it is what constitutes an object as a knowable phenomenon. It concerns the necessary and unavoidable presuppositions of knowledge which are *a priori* and it is these that transcend experience as such; they are the lens through which we see the world and enable us to make sense of the world. 'I entitle *transcendental* all knowledge which is occupied not so much with objects as with the mode of our knowledge of objects in so far as this mode of knowledge is possible *a priori*' (A12).

In contrast to the transcendental, as a necessary presupposition or conditions of empirical knowledge, transcendence refers to another level of reason beyond empirical knowledge as such. It includes ideas such as God, Freedom, the Immortality of the Soul or a 'future world,' ideas of Reason that are not knowledge claims as such but as regulative ideas or principles, they are major sources of orientation in the world. These are also necessary presuppositions for human cognition and are universal, making it possible for us to think beyond the immediately given and what can be reasonably known.

What sense can we make of this distinction between two kinds of transcendence? For Kant neither is derived from sensory experience and both are expressions of reason, which proceeds in two directions. The conception of the transcendental is fairly clear and concerns the possibility of knowledge confined to the bounds of experience but not derived from it. The notion of transcendence can be understood to be a higher level of reason beyond anything that is empirical but serves as a guide for us in the world, as in providing sources of inspiration or ideals to pursue. So while it is beyond experience and is not a source of knowledge about the world we need it to reach beyond the limits of knowledge. It is the key to thinking about future possibility.

Toward the end of the *Critique of Pure Reason* Kant concedes that while the sole use of philosophy in the end is 'only negative' in 'guarding against error,' this cannot be enough: 'There must, however, be some source of positive modes of knowledge ... How else can we account for our inextinguishable desire to find firm footing somewhere beyond the limits of experience?' (A 796). The *Critique of Pure Reason* provided no satisfactory answer to this question, since his three ideas of reason were somewhat limited. It is clear that a fuller answer would need to take into account his later two major works on critique, the *Critique of Practical Reason* [1788] and the *Critique of Judgement* [1790]. The famous words of the conclusion of the *Critique of Practical Reason* give a hint as to how Kant saw reason as transcendental: 'Two things fill the mind with ever new and increasing admiration and reverence, the more often and more steadily one reflects on them: the starry heavens above me and the moral law within me' (Kant 2015: 5: 162). The human mind is deeply affected by ideas that transcend the world but nonetheless derive from the human condition itself in its capacity for wonder. It may thus be the case that the source of reason itself lies within the human condition. In the passage that follows the above quote, Kant makes clear that these forces do not lie in a transcendent domain beyond the horizon or are veiled in obscurity but can be felt to lie deep in the fact of human existence and consciousness. In this way, the source of transcendence is ultimately within the human condition.

The received view of Kant is that he was primarily concerned with transcendental knowledge, that is, a conception of reason as something structured into human thought and which enables us to know the external world, even not as it is in itself (as rationalists would have). In this way, Kant also avoided the trap of idealism, even if his philosophy was a version of idealism (transcendental idealism, a modified form of idealism that made concessions to rationalism). This notion of the transcendental had a critical function in keeping reason in check and avoiding the pursuit of illusions. It is sometimes thought that Kant was trying to preserve a space for religious faith.[4] The domain of transcendence is less elabo-

---

4 In the Preface to the Second edition of the *Critique of Pure Reason* he found it necessary 'to deny knowledge to make room for faith' (B xxx).

rated, but it is precisely where some of the most important nonreligious ideas of reason also find their expression. For Kant, it was a domain of necessary assumptions, for example, that there is an ultimate cause, a human subject (the soul), and that freedom exists. The notion of the immortality of the soul can be taken to mean an enduring human subjectivity. The idea of God was another idea of reason, though it appears that Kant later reduced the significance of this as an explanation of the final cause of the world.

Of particular salience for the idea of the future is his interest in 'hope of a future life' – sometimes rendered immortality – as a universal idea to express our sense of a beyond. Ideas of reason, for Kant, are necessary ideas in that we cannot do without, yet they do not provide us with empirical knowledge as such. This goes to the core of the problem of the future: we cannot do without future-oriented ideas, though we cannot take them to provide us with knowledge of the future (which is not for Kant a transcendental idea of reason). Taken together, the two notions of transcendence, the *transcendental* and the *transcendent*, are two sides of reason and have a critical function in playing a role in creating the conditions of the possibility of the future. We cannot know what the future will be, but we must assume there will be one and we should strive toward it in the quest for moral perfection.

In sum, then, in relation to the question of how the idea of the future should be understood, it is clear that it firstly concerns the domain of the transcendental, in the sense of necessary presuppositions; yet, it also relates to some of the most fundamental of all questions, such as what for what should we hope. This dimension would appear to be more interesting, but for Kant it is separate from reason and not an idea of reason. As noted in Chapter 4 in relation to Koselleck's somewhat limited interpretation of Kant as a philosopher of progress, in the closing passages of the *Critique of Pure Reason* Kant said the most important question after 'What can I know?' and 'What should I do?' is 'What may I hope? (A805/B833). This question, which goes beyond the notion of progress, unavoidably pertains to transcendence, namely how we can transcend our situation and create a better world.[5] Yet, for Kant, hope lies outside the sphere of reason and not part of the transcendent ideas of reason, since it does not take the form of a principle but rather a capacity or a yearning that people have. It is clear that the concern with transcendence – that is, with ideas that make transcendence possible – was of major importance for Kant and indispensable so long as false claims were not made in its name. Kant's answer to the question 'for what should I hope,' like many of his answers to his questions, raised further questions since

---

5 On Kant's concept of hope, see Bloeser (2022), Goldman (2023), and Speight (2021).

he said the aim of hope was to achieve happiness, which is 'the satisfaction of all our desires.' But underlying it is the pursuit of 'the ideal of the highest good.' Despite the unsatisfactory treatment of hope, it would appear nonetheless to be a more important conception of future possibility than the notion of progress.

Kant was not very clear on the relation between his two notions of transcendence, other than as mentioned that they do not derive from sensory experience and are products of reason that emanate from its two main sources in the categories of the understanding and in ideas of reason. This problem is also complicated by the fact that he wanted to criticize the misuse of transcendent ideas as if they were empirical phenomena or objects of experience and much of the *Critique of Pure Reason* was dedicated to this task.

However, it is clear that the question of transcendence remained a pressing one. In *Perpetual Peace* [1795] the problem of hope remains and is related to his philosophy of morality – in that it enables its pursuit – and to his political philosophy of hope for a cosmopolitan peace, which was an ideal that in turn was influenced by reason (Kant 1991a). In one of his last writings in 1798, 'A Renewed Attempt to Answer the Question: "Is the Human Race Continually Improving,"' Kant discussed the possible future of humanity and what a 'history of future times' would look like. What can be predicted about the future on the basis of *a priori* possibilities? Such a prediction of the future, he notes, cannot be as in astronomy where reliable predictions can be made; it can only be 'prophetic.' 'The human race is either continuing regressing and deteriorating, continually progressing and improving, or at a permanent standstill' (1991b: 178). He argued that all three scenarios are problematical. But whatever the outcome, which cannot be known, 'there are no grounds for giving up hope.' For Kant, as he makes clear in the essay, in view of the fact of human freedom there is no absolute position from which we can know what will happen with certainty. He does infer that humanity will progressively improve in that it has the capacity to do so and progress may be interrupted but does not cease. But hope is independent and can help to make possible that which is potential. The realization of a republican order and constitutional law will happen one day, he believed, because the idea upon which it is based is there and thus a source of motivation and inspiration that will not go away. This goes back to his famous claim in 'What is Enlightenment' [1784] that while we do not live in an enlightened age, we live in an age of enlightenment, by which he meant that enlightenment – the presence of reason – exists in the world but the world in its present state in not coeval with reason since it is incompletely actualized (Kant 1991c: 58). In other words, the transcendent is always there on the level of ideas of reason, since it is necessary and universal, and is also variously engrained in the historical present, depending on how it is taken up in historically contingent circumstances, but also in the ways it is present in the macro-order of society, as in cultural models that provide society with frameworks of meaning (for example, the nation, a republicanism, democracy, cosmopolitanism, including ideologies and utopias).

Kant had very important insights into the idea of the future. These come especially to light in his later work. In one of his final publications, *Anthropology from a Pragmatic View* [1798], he goes so far as to say that the faculty of memory is there to serve as an orientation for the future: 'Recalling the past (remembering) occurs only with the intention of making it possible to foresee the future; we look about us from the standpoint of the present in order to determine something, or be prepared for something' (1978: 35: 197).

It is clear nonetheless that Kant's critical philosophy provided no firm foundation for critical theory, but established some of the most important ideas, above all that there are universal aspects to human knowledge about the world and that while transcending particularity they are also immanent in the world as necessary systems of reference. Reason transcends the world while at the same time it is present in the world enabling it to reach beyond the present. His philosophy drew attention to abiding questions that are all highly pertinent to how the future is to be understood as a form of transcendence and an immanent aspect of human cognition and orientation in the world.

The Idea of the Future in the Critical Theory of the Early Frankfurt School

A distinctive feature of critical theory as espoused in the work of the thinkers collectively known as the 'Frankfurt School' – Theodor Adorno and Max Horkheimer in particular but also including Walter Benjamin and Herbert Marcuse and others such as Erich Fromm – was a concern with how a better world might be possible, especially in the context of a situation that seemed to be bleak. The circumstances of the early to mid-twentieth century gave little ground to believe that the Enlightenment ideas might be realized. With the drift toward totalitarianism and the rise of fascism, these German Jewish thinkers abandoned the older Marxist belief in a historical subject that would bring about a revolutionary transformation of modern society. The future remained very much a forlorn hope, a promise yet to come. The strong orientation to the future that was present in the writings of Kant, Hegel, and Marx remained and for this reason the critical theorists did not retreat into the past or see only a perpetual present devoid of a future.

The visionary writings of Walter Benjamin provide some of the most original and inspiring thoughts on the idea of the future. In his work the future is revealed only by revisiting the past where 'traces of what was yet to become' can be found in fleeting moments of memory. It is a redemptive conception of the future. These 'fleeting moments' are often expressed in an allegorical form and provide a basis for hope.

One of the most well-known conceptions of the future in Benjamin's work was his interpretation of Paul Klee's 1920 modernist painting 'Angelus Novus,' which Benjamin had himself purchased in Munich in 1921.[6] This painting remained an inspirational icon for critical theory after Benjamin's death at Port Bou in 1940, when Adorno acquired it. It later came into the possession of Gerholm Sholem, who brought it to Israel after Adorno's death. Today it is in the Israel Museum in Jerusalem. The painting depicts 'The Angel of History' and captures an aspect of the Jewish Talmudic mystical tradition in which angels made their appearance in the present as a reminder of the past. In his 'Theses on the Philosophy History,' written in 1940, he applied the Jewish tradition of mourning and remembrance to the problem of history and redemption with the argument that historical progress does not move from the present to a future, but rather proceeds by the present looking backward at the catastrophes of the past. This allows us to have a view of the future. Benjamin describes the Angelus Novus as moving toward the future, possibly even being hurled toward it by the tumultuous times in which he lived. Yet, his face is not looking to the future but to the past. His mouth is open as if with an expression of horror. For Benjamin, Klee's painting gave expression to the problem of historical redemption: the present can redeem the past by confronting it rather than by fleeing from it. In the famous words of the ninth thesis in the 'Theses on the Philosophy of History:' 'Where we perceive a chain of events, he sees one single catastrophe which keeps piling wreckage upon wreckage and hurls it in from to his feet. The angel would like to stay, to awaken the dead, and make whole what has been smashed. But a storm is blowing from Paradise; it has caught in his wings with such violence that the angel can no longer close them. This storm irresistibly propels him into the future to which is back is turned, while the pile of debris before him grows skyward. This storm is what we call progress' (Benjamin 1970a: 259).

The essay also gives a clear statement of Benjamin's critique of the idea of progress, which can also be found in the *Arcades Project:* 'Overcoming the concept of "progress" and overcoming the concept of "period of decline" are two sides of the same things (Benjamin 1999: 460). He wrote that 'the concept of progress must be grounded in the idea of catastrophe' (p. 472).

Progress had to be measured by recognition of the catastrophes of history. Despite the catastrophes of history, there is still a future to be found, even if it could

---

6 Some of the following derive from Chapters 1, 9, and 12 in Delanty (2021).

not be identified. As he wrote in his study of Goethe's *Elective Affinities:* 'It is only for the sake of the hopeless that we are given hope' (cited in Jay, 1996/1973: p. 105). It is important to appreciate that despite the note of despair in his work, Benjamin was opposed to nostalgia, for the past offered little refuge, and he believed in future redemption. This was expressed largely in the form of mystical hope.

In his critical historical theology, the present can face the future only if it liberates itself from the past. The past with its memories and conflicting histories is like a theatre for the present to emancipate itself. As he wrote in *A Berlin Chronicle:* 'Memory is not an instrument for exploring the past but its theatre. It is the medium of past experience, just as the earth is the medium in which dead cities lie interred. He who seeks to approach his own buried past must conduct himself like a man digging' (1978: 25–6). Benjamin's critical theory of memory was thus an integral part of his theory of revolution as redemption. In this vein, he wrote in the second thesis, 'our image of happiness is indissolubly bound up with the image of redemption.' The same applies to our view of the past, which is the concern of history: 'The past carries with it a temporal index by which it is referred to redemption. There is a secret agreement between past generations and the present one. Our coming was expected on earth. Like every generation that preceded us, we have been endowed with a weak Messianic power, a power to which the past has a claim.' Memories are not then to be dismissed by history. To articulate the past, he wrote in the sixth thesis, 'means to seize hold of a memory as it flashes up at a moment of danger.' Benjamin's preoccupation with the fragments of the past contained in the present is to be seen as an interpretation of revolution as a mystical redemption for the present 'as the "time of the now," which is shot through with chips of Messianic time' (Benjamin 1970a). The category of experience, so central to Benjamin's thought, is also present in everyday life and is an integral part of both collective and individual memory. Commenting on Bergson and Baudelaire, he wrote that experience 'is less the product of facts firmly anchored in memory than of a convergence in memory of accumulated and frequently unconscious data' (Benjamin 1970b: 159).

Benjamin's writings greatly influenced T. W. Adorno, who shared with him a skepticism of the future in terms of progress. Adorno, in a late essay, wrote that the 'concept of progress requires critical confrontation with real society' (Adorno 1998a: 148). In his view, the concept of progress lacked conceptual clarity: 'Even more than other concepts, the concept of progress dissolves upon attempts to specify its exact meaning, for instance what progresses and what does not' (p. 143). He observes that the idea of progress articulates both the movement of society and at the same time contradicts it: 'Having arisen societally, the concept of progress requires critical confrontation with real society. The aspect of redemption, no matter how secularized, cannot be removed from the concept of progress. The fact that it cannot be reduced neither to facticity nor to the idea indicates its own contradiction' (1998a [1969]: 148).

His critical theory bore the influence of Benjamin's redemptive critique. A famous expression of this can be found at the end of *Minima Moralia:* 'The only philosophy which can be responsibly practised in face of despair is the attempt to contemplate all things from the standpoint of redemption' (Adorno 2005 [1955]: 245). His somewhat Kantian stance on everything was that 'wrong life cannot be lived rightly' (2005: 39). The premise of his philosophy was that while we cannot know the good, we can know what is wrong and that this is enough to provide us with hope for the future. So a good future is possible in the absence of knowing what it consists of. This argument is in line with Kant's own thinking in that a concept of pure reason cannot be a basis for knowledge, it cannot be known in the way we know empirical things, but it is nonetheless a key component of reason. In this way, Adorno's philosophy preserved the possibility of transcendence even if historical reality appeared to deny its possibility, since it was a projection into the future. As he also put it in an essay unpublished in his lifetime, 'the concept of the transcendental is a reminder that thinking, by virtue of its own immanent elements of universality, transcends its own individuation' (1998c: 257).

Adorno wrote an important essay in 1959 that is highly pertinent to how the present should relate to the future. It is also a good example of a practical outcome of his more abstract writings. In 'The Meaning of Working Through the Past' he discussed how Germany should relate to the Nazi past (Adorno 1998b). Against widespread complacency in the 1950s about the past, he argued that the past needs to be worked through in a way that overcomes the survival of many aspects of it under the conditions of democracy. The future cannot be reached through the forgetting of history: 'I consider the survival of National Socialism within democracy to be potentially more menacing than the survival of fascist tendencies against democracy' (1998b: 90). Adorno put forward an argument for taking responsibility for the present as an alternative to philosophical resignation. In *Negative Dialectics* [1966] he warned about political complacency and the illusion of progress: 'Universal history must be construed and denied. After the catastrophes that have happened, and in view of the catastrophes to come, it would be cynical to say that a plan for a better world is manifested in history and unites it. Not to be denied for that reason, however, is the unity that cements the continuous, chaotically splintered moments and phases of history – the unity of the control over nature, progressing to rule over men, and finally to that of men's inner nature. No universal history leads from the savagery to humanitarianism, but there is one leading from the slingshot to the megaton bomb' (Adorno 1973: 320). In this work he brings a further dimension to the present to bear with the argument that the experience of suffering should provide an orientation for the future.

'The need to lend a voice to suffering is a condition of all truth. For suffering is objectivity that weighs upon the subject; its most subjective experience, its expression, is objectively conveyed' (Adorno 1973: 17–18).

A theme in the writings of Adorno, Benjamin, and Marcuse was that memory, especially the traumatic memory of suffering, makes possible hope, which in turn is what opens the present to the future. Marcuse also made this argument in *One-Dimensional Man:* 'Remembrance is a mode of "mediation" which breaks, for short moments, the omnipresent power of given facts' (Marcuse 1964: 98). His book concludes with the statement that sums up the critical theory of the Frankfurt School: 'The critical theory of society possesses no concepts which could bridge the gap between the present and the future; holding no promise and showing no success, it remains negative.' Marcuse then cites Walter Benjamin's famous statement, mentioned earlier: 'It is only for the sake of those without hope that hope is given to us' (Marcuse 164: 257). As Max Horkheimer also wrote, hope offers emancipation from despair: 'the hope of Reason lies in emancipation from our own fear of despair' (cited in Jay 2016: 100).

Marcuse's work was also concerned with the idea of utopia, which he saw, following Freud, as the promise of something that was not fulfilled, a promise of happiness that made it possible for hope to still exist. For Freud, happiness was something irretrievably lost and, as he argued in *Civilization and its Discontents* [1929], incompatible with civilization, which requires its repression. Marcuse in contrast believed happiness was a desire that could be fulfilled but required revolution.

The utopian idea was more developed in the writings of the Marxist philosopher Ernest Bloch, though not a figure of the Frankfurt School as normally understood he can be considered here as he was a key influence on critical theory. In any case, the Frankfurt School was neither a school nor based only in Frankfurt, but a diverse group of German Jewish philosophers writing in the Hegelian-Marxist tradition and mostly in exile in the USA. Bloch, writing also in the tradition of Hegelian Marxism, differed from the critical theorists in his firm belief in the transformative power of political action (Hudson 1982). In his three volume *The Principle of Hope* (1995 [1938–1947]), he provided a comprehensive outline of utopian politics and its sources. In the Marxist tradition, the idea of utopia was always regarded with a certain skepticism ever since Marx's critique of the French Utopianists and utopianism in general. However, it is clear that Marx was also a utopian thinker even if utopia as a realizable ideal had to be perpetually postponed, a deferment that seems to be part of its definition. An important and influential concept in the work of Ernst Bloch was the notion of the 'Not-Yet-Consciousness,' which can be seen as a way the future is always anticipated by the present. He was concerned with how newness arises, the '*Novum*,' which is to be understood as radical newness, not simply what is new. Utopia expresses the quest for newness as a real possibility and not therefore to be equated with just optimism. In that respect the principle of hope that underlines the utopian impulse builds on Kant's notion of hope as a latent force (see Goldman 2023).

We can finally mention Erich Fromm, who was a central figure in the Frankfurt School in exile at Columbia University, where Max Horkheimer had set up a working group. While he later broke from Horkheimer's circle, he played a key role in Freudian Marxism in works such as *Fear of Freedom* in 1941 and *Beyond the Chains of Illusion* in 1962. One of his important contributions was the study of social pathologies. In his work, social pathology brings about the loss of a perspective on the future and the destruction of the capacity for renewal. Pathologies entail regression and stagnation; they are moribund structures. The critique of social pathologies seeks to recover a sense of the future. Fromm, writing in the early 1960s, was also more attuned to the reality of nuclear war and the possibility of the death of the future as a result of human self-destruction.

In sum, the critical theory of the first generation of the Frankfurt School provided an important alternative conception of the future to the dominant traditions in modern thought. Drawing on Kant and the Hegelian Marxist tradition as well as Freud, they offered a conception of the future in terms of an unrealized potentiality for transcendence. Their ideas went far beyond the notion of progress, utopia as an unrealizable aim, or hope only as an aspiration. Hope and utopia were now connected with the possibility of transcendence as potentially immanent in the present. In the case of Bloch and to an extent in Marcuse, there was the additional emphasis on political struggle, since a desirable future has to be fought for and not just passively wished for. The logic by which potentiality becomes possibility is thus the key to the conception of the future. However, in the work of these thinkers it remained a largely negative undertaking since it could not be easily related to political goals and thus lacked a positive dimension. The sociological ramifications of the philosophical arguments were never fully developed.

Habermas and the Communication Paradigm

As the older critical theory associated with the thinkers of the Frankfurt School went into decline in the late 1960s, a new generation of critical theorists advanced critical theory away from purely negative critique to a form that aimed to locate the source of transcendence within the social struggles taking place in society rather than a more general invocation of immanence. The most significant of these theorists was Jürgen Habermas, whose communication paradigm changed the conception of critical theory, bringing it closer to sociological theory and thus reviving the initial aim of the older critical theory to link philosophy and sociology. We are concerned here only with his work in so far as it has a direct bearing on the idea of the future. The idea of the future has not in itself as a concept played a major role in his work.[7] However, it is indirectly bound up with most of his writings, which in one way of the other are concerned with future possibility.

His major work of 1968, *Knowledge and Human Interests*, provided a new direction for critical theory with its focus on emancipation as guided by the human interest in emancipation from domination (Habermas 1972). The interest in emancipation leads to a different kind of knowledge, which should be the aspiration of the social sciences, in contrast to the interest in technical knowledge, as in the prediction of the future. Now, while this has been taken to be his main theoretical contribution to a critical theory of the future, it is limited as an account of critical social theory (as in for example Gidley 2017). To appreciate the relevance of Habermas's social theory for the idea of the future, it is necessary to go beyond the perspective on emancipation which he invoked as an alternative to domination without adequate consideration of the problems associated with the notion of emancipation. Since Foucault, we now know that emancipation is contested and may be a source of domination. In any case, Habermas too readily assumed that the natural sciences were based on a 'cognitive interest' in control, in contrast to the cognitive interest in emancipation in the social sciences and the interest in understanding in the humanities.

Knowledge and Human Interests was an important work in reviving the old Hegelian-Marxist conception of human emancipation in a new key and advancing an anti-positivist conception of social science as well as a call for critical hermeneutics. However, beyond a critique of prediction as a way of knowing the future, the work otherwise is limited. Of greater significance was the advancement of the communication paradigm with the *Theory of Communicative Action* in 1981 and in related publications since the late 1970s (Habermas 1984 and 1987). This work was and remains of seminal importance for many fields of inquiry and still offers one of the most original ways to theorize the future. The *Theory of Communicative Action* is based on the argument that modernity entails the progressive extension of two forms of rationality – instrumental rationality and communicative rationality – which are perpetually in conflict with each other. In line with Marx and Weber and the theorists of the older Frankfurt School, Adorno and Horkheimer, Habermas sees modernity shaped by the rise and growth of instrumental rationality, as reflected in capitalism, industrialization, and bureaucratization. However, unlike these theorists there is also a counter-rationality, namely communicative rationality, as reflected in the expansion of spaces of communication (the various

---

7 An exception, but on a specific issue is Habermas (2003).

sites of the public sphere, democracy). Society is shaped by these two forms of rationality. In more formal terms, he describes these two kinds of rationality in terms of system and life-world, with the former 'colonizing' the latter, which resists by mobilizing social movements that can be understood as expressions of communicative reason. An aspect of communicative rationality, which derives from the nature of communication, is that it makes learning possible: societies learn through the advancement of their communicative capacities. The notion of rationality at work here is hermeneutic in that it is interpreted as structured by reason, in the sense that goes back to Kant's conception of reason as bearing the possibility of transcendence. In other words, reason enters into all aspects of social life but does so incompletely.

Without further elaboration of this approach, we can see how it informs a new critical theory of the future. It does not rely on a notion of emancipation as such, though that continues to be important as a commitment to identifying progressive forms of social organization. Today, such notions of emancipation will have somehow to incorporate the relation to nature, a complex and contested question in Habermas's social theory which will not be discussed further here (see Eckersley 1990; Vogel 1996). The more important point is that the communication paradigm opened a perspective on the future as a product of social struggles and, in particular, ultimately the future is to be seen as a consequence of communicative rationality – shaped by transcendental principles of reason, as necessary presuppositions – rather than an entirely an outcome of instrumental rationality or communication devoid of the input of reason. This means that the future is not settled nor something that can be calculated or predicted. Instrumental rationality may 'colonize the life-world' but not to the point that it is incapacitated, since people always have sources of resistance to draw on and it is these that enable them to transcend their situation. In the *Theory of Communicative Action* social movements were given a specific role in shaping the future, in particular the key movements of environmentalism and the women's movement. These movements are seen by Habermas as having 'emancipatory potentials' as opposed to movements that only have 'potential for resistance and withdrawal' (1987: 393). The future is thus something that is opened up by the life-world in its resistance to instrumentalization.

While Habermas has been criticized for having a somewhat rigid separation of system and life-world as well as the dualism of communicative and instrumental rationality (work for example is seen only as instrumental), it was an approach to future possibility that gave a central place to collective agency in the context of crises and especially legitimation crises (Habermas 1975 [1973]). Power can't avoid the problem of conversion into authority, which rests in part on a claim to legitimacy and this entails appeals to reason (justice, appropriateness, truth, *etc.*). Without this transcendental dimension, power would be indistinguishable from acquiescence. Despite the erosion and even destruction of legitimate applications of power, modern democracies cannot avoid the appeal to reason. In this book and others from the period, he also made a crucial step in incorporating a perspective on collective learning into social analysis. This led to a vision of future possibility as a product of collective learning. The future is possible because societies learn; like individuals, but in different ways, societies also learn and it is this that makes possible for them to have a future. Novelty is thus produced through collective learning processes leading to social and cognitive evolution (see also Habermas 1979). His social theory has an evolutionary dimension, in the sense of cultural evolution: the historical development of societies, especially with modernity, constantly expands the limits of actuality to create new possibilities. In this way the future is constantly produced (see Kompridis 2006). The future is a product of the learning outcomes of history; it does not simply come from social practices alone, but is shaped by deeper generative forces that are also to be found in spaces of reason in modern society.

Habermas's social theory entailed a philosophical defense of modernity as 'incomplete' (see Habermas 1987 [1985]). As a future-oriented time consciousness, modernity contains unrealized potentials that are realized at least partially on the macro-level of society and also penetrate down to the meso order (collective actors) and the micro order (individual subjectivities). While modernity was a break from the past, the future in this view is not fundamentally a break from the present. This is possibly a limitation of Habermas's theory in that he sees the future as tied to the present. However, since the present is always a starting point, as it is where one is, the future can only begin from it. Modernity entails the clash of the present with the past and the present with the future. A key question is whether the future is to be seen in terms of the conflict between communicative and instrumental rationality. Electronic communication and AI, for example, are not easily located in these categories since they are not just simply forms of instrumental rationality (see Chapter Seven).

One reading of Habermas might lead to the view that he sees the future as too embedded in the present and thus lacking a sense of rupture. While there are some grounds for such a view, especially since his later discourse theory of law and democracy which emphasized politics as a discursive activity, it is also evident that he sees the future in more open terms (Habermas 1997 [1992]). In 'The Past as Future,' an interview in 1991 with Max Haller, he criticized a pattern he saw in the new politics in Germany following unification: 'the temptation to choose models from the past for the interpretation of the future seem impossible to resist. The futurity of the past could have been worked through with a self-aware creation of a constitution. Instead, the future is being perceived in the form of the past:

"Let's get it over with, just like we did once before' (p. 66). He refers here to an election slogan, 'The past as future,' of Ludwig Erhard in the 1950s. He also criticizes the failure of 'collective power of imagination whose flexibility and creativity are essential for dealing with the problem of the future' (p. 66).

On the question of transcendence and the legacy of Kant, whose importance for critical theory has been emphasized by Habermas, he has drawn on the two notions discussed earlier, the transcendental and transcendence. The former is reflected in this theory of communication, which reflects a Kantian perspective in that for Habermas communication – or more precisely the linguistic competences that make it possible – is an intrinsic feature of the human condition. In sociological and historical terms, such capacities led to modern society developing in a way that communicative rationality became an intrinsic and irreversible feature of social institutions and social possibility. In this way, individuals in modern society are able in principle to transcend social circumstances. However, this perspective only tells us what is in principle possible, that is, what the conditions of the possibility of the future consist. It does not lead to a real sense of what an alternative future might be, other than that it is a potential built into the nature of social relations.

As a clarification of this, he explained, 'it is not the case that I oppose a radiant future to a devalued past. The proceduralist concept of rationality that I propose cannot sustain utopian projects for concrete forms of life as a whole.' His theory of society at least leads to 'diagnostic descriptions which allow the ambivalence of contrary tendencies of development to emerge more clearly' (2002: 87). As a concession to those who want a stronger notion of transcendence, he agrees that we need a notion of 'going beyond,' a notion that was already implicit in his work, but it can only be 'transcendence from within,' which approximates with Kant's Ideas of Reason, as a opposed to a 'transcendence from beyond' (Habermas 2002). It is possible to see this domain consisting of general concepts of ideas as the source of visions of future possibility. Such ideas transcend the present, the level of experience and include the imaginary. In this view, the social world is mediated by future-oriented thinking. Habermas refers to this as a transcendence 'within' to emphasize that it is not of a religious nature, even if religious thought is one such expression of transcendence, as William James claimed in *Varieties of Religious Experience* [1902]. It is a 'transcendence in this world' and engrained in processes of communication, as systematically outlined in the *Theory of Communicative Action*.

The Responsibility Paradigm and Cosmopolitanism: Jonas and Apel

As discussed, Adorno made the principle of responsibility a central feature of his work. In his case, the intellectual has a responsibility to help the present to face the future by working through the legacy of the past. However, in Adorno, responsibility was essentially the responsibility of the intellectual to engage in critique. The intellectual has a responsibility to enlighten society.

The responsibility theme took on a new and more global significance in the era of fears about nuclear war. In an influential book on moral and political philosophy, published in 1979, Hans Jonas developed the case for a global ethics of responsibility (Jonas 1984). In the *Imperative of Responsibility* he wrote about how the future of humanity is in grave danger due to technological developments, in particular the creation of nuclear weapons. Jonas was, along with Arendt and Marcuse, one of Heidegger's German Jewish students. He shared Heidegger's fear of modern technology but unlike Heidegger he had good grounds for seeing what the real consequences could be rather than just a general suspicion of technology. While not a figure within the critical theory as such, he influenced critical theory. In the work of Karl-Otto Apel, a key figure in shaping the communicative turn in critical theory, his ideas played an important foundation in bringing critical theory in a more cosmopolitan direction, though Apel had arrived independently at his own theory of responsibility since the late 1960s.

Jonas argued that traditional ethics is unable to address the problem of our time in a situation in which technology has endangered the future of humanity. Traditional ethics is limited in scope to a relatively short time span, essentially to the lives of those living now. It is unable to address challenges that pertain to the wider future and to future generations; above all it cannot deal with problems that pertain to the very survival of humanity. What is called for is a new kind of ethics, one that is not addressed to the solitary individual. It must be collective. This is because the problems of our time pertain to all people and are cumulative, thus requiring a collective rather than an individual response. Another major difference today, he argued, that compels the need for collective responsibility is the vulnerability of nature. Because human life and the very possibility of society rests on nature, the destruction of nature for the first time raises moral questions. Jonas admits that the concern with the preservation of nature is for human survival and is thus anthropocentric. However, he does leave open the question of the rights of nature (p. 8). Until now, 'the presence of man in the world' was taken for granted, but it is now in question. This leads to a fundamental axiom that in turn leads to a moral imperative that 'there ought to be through all future time such a world fit for human habitation, and that it ought in all future time to be inhabited by a mankind worthy of the human name' (p. 10). Jonas, a philosopher in the Kantian tradition, argues the changed situation today requires abandoning Kant's famous Categorical Imperative[8] for a new one: 'Act such so that the effects of your action are compatible with the permanence of genuine human life;' or, expressed negatively, 'Act so that the effects of your action are not destructive of the future possibility of life' (p. 11). So, for Jonas the primary challenge is that we need to act today to ensure that there will be a future; we have a responsibility that 'there will be a future mankind – even if no descendants of ours are among them – and second, with a duty towards their condition, the quality of their life' (p. 40).

Much of his book is devoted to the analysis of the idea of collective responsibility to ensure the future existence of humanity. He sees this as more important than utopian ideas or ideas of progress. 'A critique of utopia has become necessary with the seeming possibility of its success' (p. 178). It is also an argument for an ethics of preservation, since the objective is to ensure that the conditions will exist for survival or future existence. The general principle is to protect 'the possibility of responsible action in the future – that is, for preserving its own preconditions' (p. 116). 'With every newborn child humanity begins anew, and in that sense also the responsibility for the continuation of mankind is involved' (p. 134). Once the future is viewed as an open and distant horizon, we have to accept limits to our capacity to know it and thus we cannot be responsible for concrete persons or engage in specific planning. We can be responsible only for the future of humanity as the 'overruling duty of collective human action in the age of technical civilization' (p. 136). With this stance, Jonas avoids the problems of utilitarianism, which is also future oriented, and some of the problems that Derek Parfit grappled with on our obligation to future people (Parfit 1984).

It is remarkable that Jonas, whose book was published in 1979, was already voicing concerns about the biosphere as integral to the survival of humanity (p. 138). His book can also be seen as a counter-argument to the pessimistic argument of Adorno and Horkheimer in *Dialectic of Enlightenment* [1944] that the Baconian program of the domination of nature by humanity as the source of its power can be reversed: 'the danger of disaster attending the Baconian ideal of power over nature through scientific technology arises not so much from any short-comings of its performance as from the magnitude of its success' (p. 140). *The Imperative of Responsibility* is one of the great philosophical works on the

---

8 'Act only according to that maxim whereby you can at the same time will that it should become a universal law.' According to this principle, the motive, not the outcome as in utilitarianism, determines what is moral.

need for future thinking. It has been very important in environmental philosophy and in shaping the cosmopolitan turn in critical theory.

The book nonetheless had its limits. The argument for collective responsibility, which it championed, had an unclear and unsatisfactory relation to individual responsibility. Jonas was not seeking to replace the latter with the former, but to make the case for a new conception of responsibility, which had to be collective. For this reason, the reception of Jonas's book in critical theory preferred to emphasize co-responsibility, to avoid this problem as well as some of the potentially authoritarian associations of collective morality (see Strydom 1999). This was also the aim of Karl-Otto Apel, who made an important contribution to the philosophical foundations of critical theory in the moral and political philosophy that he developed toward a 'discourse ethics' (Apel 1980a [1973]). Until his intervention, critical theory was primarily concerned with the apparently blocked nature of socio-cultural evolution, but other than in the social theory of Habermas, there was little of a systematic nature on how we should approach the future. Due in no small part to Hans Jonas's work, Apel developed independently a critical philosophy of the future when he wrote about the need for a macro ethics of responsibility (Apel 1987, 1990, 1993a, 1993b, 1996, 2001). In his work, he also corrected the tendency in Jonas to see the problem of the future exclusively in terms of survival. Jonas probably over-played the prospect of humanity being wiped out.[9]

In his assessment of Jonas's book, Apel argued that the task today is more than only the preservation of humanity (Apel 1987). Moreover, he sees the problems not entirely in terms of dangers coming from technology as such. Jonas undoubtedly remained too close to Heidegger's disdain for modernity and technology. But modern technology is not something that can be just walked away from. As the nuclear physicist Robert Oppenheimer, who was instrumental in the invention of the atomic bomb, was well aware that once atomic weapons were invented they could not be stopped but only controlled (Bird and Sherwin 2005). Jonas's position seemed to be that future progress must be stopped and we stay where we are so as not to make things worse and all that is needed in a collective ethics of global responsibility. Apel was undoubtedly correct in saying that preserving the existing state of affairs is not necessarily going to solve matters since it is that situation that has given rise to the problems, which will not simply go away. The challenge of macro-ethics for humanity is not then about the 'priority of the survival of humanity.' He argues furthermore that this position ultimately is no different from Social

---

9 Apel (1980b) did nonetheless remain fixed on the problem of the survival of humanity, which he tried to link to the problem of emancipation: 'the strategy for survival acquires its meaning through a long-term strategy for emancipation' (1980b: 282).

Darwinism, which is about survival and compatible with the neo-liberal political philosophy of F. A. Hayek. This, of course, was not Jonas's intention.

Jonas was clearly responding principally to the nuclear arms race and the prospect of the end of humanity as a result of nuclear war. It is probably the case that this led to his ecological concerns. This is a position that does not offer a satisfactory response to the ecological crisis, which is obviously not due to nuclear weapons. Apel, no less concerned with nuclear war, was more attuned to the emerging climate crisis, especially since the *Limits to Growth* publication in 1972 (Meadows *et al.* 1972): 'The ecological crisis shows us that nature, as a background presupposition for human productive forces and as the living-space for human beings, cannot be exploited and encumbered without limit; rather, as regards its utilizable resources, nature is in many respects limited; and, above all, as the ecosphere of man, nature is a vulnerable, functional system of equilibrium whose destruction affects the very conditions for the possibility of human life. To that extent there arises from the wholly novel challenge presented by the ecological crisis the following, equally novel, basic question for an ethic of responsibility: "Must we live differently in order even to survive?" ' (Apel 1987: 5–6).

Apel sees the Principle of Responsibility as expressing a new stage of moral consciousness that is now planetary: 'At issue here are rather a universalistic ethic of reason and a planetary macroethic in which the "internal morals" in many respects still taken for granted within national and other social systems of self-assertion would have to be transcended' (1987: 15). For Apel, what is needed is more than an ethics of responsibility but a universalistic global ethics: 'All previous types of rational, philosophical ethics, from Aristotle to Kant, fail to fulfil what has today become the indispensable function of a responsibility to the future because they still take their bearings by the unquestioned presupposition of a constant *conditio humana*. This is to say that these ethics do, indeed, postulate a principle of universalization valid for all human actions that can be brought into relation with one another in a given present; they do not, however, reckon with the irreversible, historical relation that human actions have to the future; in particular, they do not reckon with the futural relation for which we, in the age of the ecological crisis, are primarily responsible and which alters the *conditio humana* itself, namely, the relation of our collective technological actions to the future' (1987:15–6). As he put it elsewhere, with Kant, as an example of traditional ethics, the individual only had to look inwards to hear the moral voice tell them what to do. Today, there is no such easy solution (Apel 1993b). It is not just a shift from the individual to the collective level that is needed. A novel ethics of responsibility is required based on 'co-responsibility.' Now, while this must aspire to universal validity, such a universal global ethics is not so easily found in the form of a ready-made morality that can be appealed to that somehow transcends the great diversity of societies and cultures in the world today. Instead, he argues for a 'transcendental pragmatic conception of co-responsibility,' which is comprised of procedures and principles that are immanent in human communication.

His global ethics, a so-called 'discourse ethics' and related to deliberative politics, is procedural rather than substantive (in other words it is not based on cultural values or beliefs). It is not only on the level of advocacy or of a highly normative nature but is also demonstrable in innumerable debates and political action throughout the world. So, all that is left of ethics today in the absence of universal ethics are principles and procedures for conflict resolution. Apel grounds global ethics, as ethics more generally, in the fundamental fact of language (which includes the logical, linguistic, and semantic systems of references that make language possible) and the fact that human beings are communicating beings. This leads to a conception of ethics as produced by an argumentatively achieved rationality and is necessarily always open and future oriented. For Apel, we always need to presuppose an ideal situation, 'an ideal communication community,' even if this will never exist as a 'real communication community;' indeed, such ideal communication cannot exist as such but serves as regulative principle or a meta reference that makes possible ethics.

Herein lies a critical theory of the future: 'in the real, human community of communication the ideal community of communication must always remain to be realized progressively' (1987: 24). This is because of the inescapable fact that ethics – along with politics in so far as it is guided by ethics – in modern society has become a matter of interpreting from reference systems (such as law, universal moral principles, *etc.*) but always within specific social contexts. The result is necessarily something elusive when it comes to making particular judgments and actions. The outcome is perpetually pushed into the future. The ideal can be pursued but never realized.

Unlike Jonas, he does not see any ready-made solution to the problem of how we should prepare for the future. It cannot be found in some kind of absolute body of knowledge or something inherited from the past. It is as much a project to achieve in the future as something that actually exists. The principle of co-responsibility is rather akin to Kant's Regulative Ideas, which he says have been much misunderstood: "Regulative ideas," in our context, are normative principles of practical reason which are binding on action in the sense that they define obligations and provide guidance for the long-term, approximative realization of an ideal. At the same time, however, they give expression to the insight that nothing which can be experienced in time can ever fully accord with the ideal. In his brief writings on the philosophy of history, Kant actually tried, with the help of this concept, to conceive the concrete relation to time exhibited by his ethical principles, albeit these principles had first been stated in an exclusively abstract manner;

in this sense, he suggested in particular a principle of ethically determined progress that entails no assured prescience concerning the course that future history
can actually be expected to follow' (p. 25).

We have here a clear sense of future possibility as always indeterminate; it
may arise from moral ideas and principles that are never fully complete but
may open up new paths depending on how they are taken up. There is then necessarily something always open to the pursuit of universal or global ethics giving to
it a certain utopian dimension. Apel, against Jonas, defends the utopian imagination as relevant to his conception of a new planetary ethics, as for instance in '…
the tendency to be ahead of oneself, as it were, in the contrafactual anticipation of
the ethical ideal, an anticipation that manifests itself in every serious attempt to
address the community of argumentation. In thus arguing with respect to the
properly human utopian dimension, I do not even mention the more harmless,
so-called utopian projects that will later be shown capable of realization' (p. 26).
These ideals, as in utopian ideals, serve as counter-factuals to the present, thereby
also opening up alternative paths.

Critical Cosmopolitanism and the Idea of the Future

Apel and Jonas established a foundation within critical theory for cosmopolitanism, which is also based on a weak notion of universality understood more as
the suspension of one's own beliefs in order to achieve a consensual agreement
that can never be absolute or fully realized. The conception of cosmopolitanism
that is at work in their writings can be characterized as critical cosmopolitanism
since it requires a transformation of the present. It is underpinned by the recognition of the need for a global ethics to address the problems of our time, which
cannot be addressed by traditional notions of ethics and politics that propose na-
tion-states as the main actors in the world. In the footsteps of Kant, who in *Perpetual Peace* [1795] established the modern idea of cosmopolitanism as a 'principle of
hospitality,' Apel argued for a universal ethics to address global problems. Such an
ethics is not simply an ideal; it is also engrained in law and politics today such that
it can no longer be ignored. It is in fact itself a 'second order globalization' (Apel
2000). In this sense, cosmopolitanism can be seen as a global political movement
that is also a critique of globalization; it counter-acts the dominance of global capitalism. However, it is also incomplete and for this reason it is future oriented.

Cosmopolitanism is a condition of openness to the world; that is, it is about the opening or expansion of horizons.[10] The logic of cosmopolitanism comes into play in the encounter of the Self with the Other whereby a shift in self-understanding takes place. It accords with the logic of dialog, since dialog entails incorporating the perspective of the other. This hermeneutic understanding of cosmopolitanism is also critical in that it goes beyond mere understanding the other to self-problematization and a questioning of what was previously taken for granted. In that sense, a cosmopolitan attitude entails a re-evaluation of the self.

With its orientation toward new ways of seeing the world, self and other, cosmopolitanism also corresponds to the communicative theory of society and the idea in the work of Apel and Habermas of the force of argument. While pointing toward the future, critical cosmopolitanism differs from purely normative theories of cosmopolitanism or those that see it as an aspiration for some kind of a supranational or world state. It seeks the transformation of the present but it is rooted in social reality in terms of people's experiences, identities, values, solidarities, and social struggles.

Cosmopolitanism was once only an ideal, but it became increasingly anchored in law and politics since 1945, as reflected in the UN Declaration of Human Rights in 1948, the Antarctic Treaty in 1959, the notion of Crimes Against Humanity, and more recently with the world-wide acceptance of the need to reduce global warming. It has a special concern with global justice and the need for a global ethics, but it is not the equivalent of internationalism or transnationalism. Cosmopolitanism furthermore in this sense can be seen as a critique of both nationalism and globalization. The cosmopolitan condition emerges out of the logic of the encounter, exchange, and dialog but always in ways that lead to self-transformation.

In line with the transcendental reasoning of critical theory, cosmopolitanism is embedded in the social world and compels a reaching beyond what is given. It is expressed in various institutional forms, such as law and international organizations, and is an ideal that many organizations and movements pursue. Cosmopolitanism, like the concept of the future, is therefore a multileveled concept, embodying universalist ideas and carried forward by a plethora of cultural models, social practices, and institutions. As critical theory since Habermas and Apel has demonstrated, the structures and forms of consciousness that enable society to transcend the given are immanent in society in various forms, such as ideals, imaginaries, and goals, while at the same time, such forms of consciousness are grounded in higher level and more abstract ideas that always contain an excess beyond any given interpretation. In this way, future possibility is always necessarily

---

10 This account of cosmopolitanism is necessarily brief. See Delanty (2009) and Delanty (2019).

open. This is also the only meaningful way to understand the concept of hope, from Kant to Benjamin and Adorno.

Despite these important developments in theorizing the future, the communicative approach adopted by Apel and Habermas leaves room for further advancement. Despite Habermas's reconstruction of modern sociological theory, there is an unsatisfactory sociological conceptualization of the future. Especially in Apel's writings, it is almost as if the force of reason compels social actors to pursue future goals in light of the demands of reason. Missing from their theories is a developed sense of the macro-level of society wherein a plurality of cultural models provide social actors in the 'here and the now' with general interpretative frameworks that are taken up by them in manifold ways in pursuing political projects and other goals. But the future is never reducible to the micro/meso levels of social action; it emerges from the more general cultural level. The future is in itself a cultural model of a general and abstract nature, but it is also present in a plurality of other cultural models that are future oriented (as for example cosmopolitanism, democracy, recognition, and not to be excluded some religious ideas). In this light, the future unfolds along three levels: a meta level, a macro level, and a meso/micro level. It is guided by universal ideas of reason that transcend the social world and constitute a meta level; it is most importantly a cultural model impregnated by reason, which in turn offers resources for a plethora of future-oriented political projects on the meso level (Strydom 2024).

It should be stressed that in this three-fold conception of the future with the macro and micro as the key levels, the meta level of ideas of reason is not a 'supra level', but 'transcendental' in the sense of necessary presuppositions.

Conclusion: Cultural Models and the Future as Possibility

In this account of critical theory I have emphasized its distinctive approach to the future. From a broadly defined emancipatory intention to see the future as offering hope for the present, it preserved a link with a specific understanding of utopianism as the imagination of an ideal alternative that could be realized at least in principle if a suitable political project emerged. But it goes beyond utopianism as such, which is just one dimension of an approach to social analysis that sees future possibilities as emerging from the present. There are at least three main points to make concerning this.

The first is that in critical theory the human subject is conceived in a way that it incorporates a conscious orientation to the future. This is more than just practices that take place in the meso order of society (as in political movements or various kinds of future-oriented agency). The orientation to the future is engrained in the macro level of society in terms of the learning outcomes of history and in cultural models but also extends to the meta level. The present is imbued with potentials that open up future possibilities. These derive from higher-level ideas that provide sources of direction and reference. As Strydom has put it: 'The future discloses the world, formally, though a complex of cognitive order concepts and principles and, substantively, through a particular situation, offering anticipatory ideal-*cum*-goal orientation complexes in the of cultural models able to lead and structure constructive activities' (Strydom 2023:165). This view implies a multileveled concept of the future, embodying ideas that transcend social life while also being taken up by social actors on different levels, ranging from ideals, imaginaries, and political goals or programs. Conceptually, the future can be thought of as the coming into being of what exceeds that which is presently actualized in the logic of current forms of social life. It thus concerns what is potential and possible.

A theory of the future needs to consider that the future is not only related to social and political possibility, but it is also relevant to the natural world, as in theories of time in physics, as discussed in Chapter Two, and that human life is ultimately part of nature. For this reason, the future should be seen as having both a constitutive dimension in making the human and the natural worlds, as well as a conscious and unconscious orientation. It cannot entirely be an expression of freedom or a product of the social world. The meta level includes the basic concepts and principles that govern the natural objective world. For example, both chance (indeterminacy) and necessity ensure that the future can never be entirely controlled or known by the present; its openness will always be contingent on future facts and events.

The emphasis on possibility does not mean that everything that is possible will be actualized or that everything that is potential will be possible. Many things are potential, but not everything that is potentially possible will become an actual possibility. In conceptual terms, there is a graduated logic of emergence in how something that is latent, becomes actual, leading to further potential outcomes that open up realizable possibilities. Possibilities emerge from potentialities. For example, reducing carbon dioxide and other greenhouse gases is now a real possibility, since the Paris Agreement in 2015 it has been a goal of many governments. A cure for cancer is not yet a possibility but is a potential development that may become possible in the future.

In a sense, possibility once realized ceases to be a possibility. The creation of nuclear weapons was known to be possible in 1940 but after the Trinity Test in July 1945 what was possible became a reality. Possibility thus pertains only to the not-yet.

Certain aspects of future possibility are, in the language of philosophy, in the realm of 'necessity,' in the sense that they cannot be avoided. Relevant there are ideas and principles such as truth, veracity, justice, freedom, and authenticity (in Kant's sense of being transcendental, i. e. necessary presuppositions or conditions of possibility). Such ideas, which reside in the human capabilities and cognition, always point beyond any given attempt to realize them and are universal. So, for example, the idea of democracy always leads to demands for more democracy; the pursuit of rights in one area opens up avenues for rights in another area. Once an idea forms, it leads to indeterminate possibilities arising from the ideals and goals it may open up.

Then, there are latent forces that are not yet actual and may become so and thus open up further potentials of future possibility. So, the future is not just about the pursuit of goals – that is, the realization of possibilities – it is also about the unharnessed potentialities of the present and also those that are hidden or latent. In this view, the future is not just something cut off from the present but derives from structures and forces that are ingrained in the present, while at the same time transcends the present. These logics are best seen in terms of the macro and the meso-micro order of society, the level of general cultural models and the level of social action. The latter never exhausts the content of the former, which in turn is shaped by higher meta principles. In sum, the future emerges from the modalities of the present as well as from the organic endowment of human beings that inclines them to think in terms of future possibility.

Second, from a critical theory perspective, the focus is very much on crises and major social transformation. Such crises might be tipping points or permacrises, concatenations of various crises, which may accelerate change already underway and serve as a catalyst of major social transformation. Critical moments create spaces of possibilities when that which was only a latent or a potential becomes a source of newness. Not every crisis is significant and leads to a major social transformation. A crisis that leads to a major social transformation is marked by developments that have some normative and qualitative significance in terms of vision of future possibility, as in the example of what Apel called co-responsibility. So, something more than social change is involved in the making of future possibilities. It will entail a transformation in the structures of society, in particular structures of consciousness, as in the example of the shift from an individual concept of responsibility to co-responsibility.

Third, following from the focus on crises as the source of change leading to future developments, critical theory places special emphasis on social struggles. This follows from the dialectical conception of reality as comprised of the constant working out of contradictions in social reality, the clash of subjective aspiration and objective reality, and the pursuit of alternatives. Social reality, society as normally understood, is never complete or given but is always being produced in the meso order of contexts of struggle. It follows from this that the horizon of the future is constantly being pushed back but is also perpetually present.

This idea accords with Henri Bergson's notion of reality as a continuous process of creativity, but places a stronger emphasis on social struggles and collective action. Adorno was highly critical of Bergson's conception of time, which he saw as 'De-temporalized' due to the absence of dialectics in '*le temps durée*' (Adorno 1973: 333–4).

Axel Honneth in his theory of recognition thus looks at social struggles of recognition as the key conflicts that will shape contemporary societies (Honneth 1996). In this approach, recognition serves as a general cultural model that is shaped by higher principles of reason. While the recognition paradigm suffers from the limitation that in it the future is effectively a continuation of the present, entailing only limited transformation (since struggles for recognition can mostly be realized within the structures of contemporary society), it nonetheless entails an important conception of micro order struggles drawing their inspiration from the cultural model of recognition.

Alain Touraine, from a social movement perspective, wrote about the struggle to control historicity or 'the self-production of society' and gave a special place to cultural models that provide social actors with interpretive resources (Touraine 1977). In a similar key, Habermas emphasized the clash between life-world and system whereby social movements, as the carriers of reason, act as the agents of alternatives to the present.

The account of critical theory given in this chapter draws attention to a range of different conceptions of the future than those that are to be found in other approaches. It thus differs from phenomenological approaches in going beyond the micro level of practices and imaginaries as the source of future possibility. It also shows the shortcoming of complexity theory and the conceptualization of the future only in terms of risk. Critical theory tells us why we need a theory of the future, what its transcendental and macro-level sources are and its modalities.

References

Adorno, T. W. 1973. [1966] *Negative Dialectics*. London: Routledge.
Adorno, T. W. 1998a. [1969] 'Progress.' In: *Critical Models: Interventions and Catchwords.* New York: Columbia University Press.
Adorno, T. 1998b. [1959] 'What Does Coming to Terms with the Past Mean?' In: *Critical Models: Interventions and Catchwords.* New York: Columbia University Press.
Adorno, T. W. 1998c. 'On Subject and Object.' In: *Critical Models: Interventions and Catchwords.* New York: Columbia University Press.

Adorno, T. W. 2005. [1955] *Minima Moralia: Reflections from Damaged Life.* London: Verso.

Apel, K.-O. 1980a. [1973] *Towards a Transformation of Philosophy.* London: Routledge, Kegan & Paul.

Apel, K.-O. 1980b. 'The a *priori* of the Communication Community and the Foundations of the Ethics: The Problem of a Rational Foundation of Ethics in the Scientific Age.' In: *Towards a Transformation of Philosophy.* London: Routledge, Kegan & Paul.

Apel, K.-O. 1987. 'The Problem of a Macroethic of Responsibility to the Future in the Crisis of Technological Civilization: An Attempt to Come to Terms with Hans Jonas's "Principle of Responsibility".' *Man and World*, 20 (1): 3–40.

Apel, K-O. 1990. 'The Problem of a Universalistic Macroethics of Co-Responsibility.' In: Griffioen, S. (ed.) *What Right Does Ethics Have?* Amsterdam: VU University Press.

Apel, K-O. 1993a. 'How to Ground a Universalistic Ethics of Co-Responsibility for the Effects of Collective Actions and Activities.' *Philosophica*, 52 (2): 9–29.

Apel, K.-O. 1993b. 'Discourse Ethics as a Response to the Novel Challenges of Today's Reality to Coresponsibility.' *The Journal of Religion*, 73 (4): 496–513.

Apel, K-O. 1996. 'A Planetary Macroethics for Humankind: The Need, the Apparent Difficulty and the Eventual Possibility.' *Karl-Otto Apel: Selected Essays.* Vol. 2. New Jersey: Humanities Press.

Apel, K.-O. 2000. 'Globalization and the Need for Universal Ethics.' *European Journal of Social Theory*, 3 (2): 137–55.

Apel, K.-O. 2001. 'On the relationship between Ethics, International Law and Politico-Military Strategy in Our Time: A Philosophical Retrospective on the Kosovo Conflict.' *European Journal of Social Theory*, 4 (1): 29–39.

Benjamin, W. 1970a. 'Theses on the Philosophy of History.' *Illuminations.* London: Fontana.

Benjamin, W. 1970b. 'On Some Motifs in Baudelaire.' *Illuminations.* London: Fontana.

Benjamin, W. 1978. 'A Berlin Chronicle.' In: *Reflections.* New York: Schocken Books.

Benjamin, W. 1999. *The Arcades Project.* Cambridge, MASS: Harvard University Press.

Benjamin, W. 2006. *A Berlin Childhood Around 1900.* Cambridge, MASS: Harvard University Press.

Bird, K. and Sherwin, M. 2005. *American Prometheus: The Triumph and Tragedy of Robert J. Oppenheimer.* London: Atlantic Books.

Bloch. E. 1995. [1938–47] *The Principle of Hope.* 3 vols. Cambridge, MASS.: MIT University Press.

Bloeser, C. 2022. 'Hope.' Standford Encyclopedia of Philosophy.' https://plato.stanford.edu/entries/hope/

Delanty, G. 2009. *The Cosmopolitan Imagination: The Renewal of Critical Theory.* Cambridge: Cambridge University Press.

Delanty, G. 2019. (ed.) *Routledge International Handbook of Cosmopolitan Studies.* 2nd Edition. London: Routledge.

Delanty, G. 2021. *Critical Theory and Social Transformation.* London: Routledge.

Eckersley, R. 1990. 'Habermas and Green Political Thought.' *Theory and Society*, 19: 739–76.

Gidley, J. 2017. *The Future.* Oxford: Oxford University Press.

Goldman, L. 2023. *The Principle of Political Hope: Progress, Action and Democracy.* Oxford: Oxford University Press.

Habermas, J. 1972. [1968] *Knowledge and Human Interests.* London: Heinemann.

Habermas, J. 1975. [1973] *Legitimation Crisis.* Boston: Beacon Press.

Habermas, J. 1979. *Communication and the Evolution of Society.* London: Heinemann.

Habermas, J. 1984 and 1987. [1981] *The Theory of Communicative Action*, vols 1 and 2. London: Polity Press.

Habermas, J. 1987. [1985] *The Philosophical Discourse of Modernity.* Cambridge: Polity Press.

Habermas, J. 1994. [1991] 'The Past as Future.' In: *The Past as Future. Interviews by Max Haller.* Cambridge: Polity Press.

Habermas, J. 1997. [1992] *Between Facts and Norms.* Cambridge: Cambridge University Press.

Habermas, J. 2002. 'Transcendence from Within.' In: *Religion and Rationality.* Cambridge: Polity Press.

Habermas, J. 2003. *The Future of Human Nature.* Cambridge: Polity Press.

Honneth, A. 1996. [1992] *The Struggle for Recognition: The Moral Grammar of Social Conflicts.* Cambridge: Polity Press.

Hudson, W. 1982. *The Marxist Philosophy of Ernst Bloch.* London: Palgrave.

Jay, M. 1996/1973. *The Dialectical Imagination: A History of the Frankfurt School and the Institute of Social Research, 1923 – 1950.* London: Heinemann.

Jay, M. 2016. *Reason after its Demise.* Madison: University of Wisconsin Press.

Jonas, H. 1984. [1979] *The Imperative of Responsibility: In Search of an Ethics for the Technological Age.* Chicago: University of Chicago Press.

Kant, I. 1970. [1787 second edition] *Critique of Pure Reason.* Translated by Norman Kempton Smith. London: Macmillan.

Kant, I. 1978. [1798] *Anthropology from a Pragmatic Point of View.* Translated by V. L. Dowell. Carbondale: Southern Illinois University Press.

Kant, I. 1991a. [1795] 'Perpetual Peace.' In: *Kant: Political Writings.* Translated by H. B. Nisbet and edited by H. Reis. Cambridge: Cambridge University Press.

Kant, I. 1991b. [1798] 'A Renewed Attempt to Answer the Question: "Is the Human Race Continually Improving.' In: *Kant: Political Writings.* Translated by H. B. Nisbet and edited by H. Reis. Cambridge: Cambridge University Press.

Kant, I. 1991c. [1798] 'What is Enlightenment?.' In: *Kant: Political Writings*, Translated by H. B. Nisbet and edited by H. Reis. Cambridge: Cambridge University Press.

Kant, I. 2015. [1788] *The Critique of Practical Reason.* Cambridge: Cambridge University Press.

Kompridis, N. 2006. *Critique and Disclosure: Critical Theory between Past and Future.* Cambridge, MASS.: MIT Press.

Marcuse, H. 1964. *One Dimensional Man.* London: Routledge & Kegan Paul.

Marcuse, H. 1971. [1941] *Reason and Revolution.* London: Routledge & Kegan Paul.

Meadows, D., Meadows, D., Randers, W., and Behrends III, W. 1972. *The Limits to Growth: A Report for the Club of Rome's Project on the Predicament of Mankind.* New York: Universe Books.

Parfit, D. 1984. *Reasons and Persons.* Oxford: Oxford University Press.

Speight, C. A. 2021. 'Kant and Benjamin on Hope, History, and the Task of Interpretation.' In: Wilford, P. and Stoner, S. A. (eds.), *Kant and the Possibility of Progress.* Philadelphia: University of Pennsylvania Press.

Strydom, P. 1999. 'The Challenge of Responsibility for Sociology.' *Current Sociology,* 47 (3): 65 – 82.

Strydom, P. 2011. *Contemporary Critical Theory: Theory and Methodology.* London: Routledge.

Strydom, P. 2020. 'On the Origins of the Left-Hegelian Concept of Immanent-Transcendence: Reflections on the Background of Classical Sociology.' *Journal of Classical Sociology,* 20 (1): 3 – 21.

Strydom, P. 2023. 'The Critical Theory of Society: From its Young Hegelian Core to the Key Concept of Possibility.' *European Journal of Social Theory,* 26 (2): 153 – 79.

Touraine, A. 1977. *The Self-Production of Society.* Chicago: University of Chicago Press.

Vogel, S. 1996. *Against Nature: The Concept of Nature in Critical Theory.* New York: State University of New York Press.

Chapter Seven
Conclusion: In The Shadow of the Future

In this concluding chapter, I address questions that have been raised but not fully answered in the preceding chapters. These concern a number of substantive topics, some of which fall beyond the scope of a book on the conceptual aspects of the future but nonetheless need to be addressed at least in a rudimentary outline. I will offer a consideration of these topics in what follows, addressing four main questions. The first is, do we actually need a theory of the future? In answering this question I offer a summary of the main elements of the theory of the future developed in the course of this book. Second, are we already in a new historical era? Third, is AI leading to a posthuman future, especially in light of the possible emergence of AGI? This concerns the related question of how open is the future. Finally, how should we see struggles for the future today?

Do We Need a Theory of the Future?

The skeptical reader may conclude that the idea of the future is irrelevant or simply too confused to be a useful or legitimate concept. I hope to have demonstrated that despite the diversity of conceptions of the future it is an important and necessary concept. That it is highly contested should not be a surprise, as almost every concept in social and political science is contested.

As noted in Chapter One a pervasive tendency in postmodernist thought from the 1960s was skepticism of the idea of the future, as a residue of now discredited Enlightenment thinking that proclaimed an inner plan to history or a view of historical time that sees us moving from the past through the present to a sense of the future that will realize the aspirations of the past. We can now see that this is not a warranted objection, as it is a very one-sided account of modernity, which includes various countercurrents. The rejection of the future also led to a view of an extended present, in effect reducing the future to the present. The consequence of postmodern theory was not anything that offered a perspective on the future of humanity but a concern with the past as if rethinking the past would be sufficient for our present.

Another objection to the relevance of the idea of the future could be the sociological argument that it does not offer anything different from a theory of social change. The fact that society is always in a constant process of change means that there is necessarily a temporal movement. We can call that movement history. So, it could be said that because of the fact that things change we do not need a

https://doi.org/10.1515/9783111240602-008

notion of the future as such. On the level of change, this could easily be accommo-
dated in a wider conception of continuity. Not everything changes; some things remain relatively unchanged over long periods, and rarely does everything change at
the same time. It is not too difficult to find examples of periods when little change
took place, as in long periods of stagnation. Now, a perspective on major social
transformation offers a somewhat different view of change, when the settled
structures collapse and new ones emerge. Such a perspective requires a concept
of the future.

The very notion of a major social transformation, as argued at the end of the
previous chapter, entails precisely an orientation to the future since it will involve
a transformation in structures of consciousness and the unavoidable pursuit of alternatives. Without a theory of the future we have no way of making sense of such
transformations when new modes of knowledge, sensibility, and self-interpretation emerge. As argued throughout this book, the future is not exclusively a temporal category but is embroiled in other dimensions of society and is integral to
the human condition. A society that does not have a sense of its future is moribund.

There is enough evidence to warrant the claim that human beings, probably
unlike other forms of life, could not live without a sense of the future. So, the future is also existential. As Heidegger showed in *Being and Time*, it is part of human
existence, which is based on forms of waiting, as expectation and anticipation, and
ultimately the anticipation of death (see Chapter Four). Samuel Beckett's 1953 play
Waiting for Godot also made the concept of waiting central to the human condition. Waiting is prior to the experience of time and space, which in his enigmatic
play are frozen and meaningless. Despite the remorseless passage of time, in another sense nothing happens and life is just waiting. Beckett's suggestion is that
there is always hope for redemption.

Heidegger and Beckett encourage us to see human beings as more oriented to
the future than to the past and it is this that gives them the sense of life as perpetual waiting. However, for Beckett in contrast to Heidegger, waiting is not primarily
about the anticipation of death but an endless condition, since time stretches out
infinitely. Our collective past is relatively short in face of a potentially infinite future of humanity.

I have also stressed that the future is spatial, in the sense that it exists in a
social and historical context and that it is part of the present. This accounts for
the tension that exists between the present and the future. People live in the present; it is where their daily life is led, but they are oriented toward the future in
ways that transcend their daily pursuits and goals. This corresponds to a tension
between what philosophers have called being and existence, with being encompassing a deeper sense of existence beyond what is manifest in the present. For

de Beauvoir in an essay in 1947, both correspond to different notions of the future (de Beauvoir 1949).

A conclusion of this book drawn from the reflections on the literature discussed is that the future is an idea that does not go away – in that sense it is a meta idea. The idea of the future is in the first instance an idea of *the future* rather than a specific view of the future (the future of capitalism, the future of the environment, the future of democracy). Kant's critical philosophy gives the best way of understanding this, namely the idea that the future, while not strictly speaking an idea of reason, exists independently of interpretations of it. It is therefore more akin to a meta concept that is based on a 'transcendental subject,' namely a conception of humanity consisting of engrained attributes and natural endowments that enable it to orient itself in the world around abstract ideas and principles which do not in themselves produce knowledge but provide the necessary means of acquiring knowledge (Strydom 2023). However, the idea of the future is more fully evident as a general cultural model within the macro level of society. It offers an orientation for acting and thinking by providing general interpretive frames of reference. It follows from this that there will necessarily be many different interpretations of it. These interpretations are expressed as cultural models in that they are not reducible to more specific appropriations. It also follows that not all interpretations of the future are good or even defensible. It is not a normative concept as such, but it does raise normative questions, such as what kind of a future world do we want? In this respect, Kant's famous question, discussed in the previous chapter, is still relevant, 'for what should we hope?'

The argument put forward here emphasizes the cognitive and epistemic nature of the idea of the future, since it always entails knowledge claims. The most obvious ones entail prediction or forecasting. Prophecies are also epistemic claims. Both predictions and prophecies, as different as they are, tend to be concerned with the very near future. Prophecies, which have made a comeback today, in the form of popular futurist cultures of Armageddon, evangelical proclamations of the Apocalypse, and conspiracy theories, locate end times scenarios already in the present, the time of the Now. What is often lost is the distant future, but also the very idea of the future, namely, what is it to speak of the future?

I have argued for a conception of the future in yet broader terms of potentiality and possibility. In the most fundamental sense, I see the future as a form of transcendence; it concerns the way the present is transcended. This perspective somewhat shifts the focus away from the question of timespans, as in when does the future begin? The future has already begun insofar as it is a category of perception and a cultural model of interpretation. In phenomenological terms, the future is something we experience or perceive, but it is more than that; as a cultural model, it also exerts a structuring effect on thought and action

(Strydom 2023). It is present on the macro level order of society and feels its way into the micro- and meso order, the sphere of social action.

Human beings are the only beings who have created transcendental structures, that is, structures or forms of thought or reason that exist independently of their actual empirical forms (as reflected in aesthetic and intellectual creations, in science, and spiritual forms). The ideas of truth, freedom, or justice are not exhausted by specific attempts to embody them. As is well established in philosophy, systems of reference transcend their interpretation by providing them with their conditions of possibility. This is also the case with the idea of the future, which also contains a relation to the meta level of reason.

As a contribution to a critical sociology of the future, this book is also a historical and philosophical hermeneutics of the future. The future is an interpretative category and calls for a critical hermeneutics. This is also why I have argued that purely phenomenological approaches are insufficient, for it is also necessary to identify the sources of transcendence, which do not entirely reside in the domain of experience. This perspective, informed by critical theory and the tradition of thought going back to Kant, sees social actors pursuing future-oriented goals and ideals, which have their source in structures and concepts that are not reducible to their concrete expressions.

As an open-ended interpretive category, the future cannot be reduced to the idea of progress or seen only in terms of catastrophe, which are specific images or imaginaries of the future. Theories of the future in terms of complexity are also unable to grasp the future as a field of possibilities emerging from the potentials of the present. While such approaches have the merit of drawing attention to limits of the idea of an open future, they suffer from a concern largely with problem-solving and risk probabilities. Social actors are necessarily involved in the selection and pursuit of goals that in turn derive from a variety of cultural models that provide ideals and imaginaries. There is also the possibility of new goals or new interpretations of existing goals leading to further routes to the future. As argued in the previous chapter, an adequate theory of the future needs to span the meta order (ideas and principles that transcend the empirical world), the macro order (general cultural models), and the meso and micro order (what social actors do as collective agents or as individuals) of society. This necessarily requires going beyond looking at social actors' own self-understanding. Uncertainty, indeterminacy, and complexity are now much more a feature of the future and a challenge to the modes of knowledge fostered by the Enlightenment. This shift in our temporal sensibility is underpinned by spatial transformation as reflected in the shift away from a world dominated by the West. In this emerging post-western world, there is greater instability, in capitalism, in geo-politics, and in the climate, and as a result there are increased threats to humanity, from nuclear war to pandemics, AI spiraling out of control and ecological destruction.

I proceed in what follows with some further reflections around three additional questions on how we should view the future today in the context of our historical present.

Are we already in a New Historical Era?

A second question that arises is a temporal one, namely, are we entering a new historical era today? Throughout history, the future was always shaped by major shifts in consciousness, which lead to new ways of seeing the world and its future direction. The Axial Age, the period around 800 BCE to 200 AD when the major world religions arose, opened up the experience of transcendence and abstract thought. This period led to fundamentally novel ways of seeing the world through new ideas in the spheres of religion, science and the arts. Karl Jaspers, in a famous book, *The Origin and Goal of History*, argued that human self-understanding emerged in this period around universalistic ideas that laid the foundations for the future by asserting human potentiality to change the world (Jaspers 2021 [1953/1947]). The scientific revolution of the seventeenth century to the French and American revolutions and the revolutions that they inspired in the following centuries was a period in which a second major shift in consciousness took shape, leading to modernity and its visions of the future. Like the first, this was not a singular movement but was highly variated with different world models. All of these entailed future projections and were tied to spiritual transformations in the understanding of the self and its relation to the world. Today, it is possible to speak of a third epochal shift in consciousness that has been emerging as a result of the crisis of what can generally be referred to as modernity. Unlike the previous two epochal shifts, the current one is characterized by a sense of fear and uncertainty and, in contrast to the outlook of modernity, it lacks confidence that the future will be both new and better. As such, it is only with some qualifications that one can speak of an epochal shift in consciousness, given that at most what we are witnessing is a rescue mission seeking the conservation of the planet rather than the creation of something new. Yet, a sense of disjuncture is present.

The Axial Age and the rise of modernity were both characterized by a strong sense of universalistic ideas, even if these all had cultural and civilizational-specific forms (Bellah and Joas 2012). The rise of the idea of the future and its various crystallizations was an outcome of these movements that all had deep spiritual roots. Karl Jaspers explored the significance of the Axial Age for the idea of the future and found in that time the seeds of transcendence (see Madsen 2012).

While the consequences of the Axial Age were momentous, as argued in this book, the idea of the future, while having premodern antecedents, is nonetheless primarily a modern idea (see Chapters Three and Four). The Axial Age thesis locates the fundamental rupture in history in antiquity, thus reducing the modern breakthrough. It is still possible to agree with Karl Jaspers' insight that the origins of transcendence emerged in the Axial Age, while modernity expanded on these and found new sources, as in reason, the autonomy of the individual, the openness of the future. Today, it is possible to see something of a similar nature going on comparable to these earlier revolutions in consciousness. The idea of the future was always related to the ability of the human mind to grasp the unity of the human and natural world, whereby a space was created for new ideas and in particular for novel ideas of the future. Such ideas produced innovative models for thinking about the world, as in the notion of the rights and dignity of human beings, but also stimulated spiritual responses to the human predicament.

Whether a new epoch of a comparable nature has begun is in part a question of where we locate the point of rupture and its major expressions. It is difficult to avoid the conclusion that our present time is one of major rupture. It leads to a sense of the future as full of uncertainty. It is possible to view this rupture in two ways. As discussed in Chapter Two, the Great Acceleration thesis sees the Anthropocene – the era of human-induced climate change – as commencing in the period after 1945, with an exponential rise in greenhouse gases, which gained increased momentum from the mid-1970s. The point of major rupture probably begins there, but in combination with other crisis tendencies that became apparent since the mid-1970s, we can see the genesis of a permacrisis by around 2010, with the financial crisis of 2007–8 leading to much rethinking about the nature of capitalism and financial markets.

In the longer perspective of history, this periodization is very short and we are not in possession of the hindsight that would be required to know when the present time can be termed a historical period. Yet, all evidence does seem to suggest that since around 2010 the paths of separate crises merged, leading to a significant crisis of stability. Of course, these crises were never entirely separate, since the climate crisis is obviously related to the economic model of continuous growth and population increase and, consequently, related to demands for more and more energy. But the crisis tendencies were for long perceived as relatively separate. This is no longer the case. The climate crisis, which has been long in the making, has now merged with several other crises, producing a mega crisis as a result of a concatenation of crises and tipping points. The most obvious expression of this situation is that, for the first time, there is general consensus that the economic model of perpetual growth is no longer sustainable if human societies are to have a future. Beyond that agreement there is little consensus other than on the need to reduce greenhouse gasses and some progress has been made in that direction. It is an open question whether ecological awareness today amounts to a major shift in consciousness to an extent that it leads to effective policies that constitute a turning point in the history of civilization in reversing what is now clear: the detrimental use of fossil fuels for energy. To answer this question we would need to do a thought experiment, as in the genre of science fiction, and look back at our historical present from a future vantage point, of perhaps a few centuries from now. More than this, it is also a questioning of the very foundations of civilization, which from an early stage began the fateful path of carbon consumption, unknowing that in so doing it was endangering the long-term future of human societies.

Other expressions of the permacrisis of the present include disease and war. The Covid-19 pandemic, discussed in Chapter Two, has been seen as a global crisis that has deeply defined the present time. The pandemic itself has probably not led to major long-term societal change, whether good or bad; for it to do so it would have to intersect with other critical moments, as in for example the climate crisis, the crisis in liberal democracy and the rise of authoritarianism, economic crisis. In these examples, there are several tipping points. However, it remains inconclusive what the long-term outcomes will be. For now, it seems Covid-19 has become 'normalized' and the crisis did not lead to the collapse of liberal democracy but accelerated change that was already on the way, as is the nature of work and an increased datification. It could perhaps be seen as a potentially dangerous experiment with emergency government as a permanent feature of the state today (see Delanty 2021). But there is an important difference between short-term and long-term control. It seems to be the case that democracies are more successful in long-term control of pandemics, as is clear from the situation in China once its zero Covid policy failed. Democracies are pulled in different directions by the need to protect liberty and provide security, which includes protection from infectious diseases. Resolving this tension is critical for the future and this can only be done through public deliberation rather than rule by experts or excessive securitization and secrecy.

It is now clear that a pandemic is entangled in almost every aspect of society and, as a result, it is not easy to separate the health issue from a vast range of social, political, and economic processes: since the lockdown was also a shutdown, it unleashed all kinds of unintended effects. In view of the likelihood of more pandemics, coming from as yet unknown viruses, liberal democracies will need to learn to respond to such events rather than waiting for them to happen. Finally, a pandemic is by definition global, so it can't be controlled nationally except for short periods of time. This means that there is a vital need for greater global cooperation. But with the world drifting toward increased authoritarianism that will be difficult.

This leads to the question of war. The aftermath of the pandemic was a war that on one level was a regional war with Russia invading Ukraine in February 2022. It soon became clear that this was a global event that has fundamentally changed global geopolitics in far-reaching ways. The Russo-Ukraine war has led to a serious wakening call to the reality of war as a seemingly permanent feature of modernity. The war reveals a deep historical fissure that goes back to the break-up of the USSR which led to the unfolding of not just different, but what became for historically contingent reasons incompatible models of modernity. The signs are currently pointing in the direction of a growing drift toward a post-western world order with the liberal democracies of the West on the one side and, on the other, an augmented consolidation of authoritarian states. The loss of Ukrainian subservience to the Russian Federation has pushed the latter closer to China. The increased authoritarianism in India and Turkey is a further sign of a shift in global geopolitics toward a wider Asian authoritarianism. For these reasons, the war in Ukraine is not just a regional conflict, even if it is primarily a European war, since it is in Europe where the war is being fought and where the direct long-term consequences will be (see Delanty 2024). The wider picture is one in which war has become a major feature of the historical present as the geopolitical order is reconfigured in a direction that is unclear but almost certainly towards a post-western world. The 2023 Israel-Hamas war is a sign of significant instability in the Middle East, as is growing tensions between the USA and China.

Authoritarianism is, of course, as Adorno noted in the *Authoritarian Personality*, also present in liberal democracies (Adorno *et al.* 2021 [1950]). Brexit in 2016, when a poorly devised referendum led to a marginal and unexpected victory for a populist demand for Britain to leave the EU, was a significant marker of a crisis that has not abated. The Trump presidency that also began in 2016 and the subsequent radicalization of the Republican Party in a direction that has openly embraced fascism is another sign of tremendous political transformation that has seen the worldwide rise of right-wing authoritarianism. That both of these events that led to considerable self-harm occurred in stalwart western democracies where the established elites lost control is an indication of a deep pathology within liberal democracy.

Finally, returning to the crisis in capitalism there can be little doubt that the model of capitalism that developed since the nineteenth century is coming to an end. This does not necessarily mean an end to capitalism, but its transformation into an increasingly dysfunctional system that no longer serves the majority of people (Jonsson and Wennerlind 2023). Capitalism also creates expectations that it can no longer meet. The crisis of stability that began in the 1970s was averted due in no small part to various measures that delayed the evitable cataclysm of 2007–8 (Streeck 2014). Since then there has been entrenched precarity and ever greater inequality (Azmanova 2020). The notion that capitalism is something every-one benefits from now is no longer a credible claim, in view of the stagnation of wages, major income disparity, and a superwealthy global elite (Turchin 2023).

The failure of capitalism is not just within the wealthy countries but is a global development. This is in part linked to population explosion over the last decades combined with increased mobility. Until a few decades ago, much of the world's population was locked within communist dictatorships or immobilized due to poverty or lack of opportunity for travel. In a situation today where extremely large numbers of people have opportunities for mobility coupled with economic crisis in the countries that they are heading toward, the result is a migration crisis that is tragically illustrated by the numbers of African and Asian migrants drowning in the Mediterranean Sea while heading for Europe, where for those who succeed in the perilous journey, they will join the increasing precariat.

In sum, the current crisis of stability is endemic to much of the world. The prosperous countries of the West are undergoing major economic crises and the geopolitical order is shifting, with a consolidation of authoritarian states and failing democracies, which possibly includes the USA. This is in the context of climate change and a pandemic that offered a glimpse of a dystopian future. Such developments point in the direction of a permacrisis or at least a mega crisis – it may be permanent or of long duration. But as a crisis, there is the possibility of resolution. This leads to two further questions.

AI and a Posthuman Future

My third question is whether the idea of the future has been rendered obsolete by the severity of the current permacrisis and other developments. What if the assumptions of most theories of the future are wrong and the future has already been lost and consequently there is nothing to hope for?

Critical theory has mostly been concerned with the dark side of the world and this has been the perspective of many intellectuals. In 1915 Virginia Woolf wrote: 'The future is Dark, which is on the whole the best thing the future can be.'[1] Darkness presupposes light, as day follows night. The notion that human beings are ultimately in control of their fate was rarely doubted in modern thought or that there would always be humans and not only machines. The sunlit uplands would always be there for the life of the world to move into, to cite Churchill's fa-

---

1 Cited in an essay by Rebecca Solnit. https://www.newyorker.com/books/page-turner/woolfs-darkness-embracing-the-inexplicable

mous phrase in stirring speech in 1940. But what if the future as a meaningful concept vanishes as a result of a fundamental transformation of reality and human subjectivity and there is only darkness? Such concerns until recently seemed to be exaggerated. There are now grounds for such concerns to be taken more seriously, for in the ultimate dire scenario humans may be overtaken by their machines. The only question is how seriously such concerns should be taken and what precautions need to be taken.

To begin, let's consider a development now more or less entrenched. The rapid expansion of conspiracy theories and posttruth politics has transformed the nature of politics in far-reaching ways, as evidenced by Trump's war against truth and the transformation of the Republican Party into extremist politics. The Putin regime in Russia relies on a systemic apparatus of misinformation and lies on a scale that helps to secure a degree of acquiescence from large segments of the population that would not be possible only through repression or docility. The denial of facts and truth in an era of unlimited information cannot be explained by rationality and may be an expression of emotions overtaking reason, at least where such emotions are not unrelated to self-interest. Whatever the explanation it is clearly connected with digital communication and the existence of digital technologies that have eradicated the distinction between reality and illusion, as in fake news, fake images, etc. Powerful digital platforms have transformed the nature of politics in ways that have been more effectively exploited by the extreme right and most kinds of right-wing populism, since most people get the news from nonmainstream internet platforms that are easily influenced by the radical right. This would appear to undermine the assumptions of the centrality of the public sphere and norms of reason and truth. It is of course the case that posttruth politics often takes more subtle forms that do not rely on crude lies, as in outright climate change denial, since it is no longer possible to deny the objectivity of climate change or even deny human causation. Instead, we find other strategies, such as misleading information on alternatives to fossil fuel, delaying strategies, and strategies aimed at creating divisions.[2] Despite the dominance of posttruth/postfact politics, the war against truth is not over and there is much evidence of successful counterpolitics (see Susskind 2020). The kinds of technology used by those who perpetuate fake news are not necessarily in itself bad but are put to bad use. This brings me to a more ominous development.

The most striking development in recent years is a significant transformation in dangerous technology, technology that is inherently harmful. Until now the most dangerous technology that humanity created is nuclear weapons, along with other

---

2 https://www.scientificamerican.com/article/climate-deniers-shift-tactics-to-inactivism/

kinds of lethal weapons of war such as bioweapons. An overall conclusion is that these kinds of technology are still the most dangerous. With the proliferation of nuclear weapons they have become more dangerous than in the era of the Cold War, when only two superpowers possessed them (in the case of the USSR, since 1949). In the face of other kinds of technology potentially emerging, there is the comforting assurance that for now such weapons are controlled still by human agents, even if, in many cases these agents are increasingly likely to be rogue states. Such possibilities are in themselves a source of serious concern, as is highlighted by the Russian-Ukrainian War. But with far-reaching developments in AI, the relation between technology and humanity is changing such that the presuppositions underlying all previous kinds of technology are now in question. Any consideration of the future of humanity will now have to take seriously the possible transformation of AI into artificial general intelligence (AGI). With its possible rise, the future may be a posthuman one as a result of what can be characterized as a movement from transhumanism to posthumanism.

Julian Huxley first used the term transhumanism in 1957 in an essay 'Transhumanism:' 'The human species can, if it wishes, transcend itself, not just sporadically, an individual here in one way, an individual there in another way, but in its entirety, as humanity. We need a name for this new belief. Perhaps transhumanism will serve: man remaining man, but transcending himself, by realizing new possibilities of and for his human nature. I believe in transhumanism: once there are enough people who can truly say that, the human species will be on the threshold of a new kind of existence, as different from ours as ours is from that of Pekin [sic] man. It will at last be consciously fulfilling its real destiny' (Huxley 1957: 17). Huxley's vision was nonetheless a humanist one, believing that the enhancement of the human condition by science is a goal worth pursuing. While many transhumanists today would see themselves in the footsteps of Huxley, there are developments in technology that go beyond the transhumanist movement and notions of intelligence amplification or augmented intelligence, such that we can speak of a posthumanist specter facing the world that in effect signals the end of human evolution.

While many developments in IT and in AI are highly beneficial for human evolution in terms of health, diet, longevity, and cognition, developments around AGI are potentially catastrophic. Where the transhumanist movement assumed that superintelligent humans will emerge as the next stage in human evolution through enhancement by science and technology, a posthuman future may quite well be one in which superintelligent technologies will take over and that human beings will surrender control to them.[3] How likely is this and how worried should we be?

Currently AI serves human ends and is ultimately controlled by human agency. It can perform tasks that humans cannot or perform tasks more efficiently and quicker, as in computer chess, the use of algorithms, almost anything that requires the collection, computation, and analysis of large amounts of data, *etc.* Until now AI is not in itself based on something akin to intelligence. AI can overtake humans in computational skills but not in intelligence. With the possible emergence of super-intelligence in the near future we are beyond the domain of what is essentially speed in the computation of vast amounts of data to a form of intelligence that is potentially not human (Bostrom 2016, Tegmark 2017).

The concept of intelligence is difficult to pin down. One key aspect of it is the capacity for self-learning and reflexivity. This is something that only humans can perform, though some kinds of AI are close to it in a number of largely mechanical tasks that they can perform better than humans. Many machine technologies today are increasingly miniaturized, mobile and networked, and fully operative in many domains, especially in the economy (Elliott 2022: 43). Many types of jobs are being done by AI-powered technologies, and in the near future vast amounts of other jobs will disappear and not be replaced by different ones, as has been the trend until now. The use of algorithms to influence voting behavior, as in the Brexit referendum in 2016, and in individually targeted advertising, is now well established and the basis of what has come to be seen as algorithmic governmentality. It has been recognized by theorists such as Wark (2019) and Zuboff (2019) that big data has already brought about a new relation to the future which can be predicted as a result of gigantic data lakes. Such developments go beyond prediction as previously understood since the algorithms generated to make it possible to control human behavior. However, it is also double edged, as digital technologies also have democratizing potentials (Berry 2014, Lingrens 2023). Perhaps AI is not a form of intelligence. According to Esposito, it is a form of artificial communication and not intelligence. The key point in her assessment is we have learned how to communicate with machines: it is now increasingly the case that our communication partner may not be a human being but a machine or an algorithm (Esposito 2022).

The digitalization of war is another such development that has changed the nature of warfare, as in the use of cyberwarfare, drones, and other kinds of automated weapons. So far humans are firmly in control of such weaponry, letting aside human error and technical faults occurring. In almost every sphere of life we are interacting with AI (Nowotny 2021). As Anthony Elliot has written: 'What

---

3 For a further and wider perspectives on this see Chernilo (2017), Fuller (2011), Manzocco (2019).

must be grasped is how lives today become structured in relation to automated intelligent machines' (Elliot 2022: 80, Elliot 2019). Human evolution, as discussed in Chapter Two, is now largely occurring as cultural evolution whereby humans are adapting not to the natural environment, as in Darwin's theory of natural section, but through adaption to the new digital environment. The Covid-19 pandemic, as the first pandemic or epidemic of the digital age, led to a massive expansion in digital governance. But all these developments do not amount to AGI.

We are at the threshold of the emergence of 'machine intelligence,' whereby machines acquire something akin to human intelligence. With the arrival of generative AI (as opposed to AGI) machines already can generate original content, e.g. images, texts, even music. However, generative AI, as in its possibly most advanced form, ChatGPT, launched in 2022, does not go much beyond pattern recognition, as in voice and image recognition.[4] Current developments at worst probably point to the emergence in the not-too-distant future of apparatuses of large-scale surveillance with serious implications for individual liberty and work, but also for cybersecurity and bioweapons. Interpretations vary from those who see the benefits of what is still part of the digital revolution and those who, like James Briddle (2019) and Bernard Stiegler (2016), see the dangers and emerging dystopia of automation or, like Habermas (2001), those who see grave danger with attempts to manipulate human nature.[5] However, these developments do not necessarily entail machine intelligence but are advanced forms of automation.

AGI presents a fundamental transformation in AI beyond automation and generative AI. Features of AGI are enhanced self-improvement, autonomous capacities, and self-learning. While elements of such features are already in evidence, the critical question is whether machine self-learning will take the form of human self-learning. Currently that does not appear to be the case, despite some developments that suggest such capabilities in problem solving amount to intelligence, even in learning to understand emotions. Yet, it does not appear possible for AI to perform moral decisions or write with advanced reasoning, unless a future emerges that eradicates the need for such capacities. Artificial intelligence is after all artificial. Superintelligent robots will probably not acquire the capacity for self-reflection and empathy, but as almost every account of AI notes, it is only a matter of time before new capabilities are developed (there are dissenting voices, such as Landgrebe and Smith 2023). These capabilities may not only be bad. In a very distant future, when humanized robots evolve through self-replication and technological evolution, it is not impossible to imagine the opposite of the dire sce-

---

4 ChatGPT uses natural language processing to create human-like conversation.
5 See also Delanty and Harris (2021).

nario of amoral superintelligent robots, namely 'Kantian' robots, that are more moral than humans. This is clearly not something that can be expected. For now, the dangers lurking in AGI are greater than the positive potentials.

AGI may take the form of radical autonomy whereby robotic technologies once created may not be shut down and may be able to self-replicate in the way that viruses self-replicate. Yet more alarming specters are forms of AGI that eventually replace human beings, who become effectively absorbed into them in possibly hybrid forms or in a world in which the distinction between humans and machines has been obliterated. This is the 'singularity'[6] thesis, which is not yet a real possibility, but may become one given the possibility that human minds – in the form of consciousness – may be uploaded onto gigantic electronic clouds.[7] It is at least a popular belief that our minds will be uploaded onto machines and that as a consequence we will no longer 'die.' Developments in nanotechnology, biotechnology, genetics, and superintelligence have the potential to considerably extend longevity. Human life will no longer be as Heidegger argued in *Being and Time* an anticipation of death (see Chapter Four). Such a prospect, even on a speculative level, has been explored by the British TV science fiction series *Black Mirror* and has considerable significance for how we imagine the future and, individually and societally, view the future.

If AGI were able to self-reproduce and acquire superhuman forms of intelligence it is possible to imagine that they could not only create deadly weapons but activate them. It is not implausible that AGI, if it existed, would create new kinds of weapons and other dangerous types of technology. One possible dystopian scenario is that such weapons may be used by rogue states or organizations working with such states. A further scenario, admittedly more the stuff of science fiction, is that a future war may be between such robotic technologies and what remains of human populations, who may have to enlist friendly AI robots. Such scenarios according to some are simply the result of fear of what is not understood. Landgrebe and Smith (2023) claim AGI is not possible because software would have to be designed to emulate the human neurocognitive system, which is not possible.

In sum, currently AI is largely doing better what humans cannot do and thus serving human needs, but there is a danger of AI spiraling out of control; AGI represents a further possible development whereby superintelligent technologies would come into existence that are independent of human control and may endan-

---

6 The 'singularity' argument is widely discussed in new popular science writings and is highly contested (Kurzweil 2005, Freita 2022). It goes back to a paper in 1993 by Vernor Vinge, who prophesized the eventual emergence of 'machine sapience' (Vinge 1993).

7 https://www.technologyreview.com/2018/03/13/144721/a-startup-is-pitching-a-mind-uploading-serv ice-that-is-100-percent-fatal/

ger humanity, if not negate it. But there is also the more positive prospect of forms of superintelligence helping to realize low-carbon futures (for an assessment, see Elliott 2023:184–88). This argument is by no means self-evident, since there is a considerable negative ecological consequences for AI (Brevini 2022).

The possible arrival of AGI challenges the assumptions of the transhumanist movement, which has been broadly in favor of technological enhancement of the human being as part of a long tradition going back to the Enlightenment of human perfectibility (Bostrom and Savulescu 2009). The dangers that result from it have been generally seen as ones of ethics and regulation. It is clear that AGI goes beyond the idea of human perfectibility and concerns developments that are not specifically necessarily aimed at the human being but with technology. According to Dévédec, transhumanism is emblematic of a depoliticized conception of human perfectibility and is not compatible with the political project of autonomy, arguably the more important Enlightenment legacy, which never saw the idea of human perfectibility as a purely technical matter (Dévédec 2018). Transhumanists do not think that there is a human essence or a defining core to human nature, and consequently it is open to new definitions by science and technology, as in the writings of Ray Kurzweil (2005). Dévédec sees this as a form of depoliticization in that humans are being forced to adapt to the demands of technology and a logic that is part of capitalist growth. Boden (2016: Chapter 7) has argued that while the probability of AGI emerging is extremely small, we should by now be sufficiently concerned about the implications such that precautionary measures need to be taken. The fact that AGI will not come about, at least not in the guise of a 'singularity,' is not to say there is nothing to worry about. Such developments may come about partially or by stealth.

The question of the future implications of AI is in part a question of how open is the future. While I have argued for the essentially openness of the future, the future – especially the deep future – is also contingent on developments that cannot be predicted or known, and possibly also not imagined. Chance and necessity shape the human world as much as the natural world and while chance opens up possibilities for human agency to pursue, the forces of necessity are also at work and not so easily negated.

Struggles for the Future

The future should not be approached as something technocratic, a product of unforeseen catastrophes, the outcome of long-run patterns, or human-created forces that have got out of control. It is also produced by human actors in the present and contingent on choices made in the present. It is the outcome of debates, controversies, and above all struggles in which different visions of the future are fought over. My final question then is, what are the main struggles over the future today?

To address this question some historical contextualization can help. In the past some of the main debates about the future were on the implications of progress. In the eighteenth century with the emergence of the modern idea of the future, the idea of progress challenged the conservative idea of the future as the continuation of the past. The revival of Renaissance notions of utopia in the eighteenth century articulated variously more critical conceptions of the future as progress while calling for radical alternative societies. In the twentieth century, the idea of the future was at the forefront of many political debates and conflicts. The theme of utopia versus dystopia was, as discussed in Chapter Five, a major way to view the future. Another debate, with the rise of totalitarianism, was the conflict between freedom and tyranny. These fueled much of the Cold War debates on the future in which the older idea of progress was allied with various scientific visions of a programmed future. Throughout the century another clash over the future that frequently took place was on the theme of humans versus technology, as in controversies from conservative critiques of technology to fears about nuclear weapons. Some of these fears have not gone away but have changed their form. There is undoubtedly today a much more pronounced sense of the fragility of the earth and vulnerability of the world than there was at any time in history. The ancients were in awe of the cosmos, but they also believed they were at the center of it. The planet earth is now seen as a tiny speck in an infinite universe, and as finite and in danger. Modern science, in mastering nature, ended up revealing how limited our knowledge really is.

Against this background of greater knowledge producing greater uncertainty, we can say that the future today has become a battleground for some of the major issues of our time. In line with the theoretical conception of the future as a multileveled idea, debates and struggles over the future take a variety of forms. On one level we can identify at the most general level a strong consciousness of the future, perhaps more so than at any other time in history. The future is now a way in which the world is viewed and experienced. This is, in the most general terms, an interpretative model; it offers a way of making sense of the world. The idea of the future in itself is thus a contrast to, for example, cultural models that are focused on the past, historical roots, and origins. Such models of consciousness still exist of course, but there appears to be a strong presence today of the idea of the future. This idea operates at a very general level. There is a plurality of other cultural models too, in which the idea of the future plays a central role, as in notions of human rights, democracy, and cosmopolitanism as well as in conceptions of end times, utopianism, and futuristic worlds. There are tensions between these different cultural orientations in terms of their different projections, origins, and emphasis as well as their scale and intensity.

While there is a degree of cultural contestation going on at the cultural level – i. e. the macro level of society – in which different visions of the future compete with each other, the general idea of the future looms large. To speak of social and political struggles requires a focus on social agency, namely on how social actors pursue future-oriented projects and how they interpret the idea of the future. It is in these meso-level battles that the future plays out in terms of different political programs and cultural politics. In these conflicts the future is shaped through the narratives and imaginaries that are produced. In my account, I see these battles over the future playing out in relation to wider cultural visions, which are variously embodied by different social actors who select different themes and codes. The cultural visions are combined and articulated in the context of public debate, competing for support from the public. Some more than others have greater resonance in the wider public. It also needs to be considered that these battles of the future ultimately involve individual persons, for whom the future corresponds to feelings and emotions that are also existential and latent in the human condition.

It is evident that today the main debate about the future relates to climate change. This is obviously not only a debate about climate but goes to the core of many problems and crises of the present. It leads to a plurality of visions of the future, for example, whether all that we can now achieve in the near future is a deacceleration of the Great Acceleration, a slowing down of global warming rather than a positively new future. Depending on where one is situated in the debate on this question, other visions of future possibility open up. There is, for example, the technocratic one of geoengineering to more radical visions that question the model of continued capitalist growth or ones that seek more pragmatic solutions to the fundamental problem of new sources of energy. Post-apocalyptical images of the future as catastrophic and irretrievable loss abound in images of the present, some of which can be a call for action while others signal quiet despair and resignation. More extreme imaginaries are around the prospects of a posthuman future discussed above and long-termism, visions of future humans in a very distant future. A controversy in this context is space exploration and whether humans are by their nature earthbound. Hannah Arendt expressed one of the main criticisms of such developments (in the context of the early NASA missions to orbit the earth) in 1958 in *The Human Condition* when she wrote, 'The earth is the very quintessence of the human condition, and earthly nature, for all we know may be unique in the universe in providing human beings with a habitat in which they can move and breathe without effort and without artifice' (1958: 2–3). Whether we are 'earth-bound creatures' or 'dwellers of the universe' is a controversy that has today taken on a new dimension with space travel. This is all despite the fact that there is 'no planet B': the nearest star, Proxima Centauri, is more than 4 light years away and would take more than 6,000 years to approach it using current space technology. Such a journey may be in vain, as the habitability of its two exoplanets is unknown. Despite the implausibility of galactic space travel, imaginaries of future worlds beyond the earth will undoubtedly continue to shape future thinking.

Future ideals and imaginaries and the political and scientific programs that they lead to are not entirely open. They are also structured by the meta level of ideas that is also part of the human orientation in the world, as in ideas of reason such as truth, justice, freedom, and authenticity. Future images and politics cannot entirely dispense with the demands of reason, which filters down to the micro level of individual subjectivities and is always there as a source of transcendence. The conceptual conditions of the human condition are necessary, i. e. transcendental presuppositions in knowledge claims cannot be entirely eradicated. In many ways, due to the mediating role of science in so many spheres of life, the future entails knowledge claims, and as such it is limited by the conditions of the possibility of knowledge. Such meta-level ideas serve as reference points for critical assessments of what is potential and what is possible, but also what is desirable and what is not.

A broad assessment of our historical present suggests a view of multiple lines of conflict forming along the fissures created by the numerous interlocked crises that constitute the current permacrisis. The most pervasive one is a growing number of people for whom the future offers little. This multitude is a potential source of mass mobilization. In western societies, this includes the increasingly growing precariat, the working class, and the nonuniversity educated. It also includes young people, including university educated, for whom the future that beckons has less to offer than what it offered to their parents. For the first time the current generation of young people will be less well off than their parents. The sources of dissatisfaction are considerable, but they are also very varied and there is as yet not a single social movement capable of voicing collective grievances. Until now, the extreme right and various bands of populist movements have harnessed collective dissatisfaction. The politics of grievance, white victimhood and resentment are currently playing a major role in western democracies, which are becoming increasingly susceptible to extremist movements that amplify and exploit such sentiments. However, these movements, which are possibly passing their peak, will not succeed in the long term since they are incapable of governing the future.

According to Peter Turchin, we are now in transition from a precrisis phase 'when the state is still struggling to maintain control of the ideological landscape in the face of a multitude of counter-elite challengers, to the next phase, when numerous contenders struggle among themselves for primacy' (Turchin 2023: 106). He is mostly referring to the turbulent situation in the USA, but the picture is broadly true of many parts of the world. From a 'Global South' perspective, Aurea Mota and Peter Wagner argue: 'The belief that there are no alternatives is no longer dominant. Rather, alternatives are created, often in the most unexpected ways in parts of the world' (2019:4).

In view of the larger climate crisis playing out across the entire canvass of the world, the conditions are ripe for a major social transformation. The premise underlying this book is that the idea of the future lies at the core of such struggles, which are often subsumed by other cultural projects, such as past-oriented ones. The future is more important than the past, yet the past holds sway. This may now be changing due to the obvious failure of global capitalism and worldwide turbulence. While we no longer naively believe in utopias, the utopian impulse is still alive in the desire for alternatives. But so too are dystopias present in the imagination of the present, some of which serve as warnings. One reason why our dystopias today are more disturbing and threatening than those of the past is that they appear to be so real.

References

Adorno, T. W., Frenkel-Brunswik, E., Levinson, E., and Sanford, R. N. 2019. [1950] *The Authoritarian Personality.* London: Verso.

Arendt, H. 1958. *The Human Condition.* Chicago: University of Chicago Press.

Azmanova, A. 2020. *Capitalism on Edge: How Fighting Precarity Can Achieve Radical Change Without Crisis or Utopia.* New York: Columbia University Press.

Bellah, R. and Joas, H. (eds.) 2012. *The Axial Age and its Consequences.* Cambridge, Mass.: Harvard University Press.

Berry, D. 2014. *Critical Theory and the Digital.* London: Bloomsbury.

Boden, M. 2016. *Artificial Intelligence.* Oxford: Oxford University Press.

Bostrom, N. 2016. *Superintelligence: Paths, Dangers, Strategies.* Oxford: Oxford University Press.

Bostrom, N. and Savulescu, J. 2009. *Human Enhancement.* Oxford: Oxford University Press.

Briddle, J. 2019. *The New Dark Ages: Technology and End of the Future.* London: Verso.

De Beauvoir, S. 1949. [1947] 'The Present and the Future.' https://www.atlasofplaces.com/essays/the-present-the-future/

Brevini, B. 2023. *Is AI Good for the Planet?* Cambridge: Polity Press.

Chernilo, D. 2017. *Debating Humanity: Towards a Philosophical Sociology.* Cambridge: Cambridge University Press.

Delanty, G. (ed.) 2021. *Pandemics, Society and Politics: Critical Reflections on the Covid-19 Crisis.* Berlin: De Gruyter.

Delanty, G. 2023. 'Introduction to the Special Issue on the Russo-Ukrainian War: A New European War? A New European War? Considerations on the Russo-Ukrainian War.' *European Journal of Social Theory,* 26 (4). https://journals.sagepub.com/doi/full/10.1177/13684310231174098

Delanty, G and Harris, N. 2021. 'Critical Theory and Technology: The Frankfurt School Revisited.' *Thesis Eleven*, 166 (1): 88 – 108. https://doi.org/10.1177/07255136211002055

Dévédec, Le, N. 2018. 'Unfit for the Future?: The Depolitization of Human perfectibility, from the Enlightenment to Transhumanism.' *European Journal of Social Theory*, 21 (4): 488 – 507. https://doi.org/10.1177/1368431017750974

Elliott, A. 2019. *The Culture of AI: Everyday Life and the Digital Revolution.* Cambridge: Polity Press.

Elliott, A. 2022. *Making Sense of AI: Our Algorithmic World.* Cambridge: Polity Press.

Esposito, E. 2022. *Artificial Communication: How Algorithms Produce Social Intelligence.* Cambridge, Mass.: MIT Press.

Freita, G. A. *The Coming Singularity: The Rapid Evolution of Human Evolution.* New York: Austin Macauley Publishing.

Fuller, S. 2011. *Humanity 2.0 What it Means to Be Human: Past, Present and Future.* London: Palgrave.

Huxley, J. 1957. 'Transhumanism.' In: *New Bottles for New Wine.* London: Chatto & Windus.

Jaspers, K. 2021. [1953/1949] *The Origin and Goal of History.* London: Routledge.

Jonsson, F. A. and Wennerlind, C. 2023. *Scarcity: A History from the Origins of Capitalism to the Climate Crisis.* Cambridge, Mass.: Harvard University Press.

Habermas, J. 2001. *The Future of Human Nature.* Cambridge: Polity Press.

Kurzweil, R. 2005. The *Singularity is Near: When Humans Transcend Biology.* London: Penguin.

Landgrebe, J. and Smith, B. 2023. *Why Machines Will Never Rule the World.* London: Routledge.

Lingrens, S. 2023. *Critical Theory of AI.* Cambridge: Polity Press.

Madsen, R. 2012. 'The Future of Transcendence: A Sociological Agenda.' In: Bellah, R. and Joas, H. (eds). *The Axial Age and its Consequences.* Cambridge, Mass.: Harvard University Press.

Manzocco, R. 2019. *Transhumanism: Engineering the Human Condition.* Chichester: Springer.

Mota, A. and Wagner, P. 2019. *Collective Action and Political Transformation: The Entangled Experiences in Brazil, South Africa.* Edinburgh: Edinburgh University Press.

Nowotny, H. 2021. *In AI We Trust.* Cambridge: Polity Press.

Stiegler, B. 2016. *Automatic Society. Vol. 1 The Future of Work.* Cambridge: Polity Press.

Streeck, W, 2014. *Buying Time: The Delayed Crisis of Democratic Capitalism.* London: Verso.

Strydom, P. 2023. 'The Critical Theory of Society: From its Young Hegelian Core to the Key Concept of Possibility.' *European Journal of Social Theory*, 26 (2): 153 – 79. https://doi.org/10.1177/13684310221130914

Susskind, J. 2020. *Future Politics.* Oxford: Oxford University Press.

Tegmark, M. 2018. *Life 3.0: Being Human in the Age of Artificial Intelligence.* London: Penguin.

Turchin, P. 2023. *End Times: Elites, Counter-Elites and the Path of Political Disintegration.* London: Allen Lane.

Vinge, V. 1993. 'The Coming Singularity.' https://edoras.sdsu.edu/~vinge/misc/singularity.html

Wark, M. 2019. *Capitalism is Dead: Is this Something Worse?* London: Verso.

Zuboff, S. 2019. *The Age of Surveillance Capitalism: The Fight for a Human Future at the New Frontier of Power.* London: Profile Books.

Index

https://doi.org/10.1515/9783111240602-009